# CAMBRIDGE LIBRARY COLLECTION

*Books of enduring scholarly value*

## History

The books reissued in this series include accounts of historical events and movements by eye-witnesses and contemporaries, as well as landmark studies that assembled significant source materials or developed new historiographical methods. The series includes work in social, political and military history on a wide range of periods and regions, giving modern scholars ready access to influential publications of the past.

## Gilbert Crispin Abbot of Westminster

Gilbert Crispin (c. 1045–1117/18), fourth abbot of Westminster Abbey, was a scion of an important Norman family. Trained at Bec under St Anselm, later archbishop of Canterbury, he was a noted scholar and theologian. Under his rule, Westminster Abbey began to expand physically and grow in importance, making full play of its position as the chosen burial site of Edward the Confessor. The necessity to raise funds for the building work probably led to Crispin's association with the London Jewish community, and this was to inspire his most important theological work, *Disputation with a Jew*. In this 1911 book, J. Robinson Armitage, then dean of Westminster, mines the abbey archives to write both a biography and a discussion of Crispin's thirty-year administration of Westminster. He also includes the texts of all Crispin's known writings, together with a selection of charters. A significant work on a hitherto neglected Anglo-Norman churchman.

Cambridge University Press has long been a pioneer in the reissuing of out-of-print titles from its own backlist, producing digital reprints of books that are still sought after by scholars and students but could not be reprinted economically using traditional technology. The Cambridge Library Collection extends this activity to a wider range of books which are still of importance to researchers and professionals, either for the source material they contain, or as landmarks in the history of their academic discipline.

Drawing from the world-renowned collections in the Cambridge University Library, and guided by the advice of experts in each subject area, Cambridge University Press is using state-of-the-art scanning machines in its own Printing House to capture the content of each book selected for inclusion. The files are processed to give a consistently clear, crisp image, and the books finished to the high quality standard for which the Press is recognised around the world. The latest print-on-demand technology ensures that the books will remain available indefinitely, and that orders for single or multiple copies can quickly be supplied.

The Cambridge Library Collection will bring back to life books of enduring scholarly value (including out-of-copyright works originally issued by other publishers) across a wide range of disciplines in the humanities and social sciences and in science and technology.

# Gilbert Crispin
# Abbot of Westminster

*A Study of the Abbey under Norman Rule*

J. Armitage Robinson

CAMBRIDGE
UNIVERSITY PRESS

CAMBRIDGE UNIVERSITY PRESS

Cambridge, New York, Melbourne, Madrid, Cape Town, Singapore,
São Paolo, Delhi, Dubai, Tokyo, Mexico City

Published in the United States of America by Cambridge University Press, New York

www.cambridge.org
Information on this title: www.cambridge.org/9781108013581

This edition first published 1911
This digitally printed version 2010

ISBN 978-1-108-01358-1 Paperback

The earlier numbers of this Series are :

1. **The Manuscripts of Westminster Abbey.** By J. ARMITAGE ROBINSON, D.D., Dean of Westminster, and M. R. JAMES, Litt.D., Provost of King's College, Cambridge. Royal 8vo. pp. viii + 108. 5s. net.

2. **The History of Westminster Abbey by John Flete.** Edited by J. ARMITAGE ROBINSON, D.D., Dean of Westminster. Royal 8vo. pp. viii + 151. 5s. net.

# NOTES AND DOCUMENTS

## RELATING TO

# WESTMINSTER ABBEY

## No. 3

## ABBOT GILBERT CRISPIN

CAMBRIDGE UNIVERSITY PRESS
London: FETTER LANE, E.C.
C. F. CLAY, Manager

Edinburgh: 100, PRINCES STREET
Berlin: A. ASHER AND CO.
Leipzig: F. A. BROCKHAUS
New York: G. P. PUTNAM'S SONS
Bombay and Calcutta: MACMILLAN AND CO., Ltd.

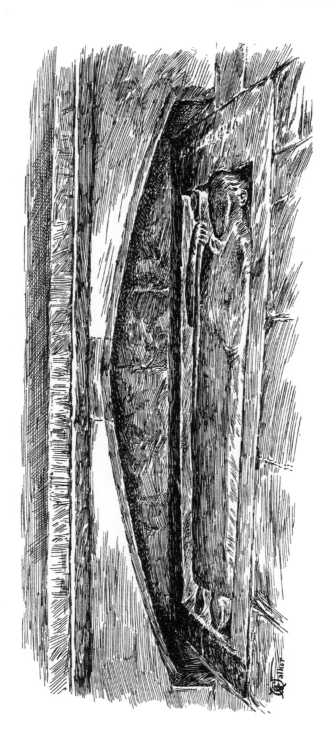

EFFIGIES · GISLEBERTI · CRISPINI · ABBATIS · IN · CLAVSTRO · WESTMONASTERIENSI

# GILBERT CRISPIN
# ABBOT OF WESTMINSTER

## A STUDY OF
## THE ABBEY UNDER NORMAN RULE

BY

J. ARMITAGE ROBINSON, D.D.
DEAN OF WESTMINSTER

CAMBRIDGE:
AT THE UNIVERSITY PRESS
1911

**Cambridge:**

PRINTED BY JOHN CLAY, M.A.

AT THE UNIVERSITY PRESS.

COLLEGIS · AMICIS

WESTMONASTERIENSIBVS

AD · WELLENSES · SVOS · REVERSVRVS

HOC · OPVSCVLVM

DE · GISLEBERTO · ABBATE

CVRIOSIVS · EXARATVM

D · D

ANTECESSORIS · TANTI · LAVDATOR · INDIGNVS

GRATO · ANIMO

# PREFACE

GILBERT CRISPIN is the earliest abbot of Westminster of whom we have any considerable knowledge : and he is one of the greatest of the line, distinguished alike by his noble descent, his high character, the fame of his learning and the length of his rule. Yet, though his effigy has been before the eyes of every generation that has trod the cloisters in the past eight centuries, no one has cared to gather together what may be known of his life and times. Even his biography of Abbot Herluin has never been edited intact, though historians draw from it all they know of the early days of Bec, which gave three archbishops to Canterbury within seventy years. This neglect seems the more strange when we remember that he was a favourite pupil of both Lanfranc and Anselm, some of whose letters to him still survive ; and that his judgment as a theologian could be appealed to on the continent more than a generation after his death.

He was a true monk and a scholar, with no desire for fame : his vocation and his instincts alike made him shrink from public affairs. His Westminster sons remembered him, as the Bec monks remembered their Anselm, chiefly for his gentleness ; and they wrote the epithet *mitis* on his tomb before they praised his justice, wisdom, strength and learning.

It has been a pleasure to restore the memory of this blameless man. As fragment after fragment of his story has revealed itself, his character has always remained without a stain. Other evidence may be found which has escaped my search; but there are few men, I think, of whom we may more safely say,

> Whatever record leap to light
> He never shall be shamed.

I owe special thanks to Dr Edward Scott, the keeper of the abbey muniments, to whose wide knowledge and unfailing helpfulness I have had constant recourse; and to the Reverend R. B. Rackham, whose work I can often hardly distinguish from my own, and who has taken on himself the labour of compiling the Index. For the frontispiece I am indebted to my friend Mr A. G. Walker, the sculptor, who took a kindly interest in Abbot Gilbert's time-worn effigy.

THE DEANERY, WESTMINSTER,
    CHRISTMAS, 1910.

# CONTENTS

# GILBERT CRISPIN.

WHEN the Conqueror came to be crowned at Westminster on Christmas Day, 1066, he was welcomed by Abbot Edwin whose contact with the Normans of Edward's court had prepared him for the new regime. After Edwin's death the king gave the abbey to one Geoffrey from Jumièges, who misruled it from about 1071 to 1075, when at Lanfranc's advice he was sent back in disgrace to his old monastery. The next abbot was chosen with more care. Vitalis, abbot of Bernay, had raised his abbey 'from little to great,' as William says in writing to demand consent to his appointment from his superior, John the abbot of Fécamp. Of Vitalis all that we know is good. He secured by the king's aid the estates of the abbey, some of which had been jeopardised in the recent changes; he seems to have pressed forward the new monastic buildings; and doubtless he enforced the improved discipline which the great reformer William of Dijon had left as the heritage of Fécamp. But he was already an elderly man, and he died, as it would seem, in the summer of 1085.

If Vitalis had come to Westminster late in life, towards the close of an energetic and successful career, the next abbot, Gilbert Crispin, was in the full strength of his manhood at the time of his appointment, and was destined to rule the monastery for thirty-two years. He must have been about forty when he became abbot of Westminster. He had spent some twenty-five years in the abbey of Bec where he was dedicated as a child. Lanfranc and Anselm had been his teachers: Anselm had set him to teach in his turn, and then Lanfranc had called him to serve as his chaplain at Canterbury. To understand his history we must read the story of the foundation of Herluin's abbey at Bec; and we are fortunate in being able to read it in Gilbert's own words, for he himself had the honour of being Abbot Herluin's biographer. Indeed it is to him that we owe almost all our knowledge of this

1

unique and exceptionally important foundation, and also of the career of Archbishop Lanfranc before he came to Canterbury. The close personal friendship between our abbot and Lanfranc's saintly successor is a further reason for dwelling on Gilbert Crispin's early monastic home.

We begin then with the story of Bec, as Gilbert has written it for us[1]. It belongs to an early period of Norman history, when the fierce Northmen were first emerging out of barbarism. They had unlearned their native language, and spoke a rude form of French; but they retained much of their primitive ferocity, and had not yet felt the constraining hand of the great duke William, who was first to discipline their forces and then to lead them to the conquest of England. The Church, as judged by the reformers of the next generation, was in a woefully backward condition. 'There were few in Normandy then,' says Gilbert, 'to point the right road. Priests and bishops freely married and bore arms as lay folk, one and all still living after the primitive fashion of the Danes.' To a man of any force of character two careers alone seemed open, the fierce life of the soldier or the austere devotion of the monk. The secular clergy counted for little: the hope of religion lay in the monasteries, and these in spite of great efforts of reform still left, as we shall presently see, very much to be desired.

In lower Normandy there is a small river called the Risle, which runs northward into the Seine: about four miles below the ancient town of Brionne it receives a tiny tributary which still bears its old Norse name of 'the beck.' This streamlet gave its name to a new monastery which suddenly became world-famous. For it revived the study of letters in the north of Europe, furnished bishops and abbots to all parts of Christendom, and within a century of its foundation gave three archbishops to Canterbury—Lanfranc, under William the Conqueror, Anselm under his sons Rufus and Henry I, and Theobald in the anarchical days of king Stephen.

In the times of which we are speaking monasteries were founded by princes or nobles, who called on well-known abbots to provide colonies of monks for the new settlements which they undertook to build and endow. But Bec was an exception to the rule and had a humbler origin. Herluin, its founder, was a soldier of good family, in the service of Gilbert, count of Brionne. In the height of his fortune

---

[1] *Vita Herluini*, printed below from the Corpus Christi Camb. MS no. 318, a Rochester book of the twelfth century.

he broke off a distinguished career to enrol himself in the *militia* of God, as it was called, and to embrace the poverty of Christ. It was with difficulty that he released himself from his service at Gilbert's court; but the crisis came when he was ordered one day to carry out a command which was against his conscience. His refusal was cruelly punished by the burning of his farms, but a reconciliation was presently effected, and he was allowed to go his own way. With two friends he retired to a part of his small property, where he began to build a little church with his own hands. He was thirty-eight years of age and had never learned his letters. He spent the days in manual labour, and the nights in teaching himself to read the psalter. Then he cast about to discover how monks should live. 'He went,' says Abbot Gilbert, 'to a certain monastery to enquire into the life of monks. Having offered up a prayer he approached with all reverence and much fear, coming to the door of the cloister as though it were the gate of Paradise, eager to learn how monks behaved and what were the holy habits of the cloistered life. He found them falling far short of what the monastic rule required: he was much perturbed, and fell in doubt what course of life he should adopt. Then the warden of the monastery, espying his entrance and taking him for a thief, caught him roughly by the neck and dragged him out by the hair of his head.' The high-spirited soldier took the rebuff with patient silence, and went his way home. On the next Christmas Day he ventured on a fresh attempt, choosing a monastery of higher reputation. But during the solemn procession he was disgusted to see the brethren as they passed along greeting the lay folk with silly smiles, and shewing off their festival attire. Then as they reached the entrance of the church, they scrambled each to get in first, and one monk smote a too insistent brother with his fist and laid him on the ground. 'So barbarous,' says Gilbert, 'were men's manners all through Normandy.'

Once more Herluin was in despair; but late that night he prayed in a corner of the church alone, after the night office had been sung. Presently a monk, who also thought that he was alone, stood near him in prayer, then threw himself flat on the ground, and thus continued praying with tears and sobs until the morning dawned. It is a fine example of the power of unconscious influence. That monk's prayer may even be said to have changed the course of history. Abbot Gilbert wisely counts it a true miracle. The enemy of souls was baffled, and Herluin returned assured that God had a purpose for his life. He finished his church, and got the bishop of Lisieux to consecrate it, and to clothe him as a monk. Presently the bishop ordained him to the priesthood, and put him in charge of his modest abbey.

But the site Herluin had chosen was waterless and unproductive; and after five or six years, when he had gained a few recruits, he was forced to come down to the side of the beck, and to build again in the meadow where it joins the main stream of the Risle. Here in 1040 his new church was consecrated, and two years later God sent him a man who was to raise his humble monastery out of obscurity and make the Bec a name in history. This was Lanfranc the Lombard from Pavia, a famous teacher who had crossed the Alps a few years before to visit the schools of France, and presently had brought his learning to the powerful but unlettered Normans. He had gained a host of pupils, but a scholar's fame could not satisfy him; he yearned for the love of God. Caught like many another by the fascinating words, 'If any man will come after me, let him deny himself, and take up his cross and follow me,' he sought for the humblest monastery, where he should be lost to the world of letters and be permitted to serve God in silence: and he found what he sought in Bec[1]. 'There was none,' says Abbot Gilbert, 'poorer or more despised: and it chanced that on his arrival the abbot was engaged in building an oven with his own hands. His humility of mind and dignity of speech won Lanfranc's veneration and love; and there he became a monk.' We may see to-day, a few hundred yards from the very spot, just such an oven as Herluin was building, a semi-circular structure of flints below and yellow clay above, set against the wall of a little shanty thatched with straw; and we may easily picture the quaint scene of the simple abbot, standing with grimy hands, half-hidden by his unfinished building, while he grants the request of the most learned man in Europe that he may become a member of his little community.

For about three years Lanfranc was a monk at Bec before the world found what had become of him. But then the place was invaded, and Lanfranc was soon lecturing again, mainly now on sacred themes, to the youths of noble families, and even to schoolmasters from all parts of Christendom. The modest abbot Herluin was suddenly famous, and the name of Bec was everywhere on the tongues of men.

Anselm of Aosta was one of those who were drawn into this magic circle[2]. He was of a noble family, said even to be of royal descent;

---

[1] Gilbert does not give the story of Lanfranc's capture by robbers.

[2] For what follows, see Eadmer's Life of Anselm. Gilbert wrote in Anselm's lifetime, and hardly mentions him at all: see below, pp. 103, 108.

born in 1034, the year in which Herluin's monastic settlement began ;
a native of Aosta, a little town in a valley south of the Alps where
the provinces of Burgundy and Lombardy met. He was a gentle,
imaginative boy, who had been dedicated by his parents in his child-
hood to the service of God. And he dreamed one night that he
climbed the mountain side above his home and reached the heaven
which was so near to his early boyhood, and sat at the feet of the
Lord, and ate the whitest bread in the royal presence. He received
a good education, and wished to become a monk ; but in this desire
he was thwarted again and again. At length, when his pious mother
died, he started for the north with a few attendants, crossed Mt Cenis,
nearly losing his life in the snow ; and then after various wanderings
found himself, at the age of twenty-five, in Lanfranc's lecture-room at
Bec. For about two years he devoted himself to study, living outside
the monastery in such rude lodgings as Lanfranc's external students
were able to procure. It was a hard life, and his delicate frame
suffered much from hunger and cold. He had some thoughts of returning to Aosta, where his father had recently died, to live on his own
estate and serve the poor. Yet he could not abandon his old desire
to be a monk. But if this were his vocation, where was he to fulfil it ?
The austerity of Cluny attracted him, but he dared not hope that his
feeble health would stand its rigours. Why should he not enter the
monastery at Bec ? His life would not there be harder than it was
already outside. In later years he made the frank confession to a
friend that he had then so little of a monk's humility that he was
unwilling to settle where the ability of which he was conscious would
be permanently overshadowed by the greatness of Lanfranc, and that
he desired to find some place where he too should be a famous teacher.
Presently, however, his hesitation came to an end, and in 1060 he
became a monk of Bec. Three years afterwards the career which he
had denied to his ambition was unexpectedly opened to him by the
hand of providence. For in 1063 Lanfranc was appointed to preside
over William's new monastery of St Stephen at Caen, and Lanfranc's
office as prior of Bec was given to Anselm.

The abbey of Bec at this moment was literally in a state of tran-
sition. The number of monks had grown so large that their buildings
were totally inadequate. Moreover, Herluin's second site was humid
and unhealthy, and suffered from frequent inundations. Lanfranc had
accordingly urged him to build afresh on a larger scale higher up the
Bec. The old abbot refused, dreading the difficulties of another

removal; but the choir of his church collapsed, and at this sign from heaven he yielded.   Lanfranc's energy planned the undertaking and found the means of its accomplishment; for, though no charge was made for his teaching, gifts were accepted from his pupils, many of whom belonged to noble families.   Thus large sums were provided for the new building.   But Lanfranc's departure for Caen was a crushing blow.   He did what he could for Bec, while his own vast church was rising at Caen; but it was ten years before the monks could enter their new buildings, and the church was not consecrated until 1077.

Anselm was now the abbot's right hand, and besides his home duties as prior he had to do most of the abbot's work in the management of the estates, and in addition to take over the responsibility of the school.   He was not a Lanfranc.   He had neither the same physique nor the same capacity for public affairs.   He disliked whatever took him away from home; and home life was so crowded that he had no time for his own studies and none of the leisured calm which is necessary for speculative thought.

A monk's life at Bec was not easy or idle.   In some of the older and wealthier houses it may have been; for the rule was sometimes ill-kept, and bad customs had relaxed salutary discipline.   But Bec in its thirty years had run rapidly through the stages of monastic development, always keeping at the highest level.   It began with extreme poverty and hardship, the day divided between prayers in church and work in the fields, the abbot sleeping in the dormitory with his monks, rising with them at two in the morning for the night services, and then after a brief repose sharing with them the full labours of their day.   After ten years or more a new element was introduced when schools were opened under Lanfranc; and Herluin himself, though no scholar, urged learning with all his might on the younger men.   By this time a more elaborate code had become necessary to supplement the general outline of St Benedict's Rule, and the Customs of Bec were developed, doubtless by Lanfranc and Anselm together, on the basis of such regulations as were in force at Cluny and in other houses of high fame.   Though the early books of Bec perished at the French Revolution, we happily possess Lanfranc's statutes which he drew up for the monks of Christ Church, Canterbury, and which found their way into many of the English monasteries under the name of the Customs of Bec.   There we can read how full and strenuous the life was, and how great was the responsibility of the position which the young prior Anselm had suddenly been called to occupy[1].

Under the strain of his new tasks Anselm was beginning to break down. This was not the life which he had looked for when he became a monk. He would fain flee to some solitary hermitage. To Maurilius, the saintly archbishop of Rouen, at whose advice he had decided to enter Bec, he now went in his distress. The old archbishop was plain with him: 'Do not give up the service of others,' he said, 'to think only of yourself. I have known instances in which that has proved the ruin of a man's own soul. To save you from that, I command you in the name of holy obedience not to quit your post except at your abbot's orders; and, if you are called to a higher place still, not to refuse; for I know that such a call will come to you ere long.' So back he went, and for fifteen years he was prior, and then for fifteen more he was abbot of Bec[2].

Amongst the boys whom Anselm found when he first entered the monastery was a youth of about fifteen. His father, William Crispin, was a soldier of distinction belonging to one of the great Norman families, and holding a castle on the border between Normandy and France. William Crispin was devoted to Abbot Herluin, and he and his wife Eva had dedicated their son Gilbert to the service of God at Bec. The boy's name stands on the roll of monks nine places before that of Anselm, who only entered the monastic life in his twenty-seventh year. After the death of William Crispin the lady Eva came to live at Bec. She devoted herself to the religious life, and regarded the monks as her sons, bestowing all she had upon their church. Anselm, in one of his letters, tenderly speaks of her as his mother, and calls himself her eldest son[3]. We shall presently see with what intense affection he regarded his younger brother Gilbert.

When William had secured the throne of England, and began to set the Church in order, he wisely summoned Lanfranc to the see of Canterbury. It was with no readiness of will that Lanfranc left his abbey at Caen. He had quite lately refused the archbishopric of Rouen. He knew no English, and was loth to undertake the responsibility of a Church which seemed to him half barbarous. William,

---

[1] Lanfranc's statutes are printed in Reyner's *Apostolatus Benedictinorum* and in Wilkins' *Concilia*. For their manuscript tradition see *Journ. of Theol. Studies* (April, 1909). Large portions of their wording are embedded in the Westminster Customary of Abbot Ware.

[2] Eadmer (Rolls S.), p. 327.

[3] Anselm, *Epp.* ii 9.

however, insisted; and in 1070 Lanfranc was consecrated as archbishop, and became the king's chief counsellor in Church and State. It was well for us that he came; but his unwelcome task weighed so heavily upon him that three years later he wrote to Pope Alexander II, at whose express bidding he had undertaken it, begging for release. He said that distractions, troubles and losses, the obstinacy, greed and immorality of those with whom he had to do, had made him tired of life itself. He yearned for the quiet of the cloister, and he pleaded his usefulness as a teacher. He was doing no good to souls, he said, where he was, or very little if any at all. While William lived there would be some sort of peace, but after his death no peace or any good could be expected[1]. And yet this was the man who, in spite of his want of sympathy with English church life, did more than any other man in the next sixteen years to weld together, by his wisdom and his justice, the conquering and conquered peoples, and to lay the foundation in the Church, as William did in the State, of a new and united England. In this mission of reconciliation he was to be followed by Anselm, who, like himself, came from the Italian side of the Alps, and, as being neither Norman nor English, exercised a strange power over both races.

Lanfranc was visited at Canterbury by the aged Herluin, to whom he insisted on shewing the humble respect due from a monk to his abbot. 'The more crowded his court,' says Gilbert, 'and the more excellent the dignity of those who waited on him, so much the more humble service did Lanfranc render to Abbot Herluin, so that all marvelled, and the English more especially, that an archbishop of Canterbury should so submit himself to any mortal man.' A few years later Lanfranc revisited Bec in order to consecrate the church which many years before he had persuaded Herluin to build. This was in 1077, and the next year the abbot passed away at the age of eighty-three, and Anselm was made abbot in his place.

For fifteen years Anselm had been prior of Bec, and during that time he had lost some of his dearest and best companions and pupils, who had been drafted off by Lanfranc, first to Caen, and then to England. Gundulf had gone to Caen to be Lanfranc's prior, and afterwards to Rochester, where he succeeded another Bec monk as bishop. Henry became prior of Canterbury, and then abbot of Battle: Baldwin and Maurice became monks at Canterbury. Lanfranc could never be refused; and at last he sent for Gilbert Crispin, whom Anselm dearly

---

[1] Lanfranc, *Ep.* 1.

loved, and probably regarded as the most likely man to carry on his work in the future at Bec.

Our first glimpse of Gilbert comes at an earlier date, in a letter which Lanfranc addressed to him about the year 1074, commending his nephew and namesake, whom he had brought from Italy and placed under Anselm's charge at Bec[1]. This younger Lanfranc was wilful, and destined to give Anselm much pain. The archbishop is anxious about him, and urges Gilbert, who is to be his teacher, to shew him a brother's love, and the more so because the Lady Eva, Gilbert's mother, has been good enough to call him her son. Lanfranc also sends Gilbert a cross, which he may set on the altar when he celebrates the holy eucharist, to be a sign and token between the two young men[2].

About six years after this, when Gilbert was some thirty-four years of age, Lanfranc sent for him to help him at Canterbury, and Anselm's correspondence reveals the pain that this new loss inflicted. 'With regard to Dom Gilbert,' he writes, 'I have obeyed your command that I should send him to you: but be assured that if anyone should cause him to remain in England he will inflict a graver loss on the church of Bec in the present and for the future, in its internal and external interests alike, than can easily be put into words. So I pray and beseech you, as earnestly as is consistent with what is right and respectful to yourself, pleading the kindness and love which I know you have for me, that if without going against God's will you see it to be at all possible, you will do your very utmost to secure his return[3].'

Later he writes to Gilbert himself, who has sent him some presents from Canterbury: 'Sweet are the gifts, sweet friend, which your sweet love sends; but they are utterly powerless to console my heart, which is desolated by your absence. No, not if you sent me all the most fragrant spices, the most glittering metals, the most precious stones, the most delicate embroidery, could my soul consent to be comforted, for it is quite beyond its power, unless its other half which has been torn away be given back to it again. My heart's pain bears me witness as I think of this; so do the tears which cloud my eyes and wet my fingers as I write. You knew indeed, as I knew, my love for you; nay, I knew it not myself. He who has torn us apart has taught me how

---

[1] Cf. Lanfranc, *Ep.* 43, to Anselm while still prior of Bec.

[2] Lanfranc, *Ep.* 45. This letter is addressed to 'G.,' which D'Achery, though not without hesitation, expands as 'Gundulfo.' But Gundulf had left Bec with Lanfranc: moreover the 'G.' here addressed came to Bec as a boy and is still 'in juventute'; and the reference to his mother makes it certain that Gilbert Crispin is intended.

[3] Anselm, *Epp.* II 13.

much I loved you. No one has real knowledge of good or evil who does not experience both. Without experience of your absence I did not know how sweet it was to me to be with you, how bitter to be without you. To you our very separation has given the presence of another, whom you love not less, yea more, than me; but I have lost you—you, I say; and none has been given me in your place[1].'

So the letter runs on to its close, revealing the pain and suffering which is so near to the purest love. And that this was no mere selfish affection is shewn by the letter Anselm writes a few years afterwards, when the separation was made permanent by Gilbert's appointment to the abbey of Westminster.

'.To Gilbert, once by God's providence his dearest son, now by God's grace his fellow abbot, brother Anselm wishes a long, holy and prosperous life here, and everlasting happiness hereafter. Though sickness has made me behindhand in writing to my loved and loving friend about the new grace granted him by God, yet it is with no lukewarmness, but with the heartiest goodwill, that I say "Glory to God in the highest," who has revealed His purpose for you which hitherto He has kept dark, although indeed I always believed that good things, as men count them, were in store for you. For in that same life of devotion in which He has preserved you, training you in wisdom and nurturing you in holiness, He has now made you a father and a teacher and a shepherd of souls.' Then, with a charming modesty and self-distrust, he goes on to say: 'Far better things may be hoped of you and the like of you, whose life has been nurtured in holy surroundings, than of me and the like of me, whose life was at one time wasted in the world. For of you it is to be hoped that, in training others to be like yourself, your own holiness will be perfected; whereas it is to be feared, when we are loaded with such a burden, that our unholiness by God's inscrutable judgment will be increased. The better our hope, then, in your accession to office, the greater and surer our rejoicing in the grace that is granted to you. May God Almighty, who has made you the keeper of others, so help and keep you that He may reward your holiness and theirs with His eternal blessing[2].'

A later letter manifests the same affection, and gives a playful account of an attack of fever which Anselm had just shaken off.

'Brother Anselm to abbot Gilbert, a servant to his lord, a friend to his friend, a lover to his lover—wishing him unending joy. If health

---

[1] Anselm, *Epp.* I 75; written when Gilbert was with Lanfranc, c. 1080.
[2] Anselm, *Epp.* II 16; written soon after Gilbert's appointment in 1085.

and welfare and prosperity be the lot of my lord abbot Gilbert, who loves me and whom I love, then indeed my heart rejoices, for my longing is fulfilled. If the kind benefactions which you bestow on us were bestowed by a stranger upon strangers, we should make a great display of gratitude lest the supply should run short. But seeing that they come from him of whom we never could have a doubt, we are content to hide our chief thanks, though ever ready to express them, in the strong-room of our heart. I know your love will want to know how I am doing. By God's protecting mercy, within my usual limits and considering these changeful times, all would have been well and prosperous, but that when I was in France, somewhat burdened by various tasks, a slight fever suddenly attacked me, frightening me more than it hurt me. But when it saw that my mind was firmly made up to send round to all my friends for the help of their prayers, after a second attack it fled just as frightened as I was. For some time since I have suffered from a distaste of food, and a difficulty in sleeping, and a general weakness in my limbs. I greet with all possible devotion, my lords and brothers, your most dear sons [the monks of Westminster], in whose kindness which takes so practical a form I rejoice as often as I think of it.'

The letter goes on to plead that Gilbert will shew indulgence to his servant Richard, who by his orders had followed him to England, and had evidently got into some trouble, but was penitent and should be restored to favour[1].

The scattered notices preserved in charters or chronicles, from which for the most part the lives of our abbots have to be compiled, give us no insight at all into the spiritual side of their character or the success with which they achieved for themselves and for others the lofty aims of a true monasticism. Gilbert Crispin offers a happy exception to the rule. We know at least what his own training was like, and how truly devotional was the atmosphere in which his youth and early manhood were spent. The devout Herluin, the wise Lanfranc and the gentle Anselm[2]—each had left his mark on the young monk, and helped to prepare him for the difficult task of maintaining the noble ideals of Bec in the wholly dissimilar surroundings of royal

---

[1] Anselm, *Epp.* ii 47. A similar account of his fever is written to Abbot Gilbert of St Stephen's at Caen: from this we learn that Anselm was returning from Caen and hoping to reach Bec before the feast of St Benedict (that is, probably, 11 July, the Translation), but was delayed by business in France (ii 44).

[2] See below, p. 26.

Westminster. The curtain of which a corner has been lifted soon falls again, and though his other writings give us an occasional glimpse of Abbot Gilbert's character and methods and reflect the spirit of his old home, we have little else to assure us that St Anselm's high hopes of his beloved pupil were not unrealised. We have to content ourselves with piecing together isolated facts and jejune references. But it is something to have caught sight of the real man, and to have learned what at any rate he must have wished Westminster to be.

## II. THE NOBLE FAMILY OF THE CRISPINS.

In writing on one occasion from Bec to his uncles at Aosta, Anselm mentions that the bearer of his letter is a son of William Crispin. This was a brother of the future abbot of Westminster, and it is interesting to note the terms in which Anselm refers to him and his family. 'He is rich, and of the first nobility of Normandy: yet his mother and brothers are so intimate with me, that his mother calls me her son, and her children call me their brother—only they say, elder brother[1].'

In tracing the history of this family, more than one of whom found a home in England, we are fortunate in possessing a curious document entitled, 'The Miracle whereby Blessed Mary succoured William Crispin senior: wherein is an account of the noble family of the Crispins.' It is printed by Luc d'Achery in his appendix to Lanfranc's works: it comes immediately after Milo Crispin's Lives of the Abbots of Bec, and is probably written by Milo Crispin himself, of whom we shall speak lower down[2].

The first of the name, says the writer, was Gilbert, called Crispin from the fashion of his hair, which stood on end—a feature which he transmitted to his descendants, who are still distinguished from other Norman families both by this peculiarity and by the surname to which it gave rise[3]. The Crispini, he assures us, were as famous among the Normans as were the Fabii and the Manlii among the Romans. With the aid of his rambling narrative we may at once construct a

---

[1] Anselm, *Epp.* I 18.

[2] *Lanfranci Opera*, App. p. 52: 'Miraculum quo,' &c.

[3] 'Antequam Normanni duce Willelmo Angliam debellarent, fuit in Neustria (quae nunc Normannia vocatur) vir egregius nomine Gislebertus, genere et nobilitate praeclarus, qui ab habitudine capillorum primus *Crispini* cognomine dicitur insignitus: nam in sua primaeva aetate habebat capillos crispos et rigidos atque sursum erectos, et (ut ita dicam) rebursos ad modum pini ramorum, qui semper tendunt sursum; quare cognominatus est Crispinus, quasi *crispus pinus*: quam capillorum rebursionem adhuc videmus in iis qui de ipsius Gisleberti genere descendunt, unde et ipsi eodem cognomine a caeteris Normannorum familiis dirimuntur.'

genealogical table, and afterwards we may comment on individual names.

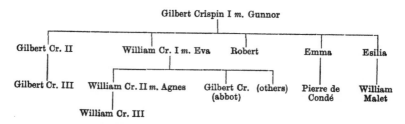

1. Gilbert Crispin I married Gunnor, the sister of Fulc d'Alnou. This is of interest as shewing the connexion of the Crispins with several Norman families of note. For Fulc's father was Baldric, who had come from Germany to serve under Duke Richard; and his mother was a niece of Gilbert count of Brionne, the over-lord of Herluin abbot of Bec. Among Fulc's brothers were Robert de Courcy and Baldric de Bocquencé (Ord. Vit. III 75).

2. In the next generation there were three sons and two daughters. The eldest son, Gilbert Crispin II, was keeper of the castle of Tillières; the youngest, Robert, died at Constantinople: of the daughters, Emma became the mother of Pierre de Condé, and Esilia of William Malet, one of the Conqueror's great men, who ended his life as a monk at Bec[1].

But the second son, William Crispin I, achieved the highest fame. Duke William had entrusted him with the castle of Neaufles, in order to check the incursions of Gautier le Vieux, count of Pontoise, who threatened the Norman Vexin. This castle passed from father to son, 'sicut usque hodie videmus,' says the writer of the *Miraculum*[2]. William Crispin was devoted to the abbey of Bec; and whenever he travelled from Neaufles to attend to his property near Lisieux ('in Lexoviensi pago') he never failed, both going and returning, to visit Abbot Herluin. One day, after parting from the abbot as usual, he suddenly

---

[1] 'Esiliam, matrem Willelmi Malet, qui miles strenuus in senectute factus est monachus Becci,' &c., *Miraculum*, p. 53. Mr C. E. Mallet in *Dict. Nat. Biogr.* speaks of 'Hesilia Crispin' as wife of W. Malet, and supposes, after Freeman, that he died in the campaign against Hereward in 1071 : but this supposition has been challenged.

[2] For 'Melfia' must be read 'Nielfia' or 'Neelfia.' 'Neaufles, canton de Gisors, arrondissement des Andelys. Il subsiste encore à Neaufles la moitié d'un château ou donjon bâti au XII° siècle' (Porée, *Hist. du Bec*, I 179).

returned to ask his blessing and the special prayers of the brethren. At the end of his journey, when he was close to his castle, the French sprang out of an ambush in the wood: his companions fled from their attack. He leapt from his horse and sat on the root of a felled tree. The Virgin appeared in answer to his prayers, and throwing the sleeve of her garment over him rendered him invisible to his enemies. His love for St Mary of Bec vastly increased, and it became hereditary in his family. On his death-bed he sent for Abbot Herluin. Before he could arrive, the brave soldier was troubled by demons; but he had a vision of St Benedict who drove them away. This was related by Herluin and his monk William, who was subsequently abbot of Cormeilles: for they arrived immediately afterwards, and had it from his own lips. He was then clothed as a monk, and dying a few days later was buried near the church of Bec, where the cloister was about to be built. His death seems to have taken place on 8 Jan. 1074[1].

Such was Abbot Gilbert's father. His mother was a French woman, Eva de Montfort, sister of Amaury III, lord of Montfort l'Amaury, a stronghold halfway between Paris and Chartres, from which in later days the famous Simon earl of Leicester had his name. She shared to the full her husband's love for Bec, where their son Gilbert had been dedicated at an early age; regarding all the monks as if they were her children, and giving precious vestments and ornaments for the service of the church. When her husband died, she made Bec her home, adopting an ascetic life. At length she received the veil from William the archbishop of Rouen. Two other ladies shared her retirement ('dederunt se in subjectionem Becci') under the rule of Abbot Anselm: Basilia, the wife of Hugh de Gournay, who himself ended his days as a monk of Bec, and Amfrida her niece. Anselm refers to these ladies several times, in letters written when he was absent from Bec: he speaks of himself as the Lady Eva's eldest son[2]. By a strange coincidence the three ladies died on three Sundays in January 1099, the 2nd, 16th, and 23rd days of the month[3]. The Lady Eva was the

---

[1] 'The year of William Crispin's death is ascertained from the *Nomina Monachorum*, the month and day from an extract from the necrology of Beaumont-le-Roger in the National Library at Paris (Latin, 13905). This document has under "Januarius, 6 idus o[biit] I$^{us}$ (i.e. primus) Will. Crispinus monachus nostrae congregationis."' M. Rule, *Anselm* i 226 n.

[2] Anselm, *Epp.* ii 9 'Mandate matri et dominae nostrae Evae quod de filio suo primogenito vobiscum audire pari desiderio expectat,' &c. This was in 1079. See also *Epp.* ii 26 and 51, iii 138 and the quotation made above (p. 13) from *Epp.* i 18.

[3] The year is fixed by the Sundays: the only other likely year, 1093, is shewn to be too early by Anselm, *Epp.* ii 51 and iii 138.

last to go: she was worn out with age and fasting. Carried into the church on St Vincent's Day (22nd Jan.), she was anointed before the altar of the Crucifix; and, as the convent withdrew, she raised her hand and made the sign of the cross over them, saying: 'My sons, I commend you to God.' The writer of the narrative adds: 'for she loved us as tenderly as if we had been her own children.' She passed away in the following night, and she was laid to rest near her husband. Brother Rodulphus, we are told, had asked her if possible to appear to him after death: she did so a few days later, and explained that she had been assigned sixty years of penance, because she had been over-fond of pet dogs and other trifles[1].

3. We come now to the third generation, to which Abbot Gilbert himself belonged. Of his brothers one only is known to us, William Crispin II[2]. Like his father he was a benefactor of Bec, and shortly after the Conqueror's death we find him at the court of Duke Robert, fiercely threatening to withdraw the gifts of his family, if the abbey should be allowed to pass into the hands of Robert of Meulan, who was claiming it as an appanage of Brionne[3]. He married Agnes, daughter of Godfrey d'Etrépagny. He took Duke Robert's side against K. Henry, and was taken prisoner at Tenchebrai in 1106. Henry in the letter in which he announced his victory to Anselm names William Crispin among his principal captives[4]. A little later he conspired with Robert of Belesme, and in 1112, according to the A. S. Chronicle, he was driven out of Normandy. A story is told of his striking K. Henry on the casque at the battle of Brémule in 1119, whereupon he was overpowered and taken prisoner by Roger fitz Richard[5]. But it is hard to believe that this William Crispin was the brother of Abbot Gilbert,

---

[1] 'Quia parvos canes et alia hujusmodi varia, quae homines pro nihilo ducunt, amavi, et ultra modum in iis delectata sum: ideo talem paenitentiam accepi' (D'Achery, *App. to Lanfranc's Works*, p. 5). The narrative is found in the Vatican MS 'no. 499, du fonds de la reine de Suède,' and in the Paris transcript of this, Bibl. Nat. lat. 5427 (Porée, *Hist. du Bec*, I 184).

[2] It is probably he who witnesses a charter (c. 1082?), in which the Conqueror grants to St Stephen's at Caen 'in Lundonia quamdam terram quae fuit Leureth, sitam prope ecclesiam sancti Petri, quietam de gelth et de scot et de omni alia consuetudine; quam dedit Wallerannus filius Ranulfi, cum decima totius terrae suae quam habet in Anglia, tam pro anima sua quam pro mea' (*Gall. Christ.* XI, instr. 67: described as 'sitam in Wodestrata prope ecclesiam sancti Petri,' in a St Stephen's chartulary, quoted by Palgrave *Eng. Commonwealth* II clxxxi).

[3] For references to the incident, see Porée, *Hist. du Bec*, I 194 ff.

[4] Eadmer, *Hist. Nov.* Rolls S. p. 184.

[5] Porée, *ut supra* 196, where references are given.

who had died two years before at the age of seventy at least. Possibly William Crispin III was the audacious hero of this fight.

4. William Crispin III fought with Geoffrey Plantagenet, count of Anjou, against Robert de Sablé who was in revolt in Dec. 1135. He was saved at this battle, so the *Miraculum* informs us, by St Mary of Bec. Afterwards he was taken prisoner, and on his release, just as he was about to start for Jerusalem in fulfilment of a vow, he died and was buried near his ancestors at Bec.

Milo Crispin, who held lands in England at the time of the Survey, chiefly in Oxfordshire, was probably the cousin of Abbot Gilbert, and the son of Gilbert Crispin II, who according to Wace's *Roman de Rou* took part in the Conquest[1]. Milo attests the Bec charter of the Conqueror (c. 1077, Porée *ibid.* I 645), though he does not appear in it as a donor. In a charter of Henry II, however, which confirms ancient grants, we find that he had given to Bec both Swyncombe (Oxon.) and also tithes at Wallingford (Porée, II 574): 'et de dono Milonis Crispini Swinecumbam et decimam de dominico de honore de Walingforde.' The Honor of Wallingford came to him through marriage with Matilda, daughter of Robert de Oleio[2]. In the *History of Abingdon* we read of 'Milo de Walingaford cognomento Crispin,' as keeping Easter with Prince Henry at Abingdon in 1084[3]. He died in 1107. Shortly before his death, in recognition of the medical services of the famous abbot of Abingdon, he gave to that abbey a hospice on their road to London[4]. He appears as attesting two charters of William Rufus to Abbot Gilbert, and also Abbot Gilbert's grant of the manor of Hendon to Gunter and his heirs. The last of these cannot be later than 1102; for in that year Robert the prior, who also attests, was appointed abbot of St Edmund's[5]. It is possible that all three belong to one date, and

[1] Porée, *ibid.* I 179. This is probably the Gilbert Crispin who attests the charter of H. Trin. Caen (1082): see *Gall. Chr.* XI, instr. 72.

[2] Dugdale, *Baronage* I 460.

[3] *Hist. Abingd.* Rolls S. II 12.

[4] *Ibid.* 97: 'Milo Crispin, pro servitio quod abbas Faritius ei in sua infirmitate impenderat, dedit in eleemosynam ecclesiae sanctae Mariae et monachis de Abbendonia quoddam hospitium in via Lundoniae apud Colebroc'...anno videlicet vii Henrici regis.' His wife Matilda is mentioned as concurring in the benefaction (*ibid.* 110). He was also a benefactor to Evesham : 'Milo Crispin dedit dimidiam hidam in Hildendone' (*Chron. Evesh.* Rolls S. 75).

[5] These charters are printed below (nos. 11—13). He attests a charter of Will. I to Lewes Priory, *Monast.* v 13 (orig. in *Cotton* Vesp. F, iii, art. 1).

Milo may have been staying at the time with his kinsman the abbot of Westminster.

Another Milo Crispin was the precentor of Bec who compiled the Life of Lanfranc, and also wrote the lives of several of the abbots of Bec. It would seem from the list of Bec monks that he entered the monastery just after Anselm had ceased to be abbot[1]: but he had seen the great archbishop on one of his visits to his old home[2]. He died about 1150[3].

In conclusion we may mention an interesting charter, in which Goscelin Crispin recites and, with the assent of his little son William, confirms the grants of his ancestors the three William Crispins: it is given at Bec in 1155[4].

I find the name of 'Fulco Crispinus' as the last witness to the Bath Charter of 1090[5]: and the name of 'Gislebertus Crispinus' entered on the Bec roll c. 1112[6].

[1] Porée i 631.

[2] *Vita Lanfranci* c. xiv (D'Achery, p. 15): 'Hoc beato Anselmo archipraesule referente cum aliis pluribus audivi.'

[3] Porée i 105, 532.                                  [4] Printed by Porée, i 656.

[5] *Bath Chartularies* [Som. Rec. Soc.] i, no. 37.

[6] Porée i 632.

## III. Gilbert at Westminster.

It is not always easy to date Anselm's letters, but it seems likely that Gilbert must have gone to Canterbury at the close of the year 1079, shortly after Anselm's return from his first visit to England. Of the time which he spent in Lanfranc's service we know nothing; but that he had proved his worth we may conclude from the fact that it was at Lanfranc's instigation that the king appointed him to Westminster[1].

The date of his appointment to Westminster cannot be fixed with certainty. There is good evidence for placing his death in 1117; and, if we may trust the writer of the *Miraculum*, he was abbot for thirty-two years. This would give us 1085 as the year of his accession: and with this as a provisional date we must at present be content[2].

[1] Flete (p. 86), quoting from a Bec document, the *Miraculum* alluded to above, says: 'ut...eum Lanfrancus ad regimen Westmonasterii provideret.' Hugh the precentor of York introduces Gilbert into an absurd story about the famous Canterbury Privilege of 1072, which he says was a forged document, issued in many copies to which the royal seal had been fraudulently affixed. The king as he was crossing to Normandy for the last time (1086) was told of this in the Isle of Wight, and repudiated the document, saying that he would do justice between the two archbishops on his return, which never took place: 'hoc plures audierunt, inter quos et Rannulphus qui nunc usque superest [†1128] Dunelmensis episcopus, tunc quidem capellanus et custos sigilli regis sub Mauricio cancellario postea Londoniensi episcopo, et Gillebertus Crispinus monachus L. archiepiscopi, postea abbas Westmonasterii; qui ambo coram multis edixerunt, et si quis dubitaret jurare parati, cartam sic confirmatam fuisse, et regem sicut predictum est inde respondisse; et quod ipse rex Gilleberto Crispino, nobili genere monacho, preceperat ut hoc testimonium Eboracensi ecclesiae perhiberet, quicquid de ipso contingeret' (*Historians of York*, II 102 f.). The same charge is repeated on behalf of Thomas II of York to K. Henry I; and of Gilbert it is said: 'iste tunc temporis Lanfranci archiepiscopi monachus et familiaris erat' (p. 122). The story is interesting for the light it throws on Gilbert's position: but it is full of contradictions. Gilbert was abbot before 1086; he was not in England at the time of the controversy in 1072. In the second passage Ranulf and Gilbert are accused of being parties to the forgery, and the king indignantly replies that they are not men of whom such things could be believed.

[2] Flete brings him in two years earlier, and puts his death in 1115: and a charter (printed below, p. 38) would confirm this, if we could trust the late copy which alone is preserved of it. But there are difficulties also as to the year of his predecessor's death: see my edition of Flete's *History*, p. 141 f.

The Conqueror's reign was nearing its close. The great Domesday Survey was being made when the new abbot was fresh in his seat; and he doubtless attended the meeting at Salisbury on 1 August, 1086, and took the oath to be King William's man against all his enemies. Later in the same year the king left England for the last time. On 26 September, 1087, Gilbert must have helped his old master, the aged Lanfranc, to crown William Rufus, and have heard the welcome pledge which the new king gave that in all matters he would be guided by the archbishop's advice. The pledge was quickly broken—'Who can keep all his promises?'—and on 24 May, 1089, the primate was released by death from his thankless responsibility. For the next four years the see of Canterbury was left unfilled, and the Red King drew its revenues. It was well for Westminster that a young and vigorous abbot had recently been appointed: for otherwise it would have shared the miserable fate of the eleven abbeys which as they fell vacant were kept in the king's hands.

It is possible that before the end of 1086 Gilbert may have received a visit from Abbot Anselm: for a charter granted to him by William (possibly the Conqueror) has for its first witness 'abbas Beccensis[1].' At any rate in the beginning of 1093 Anselm was at Westminster. In a letter written to Baldric his prior at Bec he commends its bearer, 'a monk of the lord abbot Gilbert, whom I would have you receive with special kindness.' He will tell them, he says, more than can be put into writing. They must know that the king still delays to respond to his request (probably for a confirmation of the English estates of Bec), though both he and all the nobles shew him love and honour beyond anything he could expect. He cannot, he says, now hope to return before Lent[2]. This was written just before the king's sudden illness and short-lived repentance. Anselm, as it proved, was not to return to Bec, until he came as the exiled archbishop of Canterbury. On the first Sunday in that very Lent (6 March, 1093), the pastoral staff was thrust between his resisting fingers, and after vain endeavours to regain his freedom he allowed himself at last to be enthroned at Canterbury on 25 September. He left England in October, 1097, and did not come back until after the Red King's death.

In the meantime Gilbert's devoted mother, the Lady Eva, died, as we have seen, at Bec on 21 Jan. 1099. The next year Gilbert was at the Easter court at Winchester, where he witnessed the king's charter

[1] Printed below, no. 17. Probably, however, it should be assigned to 1093.
[2] Anselm, *Epp.* II 51.

to the monastery of Evesham[1]. That same year brought Henry's hurried coronation in the abbey, performed by the bishop of London on 5 August, 1100. Anselm's return soon followed.

At Michaelmas, 1102, Anselm held a council at Westminster with a view to the enforcement of reforms in the Church. A canon was passed against clerical marriages, and several abbots were deposed for simony and other causes[2]. A strange scene is recorded as having taken place before the session of the council. Gerard the archbishop of York had come; but, as Hugh the precentor of York relates, 'the monks having prepared for their archbishop a seat singularly high, Gerard was wroth, and, publicly invoking God's hate on him who had so set it up, he kicked it over, nor would sit down till a seat of equal dignity had been prepared for him; desiring to make it perfectly plain that he owed him no subjection[3].' This was an inherited quarrel, and Gerard was a passionate Norman, the kinsman of our Norman kings who frequently were carried away by uncontrollable anger. Seventy years later St Catharine's chapel in the infirmary witnessed a yet more distressing episode of the same struggle.

Six months after this council Anselm's difficulties with the new king led him to leave the country again, and he did not return till towards the end of 1106. The king meantime had seized the revenues of the archbishopric, and in other ways had pressed hardly upon the church— so hardly, indeed, that Gerard and several of the principal bishops, who had hitherto refused to support Anselm, wrote earnestly intreating him to come back. The question of the Investitures was not a simple one, and the minds of English churchmen were seriously divided upon it. The time-honoured customs of England pointed one way: the recent legislation of councils, anxious to secure the Church against simoniacal appointments, pointed the other way. We should have been glad to know what a quiet and thoughtful churchman like Abbot Gilbert felt about the merits of the controversy. The question had not

---

[1] 'In quarta feria Paschae,' *Chron. Evesh.* Rolls S. p. xlix. He had witnessed the charter of Lincoln, sometime previous to Sept. 1090 (*Linc. Cath. Stat.*, Bradshaw and Wordsworth, II 5).

[2] This is the 'Council of London,' held (as Anselm says) 'in ecclesia beati Petri in occidentali parte juxta Lundoniam sita' (Eadmer, *Hist. Nov.* Rolls S. p. 141).

[3] 'Postea placuit Anselmo et Girardo archiepiscopis concilium celebrare: quo in Westmonasterio congregato, cum monachi archiepiscopo suo sedem singulariter celsam parassent, Girardus indignatus, et dei odium ei qui sic paraverat vulgariter orans, pede subvertit, nec sedere voluit donec sibi cum archiepiscopo sede pari parata, liquido volens ostendere ei nullam subjectionem debere' (Hugo Cantor, Rolls S. p. 110).

arisen for England when he received his pastoral staff from the Conqueror; and the matter had therefore no practical bearing for himself. But from his central position he was able to see the disaster which the prolongation of the controversy was bringing on the Church: and we are fortunate in possessing a copy of verses addressed to Anselm, in which he deliberately warns him of the perilous responsibility which he is incurring by his continued absence. They are an instructive comment on the situation, coming as they do from one of Anselm's most devoted sons[1].

> The tuneful pipe that loved to chant your praise
> Is hoarse and mournful now. Shepherd, it cries,
> Why is the Shepherd absent from the fold?
> The flock is wandering leaderless astray:
> None brings it back. Pastures it vainly seeks,
> And knowing not its good takes hurtful food:
> Wherefore 'tis wholly sick and near to die.
>
> The cunning foe creeps round, and sees the fold
> Abandoned: enters here and goes out there
> Unhindered, finding none to drive him back
> Or check the full glut of his wolfish rage.
>
> He scatters all, and all are slain—fat, lean,
> And old and young. The appetite of wolves
> What can abate? One wolf will count too few
> A thousand thousand sheep: when many come,
> See how the abandoned fold is given to death!
>
> I say, their Master will demand them back:
> Who asks not back what he has given in charge?
> I say, these sheep 'tis you who must restore
> To whom they were committed: none disputes
> Recovery of a trust: therefore beware!
>
> Oh, many a thousand, trusted to your care
> And lost, He asks again. All England first—
> How great a multitude: all Scotland next;
> And then that further distant island, where
> The populous Irish dwell. These ample realms,
> When were they visited? None visits them:
> A year, nay years have passed. Therefore beware!

We know from Boso's language in the opening of the *Cur Deus homo* what liberty of speech Anselm had encouraged in his pupils at Bec. But this is plain speaking indeed; and it must have wrung his

---

[1] For the text see below, p. 83.

tender heart more than any of the remonstrances that reached him from other quarters[1].

The controversy ended at last with an English compromise. The king should no longer give the staff, the symbol of a spiritual responsibility: but the bishops and abbots should still do homage for their temporal possessions.

On Sunday, 11 Aug. 1107, Anselm consecrated five bishops at Canterbury: and a few days later Robert, Gilbert's former prior, was blessed as abbot of St Edmund's. The new abbot of St Augustine's was deferred, as he was not yet ordained. He would have been blessed shortly after Christmas, but that he demanded that the ceremony should take place in his own church. When Anselm was near London ('juxta Lundoniam') at the beginning of Lent, the monks of St Augustine's persuaded the king to command the archbishop to consecrate Hugh in his own monastery. A deputation was sent by the king to urge Anselm to consent. It consisted of the bishops of Winchester, Sarum and Exeter, together with Gilbert the abbot of Westminster[2]. Anselm would not yield the point; and in the end he consecrated Hugh at Lambeth on 27 Feb. 1108. This is the last occasion on which we see the master and the pupil together: on 27 April, 1109 the saintly archbishop passed away at Canterbury.

Gilbert had dedicated to him three of his works: the famous Disputation with a Jew, and the treatises on Simony and on the Holy Spirit. Each dedicatory letter is addressed to Anselm as archbishop, but none makes reference to his troubles or his absence[3].

We have anticipated the course of events in order to complete the story of Gilbert's relations with Anselm; and we must now return to consider a notable incident of the year 1102. It is recorded by Ailred the abbot of Rievaulx in the Life of St Edward which he drew up by request of Abbot Laurence on the occasion of the canonisation or the translation of the king (1161, or 1163). But Ailred was merely recasting the earlier Life which Osbert the prior had written in 1138;

---

[1] Anselm, *Ep.* III 121. The pressure which was put upon Anselm at this time to return is fully described by Eadmer, who quotes some striking letters of remonstrance (*Hist. Nov.* pp. 159—168).

[2] 'Hujus mandati Willelmus episcopus Wintoniensis et Rogerius Serberiensis et Willelmus Exoniensis, cum Gisleberto abbate Westmonasterii, a rege ad Anselmum nuncii fuerunt' (Eadmer, *Hist. Nov.* p. 189).

[3] The years in which he was in England are 1093—1097, 1100 (Sept.)—1103 (April), 1107—1109 : to the first two periods the dedications most probably belong.

and, as this Life has not yet been printed, I have here translated the following passage, which is in fact our ultimate authority for the story of the opening of the Confessor's tomb in 1102[1].

Inasmuch as it hath pleased our Lord God to disclose to many mortal eyes the fair beauty which adorned this sacred Prince in the flesh, his temporal glory is sufficiently attested by that holy company who on the day of his translation found the king's body whole and incorrupt. Gilbert the lord abbot, whose patronymic was Crispinus, had called to the great solemnity many men of note, chief among whom was Gundulf the venerable prelate of Rochester. Six and thirty years had King Edward lain in the tomb, and many thought that like other men he had fallen to ashes after our common mortal lot. But some there were whose loving thoughts gave them a holy presentiment of somewhat divine attending one whose limbs had never known the loss of virgin purity, and whose body they could not doubt remained in a kind of resurrection glory. Other devout religious men were moved by a great longing to look upon his face, men who had seen his beloved countenance while he yet lived in the flesh. For in his service they had been enrolled, and therefore burned the more ardently in this holy purpose, that with their very eyes they might behold him after so long a time in the tomb.

So then the upper stone is lifted from the sarcophagus, and his glorious body is found wrapt in a costly robe : slender hands and flexible joints, the finger with its royal ring, the sandals—all are plainly seen to shew no sign of corruption : the sceptre at his side, the crown upon his head, all the regal ornaments of his noble burial are shewn uninjured by the touch of time. So firm and bright was the flesh, so perfect all the garments, that their soundness told that God in truth was magnified in Edward, setting forth in his flesh an image of the resurrection of the saints.

So great fear fell on all, that none could dare uncover the king's veiled countenance, nor disclose on any side the face they longed to see. One man alone, God's holy and righteous bishop Gundulf, was so kindled with the flame of yearning love as to cleave the covering beneath the chin, draw out the beard and arrange it in comely wise betwixt his hands. Then, when he felt it firm set in the flesh, was this great man astonished at the strange miracle. But yet he essayed to draw gently forth a single hair, if perchance it might yield to his touch, that so of the relics of the holy king he might thus be allowed an abundant enrichment.

But as the lord abbot Gilbert stood and watched, 'What is this,' he cried, 'good bishop, that thou dost? In the land of the living he hath attained an eternal inheritance with the saints of God : wherefore then dost thou seek to diminish his share of temporal glory? Cease, honoured Sir, so to presume : vex not the king in his royal bed.' Then was Gundulf wholly resolved in tears, and said, 'Venerable abbot, thou hast spoken aright. Yet know that not any bold presumption sped me to this deed. The flame of holy devotion, wherewith I burned for love of the glorious king, urged me to take but one hair of that snowy beard, to keep it with solemn reverence in his memory as a treasure more precious than gold. But since my hope is gone, and my wish could not be granted, let him keep his own by his own right in peace. Let him rest in his palace, virgin and incorrupt, till with

---

[1] Brit. Mus. Add. ms 36,737, f. 156 b.

triumphant joy he shall meet the advent of the Judge, and receive in this his flesh the abiding glory of a blessed immortality.'

In the tomb therefore they shut that sacred body, which they had found in its solid perfection, and from whence already such fragrant odours had exhaled as to fill with sweetness the whole house of God.

The florid magnificence of Osbert's style need not make us distrust entirely the tradition which he records. It is probable that the tomb was opened, though the motives of curiosity or affection are insufficient to account for the disturbance of the royal remains. The rubric which heads the chapter speaks of this as 'the first translation' of the saintly king; and though this may not come from Osbert's pen, yet he does use the word 'translation' in his first sentence; so that it is possible that a new shrine may have been made, or the tomb may have been moved to some position more suitable for one who was already working miracles of healing. It would seem that Anselm was not present: possibly our date is incorrect, and he may have been out of England at the time. But no one had a higher reputation for holiness than Gundulf, Anselm's bosom friend at Bec, who had been twenty-five years at Rochester and had known Gilbert for more than forty years.

Gundulf's rash act is explained when we remember that a bishop who presided over the translation of a saint carried off as his due some fragment of his body to add to the store of his church's relics. We may here recall a story of Archbishop Thomas who translated our saint in 1163: for it seems to have escaped attention, and it illustrates the common practice[1]. Whereas the archbishop's due was the saint's right arm, St Thomas preferred to take the stone which covered his coffin. Nor need we wonder at his choice. For his conflict with the king had well begun, and this stone was the memorial of an earlier struggle. Had it not received and held the staff of Wulstan when he had refused to yield it at the Conqueror's bidding? The stone, then, went to Canterbury, and for many years it stood by the tomb of the martyred prelate; until at length, when King Henry IV made a chapel of St Edward in the cathedral, it was used for the altar slab. Once more St Edward was left to us intact, escaping the common lot of saints— partly perhaps because he was a king.

There are no further incidents of general interest to record of Gilbert's tenure of the abbacy, save that on 19 Sept. 1115 a bishop was for the first time consecrated within the abbey walls. At a later date St Catharine's chapel in the infirmary saw many such consecra-

---

[1] Continuator of Gervase of Canterbury's *Gesta Regum*, Rolls S. II 285.

tions: but in these earlier days the archbishops were peculiarly tenacious of their right to bring the bishop-elect to Canterbury, or at least to some chapel of their own. Ralph was no less jealous on this point than Anselm had been, and it was only because he was the chaplain of the good Queen Maud, and because she specially desired to be present, that Bernard, the bishop of St David's, received his consecration in the abbey church[1].

Gilbert died on 6 Dec. 1117, and he was laid in the south cloister close to his predecessor. The grave of Vitalis was marked by a plain flat stone, on which year by year a carpet and tapers were set on his anniversary. Gilbert is figured with his pastoral staff in high relief on a slab of black Tournai marble—the oldest sculptured monument of the abbey[2]. The features of the face are wholly gone, worn by the tread of thousands of Westminster boys before the slab was shifted in the eighteenth century to a securer place beneath the long stone bench. But the delicately carved ears remain; for the deep recesses on each side of the head had been filled in with Roman cement to save the passing foot from tripping. The epitaph has long since disappeared, but Flete records it; and, though hardly worthy of one who could write such good verses as our abbot, it is not so insipid as these things usually are, and it has the rare merit of truth.

> Hic pater insignis genus altum, virgo senexque,
> Gisleberte, jaces, lux via duxque tuis.
> mitis eras justus prudens fortis moderatus,
> doctus quadrivio, nec minus in trivio.
> sic tamen ornatus nece, sexta luce Decembris,
> spiramen caelo reddis et ossa solo.

An anonymous monk of Gilbert's former monastery characterises the three great spiritual builders of Bec in the brief sentence: *Anselmum mitem, Herluinum devotum, Lanfrancum sapientem*[3]. 'The gentle Anselm' was the man whom the Bec monks knew, though the

---

[1] 'Proposuit itaque illum in ecclesia hospitii sui apud Lambetham consecrare. verum quoniam ipsi officio regina interesse volebat, postulatus ab ea sacravit ipsum in ecclesia beati Petri Westmonasterii xiii Kal. Octobris...huic consecrationi interfuerunt et cooperatores extiterunt suffraganei ecclesiae Cantuariensis episcopi videlicet hi, Willelmus Wintoniensis, Robertus Lincoliensis, Rogerus Serberiensis, Johannes Bathoniensis, Urbanus Glamorgatensis, Gislebertus Lumniensis de Hibernia' (Eadmer, *Hist. Nov.* Rolls S. pp. 235 f.).

[2] For the graves of the abbots in the cloister, see the Introduction to Flete's *History*, pp. 22 ff.

[3] Porée, *L'Abbaye du Bec et ses écoles*, p. 66: cf. *Hist. du Bec* I 536. The letter in question was written c. 1130—50.

world has wondered at his inflexible will and the daring originality of his thought. In the verses above cited the epithet *mitis* is happily chosen to express the leading trait of Abbot Gilbert's character: we shall find its justification presently in his writings.

When an abbot died a mortuary roll was carried from abbey to abbey to ask for the prayers of the brethren. Each monastery made its own entry, promising prayers and asking prayers in return on behalf of its own departed brethren or patrons, the chief of whom were commonly mentioned by name. Abbot Gilbert's mortuary roll has not survived; but the roll of his contemporary, Abbot Vitalis of Savigny, has been fully published in facsimile by the late M. Léopold Delisle[1]. Vitalis had come to England on a preaching tour: for he was a famous revivalist. We learn from this roll that he had visited our abbey. He died 16 Oct. 1122; and the Westminster entry on his roll is of interest, not only because it names those for whom the prayers of a foreign abbey were desired, but also because it offers a specimen of the hand which was then written by our precentor or in our scriptorium. The entry is as follows:

### TITVLVS ꞉ SCI ꞉ PETRI ꞉ WESTMONASTERII

Anima eius et anime omnium fidelium defunctorum Requiescant in pace
Offa. rege. Ældgaro. rege.   Matilda. regina.   crispin.
AMEN. Orate pro nostris. ᴧ ÆDWARDO. REGE. ᴧ Vital'. abb'. Gisleberto. abb'.
Riculfo. Turstino. Turkillo. Ægeluuardo. Mauritio. Willelmo. et pro omnibus. aliis. Concedimus sibi plenam fraternitatem et societatem ęcclesię nostrę꞉ sicut concessimus illi cum fratribus qui secum ad nos uenerant. Hęc igitur renouantes obnixe uos petimus. ut eadem nobis concedatis꞉ quatinus in supernę civitatis arce mereamur abinuicem in lęticia sempiterna uideri. AMEN.

We note that after the entry had been made it was evidently supplemented at the bidding of authority. Offa and Edgar were prefixed, and the good Queen Maud was added: and Crispin was inserted above Gilbert's name, that none might fail to recognise the well-known personage. Of the monks Riculfus, Turstin, Turkill and Aegelward no other record remains. There was a monk named William in the early days of our abbot; but the name is too common to allow of a certain identification. We are on more sure ground with Maurice, who is doubtless Bp Wulstan's chaplain, of whom Osbert has told us[2].

---

[1] The last gracious gift which I received from the illustrious scholar was this beautiful product of his declining years, with which he reprinted one of the essays of his youth. Within a year has followed the 'Priez pour Lui.'

[2] See below, p. 31.

## IV.  Details of Administration.

### 1.  *Domestic Rule.*

When Lanfranc came to Canterbury, he drew up for the regulation of the monks of Christ Church a book of Customs, which found its way into many of the English monasteries and was known sometimes as the Customs of Canterbury and sometimes as the Customs of Bec[1].  It represented the result of the experience of Lanfranc and Anselm, as gained and formulated in the eager life of Herluin's new foundation; but it rested largely on earlier codes which can be traced back through Fécamp and Dijon to Cluny and even to that strenuous reformer Benedict of Aniane.  Lanfranc made some modifications in detail in deference to English traditions, though in general he was not sympathetic in dealing with the religious life of his new fellow-countrymen.  We can hardly doubt that this code, which Gilbert must have seen in force at Canterbury, was brought by him to Westminster.  As a matter of fact, considerable portions of it are embodied word for word in the thirteenth century Customary of Abbot Ware.  Vitalis, who had come to Westminster from Bernay, which was a cell of Fécamp, must have paved the way for the peaceable introduction of the new regulations.  From Lanfranc's book a picture might easily be drawn of the daily life of Westminster Abbey at the close of the eleventh century; but we must confine ourselves here to the more laborious task of gathering together such scattered notices as can be found in charters or elsewhere of Abbot Gilbert's rule.

Much of an abbot's energy was of necessity expended on the troublesome business of managing and safeguarding his abbey estates; and what is perhaps the earliest of all the charters addressed to Abbot Gilbert reminds us that he came to his task just when the great Survey

---

[1] Lanfranc's Monastic Constitutions were printed in Reyner's *Apostolatus Bene-dictinorum* (1626), and thence by D'Achery, *Lanfranci Opera* (1648): they were printed again by Wilkins, *Concilia*, i 328, in 1737.  I have discussed their title and manuscript tradition in *Journal of Theol. Studies*, April 1909.

of England was being completed[1]. Gilbert indeed found time, as we shall presently see, for a good deal of literary work; and we cannot doubt that he would take a share in the teaching of the more capable of his younger monks.

All the details of domestic management were in the hands of the prior; and we are fortunate in knowing something of one of Gilbert's priors. Two charters remain which are attested by 'Robertus prior[2].' Towards the end of the year 1102 this Robert succeeded another Robert as abbot of St Edmund's. The story given by the Bury annalists is as follows. Immediately on his accession in 1100 King Henry began to fill up the abbeys which the Red King had kept vacant in order that he might draw their revenues. He appointed to St Edmund's Robert, the illegitimate son of Hugh, count of Chester. The appointment was against the will of the monks, and Anselm wrote to Abbot Roger of St Evroul warning him and his monk Robert of the wickedness of such an intrusion, and refusing to consecrate the abbot-designate[3]. At the council held in Westminster at Michaelmas, 1102, Robert was deposed. Then 'Robertus, prior Westmonasterii, vir magnae religionis, abbatiam suscepit[4].' Robert had not been consecrated when Anselm's second exile began in April, 1103: but he ruled his abbey, none the less, for more than four years; and he built 'claustrum, capitulum, refectorium, dormitorium, et cameram suam.' At last he was consecrated by Anselm on 15 Aug. 1107: but after four weeks and four days he died (16 Sep. 1107). He was remembered as a model administrator: 'qui quidem inter omnes abbates optimus custoditor et adquisitor terrarum laudatur[5].' We hear of him long afterwards in one of Jocelin of Brakelond's gossipping stories. To annoy Abbot Sampson, we are told, Robert's anniversary was celebrated in 1197 with unusual bell-ringing,

---

[1] This is the famous Charter no. xxiv, exhibited in the Chapter House :

W. rex Anglorum R. vicecomiti et omnibus ministris suis in Suthreia sal'. Sciatis quia pro salute animę meę concedo deo et sancto Petro Westmonasterii et abbati G. viii hidas de manerio Piriford, quę in dominio meo sunt infra forestam de Windlesores, quietas amodo semper et liberas a scoto et ab omni mea consuetudine et censu pecunię quę geld vocatur anglicę. T'. W. episcopo Dunel' et I. Taileb'. Post descriptionem totius Anglię.

For Rannulf sheriff of Surrey, see below, charter no. 2: for William bp of Durham and Ivo Taillebois, no. 4. Henry I's confirmation of this charter (no. 19) mentions the new geld 'propter hidagium.' Another charter which has 'post descriptionem Anglie' (D. f. 489 *b*) is printed in my edition of Flete's *History* (p. 141); but it is obviously not genuine in the form there given.

[2] See below, p. 38, and charter no. 13.   [3] Anselm, *Epp.* iv 14.

[4] *Ann. S. Edmundi*, Rolls S. ii 4.   [5] *Ibid.* iii 355 f.

on the ground that he had done a noble deed—'qui distinxit res et redditus nostros a rebus et redditibus abbatis[1].'

Returning now to Westminster, where Robert had learned the art of administration which he exercised so well, we find that Abbot Gilbert himself was specially remembered on his anniversary for having 'extended the *camera*,' making assignment for the clothing of eighty monks[2]. This notice has a twofold interest. For, first, it is the only information we have as to the number of the monks in the Norman period, and in this respect it matches well with the great scale of the abbey buildings, especially the dormitory, refectory and cloister. The number, so far as we can tell, never rose above this figure: our earliest lists of names in the chamberlain's rolls shew us that in the fourteenth century the average was about fifty-two[3]. And, secondly, this is our first express notice of the system by which the various obedientiaries had their own endowments out of which they discharged the responsibilities of their offices. That the almoner, as well as the chamberlain, was thus endowed is suggested by a charter of Gilbert's which mentions the 'domus elemosinaria[4].'

As to the extent of the abbot's own household we have little to guide us; but among witnesses to charters we find names of persons 'de familia abbatis'; and these include William the chaplain, Herbert the steward (*dispensator*), and William the chamberlain[5].

We may also note at this point a royal confirmation to Hugh de Coleham of the office of 'dapifer' of the abbey—'videlicet, ut ipse Hugo totius praedictae abbatiae sit dapifer et sub abbate procurator, et heredes sui post eum...sicut unquam aliquis ante eum illud officium melius ac liberius tenuit[6].' This office, which was even then not a new one, has waxed and waned in importance in the course of the centuries: it reached its zenith when it was held by Lord Burleigh in the days of Queen Elizabeth, and it survives to-day in the honourable sinecure of the Lord High Steward of Westminster.

---

[1] Jocelin, *ibid.* I 291 f.　　　　　　　　　　　[2] Flete, p. 87.

[3] Thus there were 51 in 1329; 52 in 1347; 35 in 1355 (the numbers having fallen owing to the Black Death). In 1429 there were 54.

[4] Below, p. 38.　　　　　　　　　　　[5] Below, no. 37.

[6] Rymer, *Foedera*, I Pt I, p. 2 (ed. 1816). By this charter K. William confirms a grant of Abbot Gilbert and the convent. The date therefore must fall between 1085 and 1100. The attestations present a curious difficulty (T'. *Roberto comite de Mellent, Rogero Bigot, Roberto de Bello Monte*), the first and third being different names of the same person. Mr Hubert Hall has kindly collated the text with the *Cartae Antiquae* from which it is derived, and finds no variant. For Hugh de Coleham, see below, no. 27, where he appears among 'homines abbatis' [c. 1088—97].

The names of but few of Abbot Gilbert's monks have come down to us. Nicholas, William and Herbert, as well as Robert the prior, attest the grant to William Baynard which is printed below[1]. These were probably all Normans: for, though there was a chapel of St Nicholas in the Confessor's church, that saint was but little known in England before the Normans stole him from Myra in 1096, brought him to Bari, and sent his fame over the world. Nor did monks in those days take new names on entering a monastery. Herbert may well be the almoner who many years later succeeded to Abbot Gilbert's place. It is possible that he followed Gilbert from Bec; for we find a Herbert on the roll of Bec monks about the year 1184[2].

We find the names of Hugh and Warner in a Malvern charter, which recites how these two monks stepped out the limits of a property which Gilbert and the convent made over to the new priory[3]. These again are not likely to have been Englishmen[4]. Of Warner we happen to know something more : for the Ely records tell us that when St Etheldreda was translated in 1107, and other saints were being moved at the same time, an accident which had occurred to St Withburga's coffin led to the discovery that her body was still incorrupt. None dared remove the face-cloth, till one of the visitors on the great occasion, a holy man, Warner by name, 'of the apostolic fold of Westminster,' ventured to reveal her fair countenance and to lift her still flexible arms[5]. Doubtless he had assisted at the uncovering of St Edward some five years before.

There is one more name, which again has a foreign sound. When King Edward and Count Leofric together saw the child Christ in the eucharist, the king bound the count to secrecy. At a later day Leofric confided the vision to his confessor, a monk of Worcester: charging him to write it down, lest it be lost, but not to reveal it in the king's lifetime. He laid up the parchment in a box among the relics, and long afterwards the box fell to pieces and the secret was disclosed. Among those who saw the document and heard it read out in the church, was Bishop Wulstan's chaplain, 'Mauricius subdiaconus sancti Wulstani Wigorniensis episcopi.' He when his master died became

---

[1] P. 38.  
[2] Porée, *Hist. du Bec*, I 631.  
[3] Below, p. 33.  
[4] We find a Warnerius among the monks of Bec, c. 1070 (Porée, *ib.* 629): this may be the same man.  
[5] *Liber Eliensis* (ed. Stewart) p. 296: 'quidam senior ex apostolico ovili Westmonasterii, Warnerus nomine.'

a monk of Westminster, and a pattern of devotion for full twenty years[1].

The narrator of this tale is Osbert of Clare, who whatever his name may suggest was probably an Englishman. This strange personage, who fills the chief place in the abbey's history after Abbot Gilbert's death, must have entered the monastery some time before that event: but his perplexing history does not concern us here[2].

One nameless monk must be added to the list—the London Jew who was converted and baptised as the result of Gilbert's discussion with the learned Jew from Mainz[3].

## 2. *Foundation of Priories.*

Soon after his appointment Gilbert was called upon to make a new departure in the history of the abbey. Geoffrey de Mandeville[4], the sheriff of London and Middlesex, who had succeeded to the functions and estates of Esgar, the staller of King Edward, had buried his first wife Athelais in the unfinished cloister at Westminster, and had granted to the convent for her soul's sake certain lands at Tilbury[5]. At a later period, having made provision to be buried by her side, he granted also the manor of Eye in the immediate neighbourhood of the abbey[6]. Meanwhile he was designing, with the concurrence of his second wife Lesceline, a benefaction on a far larger scale. Among the possessions of Esgar to which Geoffrey had succeeded was the manor of Hurley on the Thames, and here he proposed to found a priory in subjection to the abbey of Westminster. There was already a church in the place, and this was probably enlarged or rebuilt. Osmund the bishop of Sarum, in whose diocese it lay, came to dedicate it afresh as the priory church of St Mary of Hurley; and he and the new

---

[1] Osbert's *Life of St Edward*, Brit. Mus. Add. MS 36,737 f. 147.

[2] I have attempted to unravel his story in an article in the *Church Quarterly Review* (July 1909); but many of his letters still await publication.

[3] See below, p. 82.

[4] He was grandfather of Geoffrey of Mandeville, first earl of Essex, the subject of Dr Horace Round's valuable study. I desire here to express my great obligation to Dr Round's works. As he did not deal at any length with the first Geoffrey, the benefactor of Westminster, I have taken the more pains to collect notices of him from the Westminster documents: see below, Selected Charters nos. 1—7, etc.

[5] See below, charter of Will. I (no. 1), granted before 1086, while Suain was still sheriff of Essex: 'pro anima uxoris que illic jacet.'

[6] See below, charter of G. de M., no. 15, and confirmations by Will. II and Hen. I, nos. 16, 20.

abbot Gilbert solemnly invoked the fate of the traitor Judas and the doom of Korah and Dathan on any who should violate this pious foundation.

The charter was written out thrice on one piece of vellum, which was then cut, so that one copy might be given to the abbey and another to the priory, while the third remained with the founder and his heirs. The middle copy of the three still exists with the founder's seal attached: it came with many other Hurley charters to the abbey muniment room when Henry VIII in 1536 dissolved the priory, and gave back its site to Westminster, in exchange forsooth for Hyde Park and other valuable lands which he took away. The charter is attested by William and Richard, the sons of Geoffrey by his first wife. It bears no date; but the foundation cannot well be put later than 1086, when the Conqueror left England for the last time: for the founder says that he had obtained the king's consent, and the confirmatory charter of Henry I refers to the grant of K. William his father.

The history of Hurley priory has been told by the present vicar of the parish, who has devoted immense pains to its investigation. In his book, *St Mary's, Hurley*, he has given an abstract of 562 Hurley charters which are still preserved among the abbey muniments at Westminster.

It is not easy to determine the origin of the priory of Great Malvern, or the date of its first connexion with Westminster. There is, however, probability in the account that it began with a local hermit named Aldwyn or Alwy in the time of Edward the Confessor, and that Urse d'Abetôt, the despotic and ill-famed sheriff of Worcestershire, founded the priory and agreed to Aldwyn's placing it under the abbot of Westminster[1]. This robber of churches may well have made some such provision for his future. As the Domesday Survey says nothing of this priory, its foundation probably must belong to Abbot Gilbert's time. This accords with a charter of K. Henry I, issued c. 1125, which grants to the monks of Malvern certain lands, 'according as Gilbert abbot of Westminster with the common consent of the chapter of the church conceded and gave them, and as Hugh and Warner the monks perambulated them[2].' Gilbert had died in 1117; Warner, one of his

---

[1] For references see Miss M. M. C. Calthrop in Victoria County History, *Worcestershire*, II 137.

[2] 'Et concedo eis illas terras de Wrdesfelde et de Limberga illa nova essarta, sicut Gislebertus abbas Westmonasterii communi consensu capituli ecclesiae concessit et dedit, et sicut Hugo et Warnerus monachi illa perambulaverunt...et concedo illis illam virgatam

monks, of whom we have spoken already (p. 31), was probably an old man when he visited Ely in 1106 ; and we may assume that Hugh, as he is mentioned first, was his senior. Abbot Gilbert's benefaction probably belongs to the moment of the attachment of the priory to Westminster, and we shall not be far wrong if we assign the transaction to the early years of his administration.

These two priories stood in very different relations to the mother church. The prior of Great Malvern was elected by his brethren on the spot, and was then sent up to Westminster to receive the abbot's confirmation ; and the loyalty of the priory to the abbey was largely due to a desire to escape the jurisdiction of the bishop of Worcester. The priory of Hurley was a smaller foundation, and much nearer home : its prior was chosen from among the senior monks of Westminster : sometimes he returned after a period of service, in one instance he came back to be abbot.

One other priory belonged to Westminster, that of St Bartholomew at Sudbury. This was founded by Wulfric, the king's moneyer at Norwich, who would seem to have died as a monk of Westminster. As the king's charter is attested at Westminster by Archbishop Ralph, it cannot be earlier than Easter 1114 ; nor can it be later than Easter 1116, for it is addressed to Herbert Losinga, the bp of Norwich, who died before the king's return from Normandy[1]. Perhaps the most probable date is the council held at Westminster in Sept. 1115, just before Bernard's consecration to the see of St David's.

Another cell of Westminster may perhaps have been contemplated in Gilbert's time, though it was actually founded under his successor, Abbot Herbert : for in the first endowment of the canonesses of Kilburn, who were superintended by a senior monk of Westminster, we find mention of a corrody of Abbot Gilbert, and they were under special obligation to pray for this abbot's soul[2].

terrae in Martuna quam Landricus de Clifford reddidit Gisliberto abbati, quam Gislebertus dedit monachis de Malvernia, sicut ipse Gislebertus abbas consensu communis capituli eam eis dedit et concessit ' *Monasticon*, III 448.

[1] *Monasticon* III 459 (from Faustina A. III, f. 79): H. rex Angl' Herberto episcopo Norwic' et Haymoni dapifero et burgensibus de Suthbery...Sciatis me concessisse deo et sancto Petro et mon' Westm' pro redemptione animae meae ecclesiam sancti Bartholomei de Suthberia, quam Wlfricus monetarius meus ad usum monachorum inibi servientium eis dederat pro fraternitate et monachatu suo quem ibidem susceperat....Test' R. archiepiscopo, R. episcopo London', R. episcopo Sarum, R. canc', Nigillo de Albineio, et aliis multis apud Westm'.

Can this Wulfric be the same person as 'Wlfricus taynus cognomine Bordewayte,' who held 'Totenhala' before William Baynard (see p. 38)?

[2] *Liber Niger Quaternus*, f. 125.

### 3. *Building.*

The new abbey of Westminster had been planned on a splendid scale. King Edward had built a great church in a style unknown before in England, after the pattern of the church of Jumièges, whose abbot he had brought over and made bishop of London[1]. We can hardly suppose that he had completed much else of the monastic buildings. The long undercroft beneath the dormitory may belong to his time; and sufficient indications remain elsewhere to shew that the general scheme had been fixed. Doubtless Abbot Edwin carried forward the work; and, if it slackened during Geoffrey's brief misrule, we may be certain that Vitalis pressed it on again. Before Gilbert came the dormitory was probably finished and the refectory well begun: for Vitalis lies in the east part of the south cloister walk, under the refectory wall.

A happy chance has preserved to us the information that Gilbert completed the cloister before the year 1100. In 1807 a piece of carved stone was found in a wall between two taverns which were then being pulled down. This wall was the only surviving fragment of a gateway in King Street, built by King Richard III in 1484, and demolished in 1706. The stone was one of the capitals from the old Norman cloister, and had a broken inscription which seemed to mean that the cloister and refectory (?) were finished under William II and Abbot Gilbert[2]. Three sides of the stone are figured in Brayley and Britton's *Ancient Palace of Westminster*, pp. 416, 445 f., and again in plate xxxv; but the stone is now lost[3]. Some similar capitals, together with other fragments of the ancient cloister, are now preserved in the Norman undercroft.

---

[1] See *The Church of Edward the Confessor*, in *Archaeologia*, LXII pp. 81—100, where I have endeavoured to describe the church as St Edward left it.

[2] The lettering on the three sides appears in the reproductions to read as follows:

*.claustru[m]. et rel*
*u. sub abb[at]e Gisle*
*Willelmo . secun*

The carving may be later than Abbot Gilbert's time; but none the less the record may be true.

[3] The drawings were made by Mr William Capon, who 'sold the Capital to Sir Gregory Page Turner, Bart. for one hundred guineas' (*ibid.* p. 446). I have failed as yet to discover the present resting-place of this precious fragment. Since the above was written a full account of all that is known of this stone has appeared in *Notes and Queries* (Sept. 3, 1910, p. 181) in a letter from Mr Robert Pierpoint.

We can have little doubt that Gilbert built the abbot's *camera* (or *capella*, or perhaps both) over the locutory which formed the entrance to the cloister at its S.W. angle. A similar arrangement is to be seen in the prior's (at first the abbot's) lodging at Gloucester, and formerly existed at Abingdon[1].

### 4. *Exemption and Sanctuary.*

To Abbot Gilbert's time belongs the first document which can pretend to any validity in the long strife between the abbey and the bishop of London. This document, if genuine, is the earliest of our genuine papal bulls, being a letter of Paschal II (1099—1118) to King Henry I, dated at the Lateran 'iv Kal. Iulii.' It falls within the last half of Gilbert's period of rule; but we cannot fix the date more nearly, or decide whether Maurice, who died 26 Sept. 1107, or Richard de Belmeis, who was consecrated 26 July, 1108, was the aggressor whom the pope restrained: both alike were ambitious and contentious prelates.

Gilbert in appealing to the pope had referred to the controversy as having originated with Robert, Edward's bishop whom he had brought from the abbey of Jumièges and who probably had no small share in directing the building of the new abbey church at Westminster. Robert had insisted, it would seem, as against Abbot Wulnoth (†1049), on the right of entry and of receiving various procurations. The pope now declares the abbey free 'ab omni servitio et dominatione episco-pali...ita ut nullus episcopus, sive Londoniensis seu quicunque aliquis alius, illuc introeat ordinaturus aut aliquid sive in maximo sive in minimo praecepturus, nisi propria abbatis ex petitione et monachorum communi utilitate[2].'

The question of the authenticity of this letter must remain at present undecided. Struggles for exemption have been a frequent source of forgery: but monastic forgery offers a problem which needs a critical investigation. It is easy to dismiss a document, and to misread history as the result.

---

[1] *Hist. Abingd.* Rolls S. II 286: Abbot Faricius (1100—1115) 'omnia a fundamentis aedificavit, sicut hodie cernitur: scilicet claustrum, capitulum, dormitorium, refectorium, lavatorium, cellarium, coquinam, *duo locutoria, unum ad orientem juxta capitulum, aliud ad occidentem sub capella abbatis.*'

[2] See the extract from the bull in Flete's *History*, p. 48; and, for a further extract, p. 17 of the introduction. This bull afterwards provided phraseology for the pretended Third Charter of the Confessor: see *ibid.* p. 15. It likewise formed the starting-point of the Second Charter which is dated 1045 (*Monasticon,* I 295).

The question of sanctuary at Westminster has never yet received a proper examination. This is not the place to discuss its origin, history or results: but we may call attention to what appears to be the earliest trustworthy evidence with regard to it which is still extant. The following are copies of writs of Abbot Gilbert, which were probably kept as precedents for the guidance of later abbots.

Gilbertus abbas et conventus Westm' omnibus fidelibus regis Angliae salutem. Sciatis quod iste Jordanus altare sancti Petri Westm' et corpus regis Edwardi requisivit: et ideo precamur ut libertatem sui corporis et pacem regis habeat. Valete[1].

G. abbod and alle tha brodera on Westmynstr' gretith N. schirerefan on estsex' godesgretyng' and owr'. And we kythath the that this man R. hafeth ge soht' Crist and seint Petr' and Edwarde kynges reste and alle thon halidom th' inne thone halighan mynstr' is. Now bidde we the for godes lofan and for thaer' sokne th' he ge soght' haueth th' thu hine ge myltsie and forgif swa what swa he gilt hafeth. God the ge behalde. amen[2].

The later hand, which has copied these writs on a blank page of the Westminster 'Domesday,' has written over them: 'De fugitivis visitantibus feretrum regis Edwardi nondum canonizati.' Two other Latin writs of Abbot 'G.' on the same page clearly belong to Abbot Gervase, as is seen by comparing a writ of his quoted in the *Monasticon* (I 310): the formula has grown by this time, and it speaks of the privilege as granted 'ab antiquis Angliae regibus.'

## 5. *Knight Service.*

The question of knight service, as affecting ecclesiastical corporations in the time of William the Conqueror, has been investigated by Dr Round, who shews that a *servitium debitum* was imposed on the abbeys by that king, the number of knights required being as a rule some multiple of five[3]. He notes that for Westminster in particular the exact number is difficult to fix[4]. It may be useful here to bring together such early references to knights of Westminster as can at present be discovered: and we may begin with a document which has not yet been printed.

[1] D. f. 82 *b*. Compare a writ of Abbot Herbert in the same words on behalf of ' Jordanus de Wygorn' (*Monasticon,* I 310).

[2] There is a similar writ of ' Gisilberd abbod ' on behalf of Deorman in *Monasticon,* I 310.

[3] *Feudal England,* pp. 296—307.    [4] *Ibid.* p. 252.

Anno dominice incarnationis millesimo LXXX° III°. Nos Gilbertus abbas et conventus Westm' concessimus Willelmo Baynard quoddam berwicum de villa Westm', nomine Totenhala, ad se hospitandum et tota vita sua tenendum, pro servicio unius militis, cum omnibus rebus illi pertinentibus, ita bene et quiete sicut unquam Wlfricus taynus cognomine Bordewayte melius de ecclesia illud tenuerat. consuetudines igitur et libertates quas nos in eodem habemus ipse Willelmus habebit ; exceptis auxiliis nostris, que inde sicut in aliis ecclesie terris de militibus nostris accipiemus ; et exceptis decimis illius terre domui elemosinarie nostre constitutis. hec vero sibi tenenda concessimus pro amore et servicio quod ecclesie nostre contulit, eo tamen tenore ut post ejus decessum terra illa predicta soluta ecclesie nostre maneat et quieta. et super eo quidem affidavit nos predictus Willelmus, quod nec terram prefatam vendet nec in vadium ponet nec alicui ad dampnum ecclesie nostre dimittet. Test', Roberto priore, Nicholao, Willelmo et Herberto monachis, Radulpho Baynard, Herlewyno fratre Grunzonis, et multis aliis[1].

The date of this document presents a difficulty which I have discussed elsewhere[2]. It is possible that it formed no part of the original document; and in any case it may be due to the error of the late copyist who has written it into a vacant space of the Westminster 'Domesday.' Even if we date the charter a few years later, it still remains a very early instance of the enfeoffment of a knight by an abbot.

The grant is made to William Baynard, and it is attested by Ralph Baynard. Who are these Baynards, and how do they stand in relation to the Baynard who gave his name to Baynard's Castle on the Thames, near the present Blackfriars Bridge? Three Baynards meet us in the records and chronicles of this period—Geoffrey, Ralph and William.

(1) *Geoffrey.* A grant of William I of land at York for a hospital is addressed to 'Galfridus Baynardus' (? as sheriff)[3]: and according to the A.S. Chron. (*sub anno* 1096) Geoffrey Bainard accused William of Eu, the king's kinsman, of treason at Salisbury, and overcame him in single combat. A list of the benefactors to Lewes Priory includes 'Geoffrey Bainard and Ralph his brother[4].'

(2) *Ralph.* Of Ralph Baynard we further know that before the Survey he was sheriff of Essex, and at the time of the Survey he held lands in several parts of that county[5]. He is one of those to whom is

---

[1] D. f. 82, inserted in a fifteenth century hand.

[2] Flete's *Hist. of Westm.* pp. 141 f.

[3] *Historians of York*, Rolls S. III 163 n.

[4] 'Ecclesiam de Essenduna dedit nobis Gaufredus Bainardus et Radulfus frater ejus' (*Monast.* v 14): see also the confirmatory charter of Stephen in Round's *Doc. pres. in France*, p. 512.

[5] For Ralph as a Domesday tenant, see Round, *Feudal England*, pp. 461, 475.

addressed a writ of William I confirming to Abbot Vitalis among other properties the mill at Stratford (co. Essex): this is previous to the Survey[1]. So, doubtless, is the famous writ concerning Church courts, which is addressed to R. Baynard, G. de Mandeville and P. de Valognes, and all the liege men of Essex, Hertfordshire and Middlesex[2].

(3) *William.* A charter printed below (no. 27) speaks of William Baynard as one of the witnesses to a restoration of lands in Worcestershire, c. 1090—1097. The A.S. Chronicle, *sub anno* 1110, says that William Baynard forfeited his lands to the king.

The Chronicle of Dunmow, cited in the *Monasticon* (VI 147) from Cleop. C. III f. 29, says, under the year 1104, that 'Juga Baynard domina de parva Dunmowe fecit Mauricium episcopum Londoniensem dedicare ecclesiam de dicta villa'; and, under 1106, that 'Galfridus Baynard filius et haeres Jugae Baynard' introduced canons with the assent of Archbp Anselm. Then, under 1111, it relates that William Baynard, 'sub quo domina Juga tenebat villam de parva Dunmowe,' lost his barony 'per infortunium et feloniam'; and that K. Henry gave it to Robert fitz Richard, who was the son of Richard fitz Gilbert, count of Clare, together with the Honor of Castle Baynard.

Information derived from this source must be accepted with caution. Geoffrey is here represented as the son of Juga (or it may be read 'Inga') Baynard. But the point which specially interests us is the descent of the Honor of Castle Baynard: for with it went the Westminster knight's fee. Robert fitz Richard had a son Walter fitz Robert, and in due course the properties came to Robert fitz Walter. Now in 1166 we find William Baynard's Westminster fee evidently held by the second generation of his successors: for in the list of enfeoffed knights of the abbot of Westminster we read: 'In Middlesex Walterus filius Roberti servicium i militis, quod difforciat[3].'

We have next to ask what is the relation, if any, of this grant to the statement as to land held at Westminster by 'Bainiardus' in the Domesday Survey. It will be well to transcribe the whole entry for the 'vill' of Westminster at this point.

Terra sancti Petri Westmon'. In Osuluestane Hundr'.

In villa ubi sedet ecclesia sancti Petri tenet abbas ejusdem loci xiii hid' et dim' Terra est ad xi car'. Ad dominium pertinent ix hid' et i virg', et ibi sunt iiii car' Villani habent vi car', et i car' plus potest fieri. Ibi ix villani quisque de i virg', et

---

[1] Printed below, no. 2.  [2] Stubbs, *Select Charters*, 85.
[3] *Lib. Nig. Scacc.* I 51, quoted in *Monasticon*, I 307.

i villanus de i hid', et ix villani quisque de dim' virg'; et i cotarius de v acris, et xli cotarii qui reddunt per annum xl sol' pro ortis suis. Pratum xi car'. Pastura ad pecuniam ville. Silva c porc', et xxv domus militum abbatis et aliorum hominum qui reddunt viii sol' per annum. In tot' valent' val' x libr'. Quando recep' similiter. T.R.E. xii libr'. Hoc manerium fuit et est in dominio ecclesie sancti Petri Westm'.

In eadem villa tenet Bainiardus iii hid' de abbate. Terra est ad ii car', et ibi sunt in dominio, et i cotarius. Silva c porc'. Pastura ad pecuniam. Ibi iv arpenni vinee noviter plantatae. In tot' valent' val' lx sol'. Quando recep' xx sol'. T.R.E. vi lib'. Hec terra jacuit et jacet in ecclesia sancti Petri.

We proceed to investigate the 'berewic of the vill of Westminster called Totenhala,' which Abbot Gilbert granted to William Baynard for the service of one knight. Is this to be identified with the three hides in the same 'vill' which Baynard holds of the abbot in the Survey?

At the first glance the name suggests to us Tottenham, of which Tottenhall is a variant in later days. But, even if the distance does not render this impossible, we are debarred from such a solution by the Westminster tradition of the twelfth century. The great charters of Edward the Confessor, though they are manifestly unauthentic, have a high value as representing current opinion in the abbey at the time of their composition; and they frequently help to interpret the brief charters which furnished them with their materials. In the 'Telligraphus beati regis Edwardi' we read (D. f. 47):

Concessi etiam et confirmavi omnes donaciones que a regibus vel ab aliquibus aliis ante me donate sunt: hoc est, in eadem villa in qua idem monasterium est iii hidas et dimidiam; in berwika quod Tottenheale appellatur iii hidas; in Tatewelle unam; in Cnihtebricge iiii; in Padington' ii; in Hæmstede v; in Heændune cum territoriis...suis que appellantur Bleccenham, Codenhlæwe et Lothereslege xx hidas....

Here we find that the 'berewika' of 'Tottenheale' has three hides, the exact number held by Baynard at the time of the Survey. But there is an evident mistake in assigning three and a half hides only to the abbey itself. Probably we should read xiii for iii, as in the Survey: and thus, with Tottenheale and also the mysterious Tatewelle added in, we should make up the number of seventeen and a half which is found in the First Charter of the Confessor (D. f. 39b):

Concessi etiam et confirmavi donaciones que ab eisdem regibus ante me donate sunt: hoc est, circa ipsum monasterium xvii hydas et dimidiam; in Heandune xx; in Heampstede v....

There can be no doubt, then, that in the twelfth century Totenhala, or Tottenheale[1], was identified with three hides of land in the immediate

---

[1] Cf. Pope Adrian's bull (D. f. 6b): In Middelsex' villam Westm', Cnichebrigg', Padinton', Totehal', villam de Eye.... [See also Addit. Note B, p. 167.]

neighbourhood of the abbey. There appears to be some connexion between Totenhala, Tatewelle, and the well-known Tothull or Tothill.

The twenty-five houses for the abbot's knights and other men suggest that the process of enfeoffment had not been carried far; and that, as at Abingdon and at Ely[1], a number of knights resided in the immediate neighbourhood of the abbey, and perhaps were fed at the abbot's table. Possibly we may find here the explanation of the rebuke administered by Pope Innocent II in 1139 to Abbot Gervase for having knights about him in the abbey: 'militarem praeterea manum et laicorum conventum procul a limitibus monasticae arceas disciplinae[2].'

In Geoffrey de Mandeville's grant of Eye we find the clause: 'super altare predicti apostoli Petri presentavi in presentia Gisleberti abbatis et monachorum, et multorum militum meorum et suorum[3].'

For further notices of knight service, see. pp. 48 f.


### 6. *Domestic Economy.*

Among the abbey muniments is a document which appears to have been written in the first quarter of the twelfth century, and which throws light on the domestic economy of the period[4]. At first sight it is puzzling, but it yields its meaning to a careful study.

Hec est firma monachorum in septimana. ad panem vi cumbas: et lx et vii sol' ad coquinam: et xx hops de brasio, et x de gruto: et iii cumbas avenae; et ad servientes i marc' argenti. et illa maneria quae longinqua sunt, et hoc reddere non poterint, reddent pro tota septimana viii ħ et x sol'.

Ad karitates et pitancias xxxii ħ, de Bienflet, de Fantone, de Pakelesam et Winetona, et de Cumbritona.

Ad ligna xv ħ.

Ad cameram et ad omnia quae necessaria sunt, omnes redditus Lundoniae, Dodintuna, et Cillentuna, et Sippeham, et Sulebi, et i molendinum apud Stretfort, et Perham. Haec est summa: lx et x ħ.

Ad servientes coquine, et pistrini, et bracini, et orti, et vineae, et infirmatorii, et portarii, de Hanewrde xxx sol', de Coueley xxx sol', de Titebirste x sol', de Merdeleya xv sol', de Elteneya xxiiii sol'. et v sol' de Okkenduna; et xx sol' de illis qui tenent terras vinearum, exceptis illis qui habent terrulas pro solidatis suis.

Ad servicium cenae domini lx sol', de Wateleya; et xx sol' de Knichtebrigge.

---

[1] See Round, *Feudal England*, p. 300. At Ely the abbot 'habuit ex consuetudine, secundum jussum regis, praetaxatum militiae numerum infra aulam ecclesiae, victum cotidie de manu celerarii capientem atque stipendia' (*Lib. Eliens.* p. 275).

[2] Quoted by Flete, p. 90.  [3] Below, no. 15.

[4] *Munim.* 5670: endorsed 'Extenta conventus Westm. Compositiones.' It is copied in D. f. 659.

The first paragraph refers to the system of 'firmae,' which is explained by Archdeacon Hales in the introduction to the 'Domesday of St Paul's,' pp. xxxix—li. 'Firma' represents the Anglo-Saxon 'feorme,' and means originally provisions supplied by various manors as a rent in kind. The manors rendered one, two, or more 'firmae,' in the sense of provisions for a week: at the end of the eleventh century 52 weeks, and something more, were thus provided for; but afterwards the 'firmae' were only 45. 'The forty-five firmae were furnished by thirteen manors. Each firma consisted of sixteen quarters of wheat, sixteen quarters of oats, and three quarters of barley[1].'

At St Alban's the same system was in force: and it is thus described for the first half of the twelfth century:

Habemus igitur de maneriis nostris quinquaginta et tres firmas. firmam vocamus quadraginta et sex solidos. tot ergo habemus firmas, quot sunt septimanae in anno, et unam in antecessum. quae hoc modo proveniunt: qualibet hebdomada quadraginta sex solidos recipiunt cellararii nostri, scilicet monachorum et curiae; tresdecim vero ex hiis recipit cellararius curiae, noster vero triginta tres. tres autem solidi pro novem sarcinariis, qui victum nostrum a Londoniis vel aliunde debent afferre, statuti sunt; triginta vero pro victu nostro. hiis vero triginta solidis per hebdomadam adjecit dictus abbas Gaufridus [1119—1146] quinque solidos qualibet septimana, scilicet annuas tresdecim libras; ita ut cotidie ad coquinam nostram quinque solidos haberemus....habemus etiam ex antiqua statutione qualibet hebdomada annuatim duas summas frumenti ad coquinam nostram, et quolibet anno sexaginta solidos de Apsa ad lac emendum[2].

The 'firma' is given here in money, but whether the commutation had been made so early is not clear. At Westminster, as our document shews us, about half of the 'firma' was rendered in money, and the other half in kind: but the distant manors paid the 'firma' wholly in money, at the rate of £8. 10s.

A charter of Abbot Gilbert, printed below (no. 13), is interesting in this connexion. The abbot grants to Gunter and his heir the manor of Hendon 'in feudo firme pro una plenaria septimana firme quoque

---

[1] *Domesday of St Paul's*, xlviii. This seems to apply to the 13th century.

[2] *Gesta Abbatum* (Rolls Series) i 74. Another document which may be compared with these is the account of the provision 'ad ministerium cellerarii' at Worcester Priory: the last named benefactor is Bp Teolwold (†1123), and the document perhaps belongs to the first half of the 12th cent. *Inc.* 'In septimana recipiet x sextarios frumenti fannatos' (*Monasticon*, i 606). To a somewhat later period would seem to belong the Statute traditionally ascribed to Abbot Aldwin of Ramsey (1091—1102): 'ad celerariam pro victu praedictorum monachorum et hospitum assignavit diversa maneria, quae vocantur firmas (*sic*) monachorum,' etc. (*Ramsey Chartulary*, Rolls S. iii 163: cf. 168 and, more elaborately, 230.)

anno[1].' Abbot Herbert confirmed this grant, apparently on the same terms: but Abbot Gervase regranted the manor to Gunter's son Gilbert for an annual rent of £20; and this grant was confirmed by Pope Innocent II on 22 April 1139. The change in the rent is noticeable. The value of the manor stands in the Domesday Survey at only £8; but in K. Edward's time it had been worth £12.

Six coombs would be a very insufficient supply of wheat for the bread of the monastery each week, if the coomb was, as now, half a quarter. Either some larger measure must be signified by the word, or we must suppose that much of the payment in wheat had been commuted for money.

By 'xx hops de brasio' we must understand 20 pecks of malt. In one of the Worcester Compotus Rolls published by Canon J. M. Wilson[2] we find such entries as 'i qr. vii estr. i hop.' and 'iii qr. iii estr. iii hop.' It would appear that the 'esteria' is the eighth part of a quarter (sc. a bushel), and the 'hoop' a fourth part of an 'esteria[3].' It is interesting to see that the reckoning in our document is not by the bushel, but by the 'peck o' maut.'

'Grutum' is defined by Du Cange as barley prepared for making beer: 'grout' and 'grout-ale' are still in use for a cheap kind of ale.

The subsequent paragraphs refer not to weekly but to yearly payments. 'Pitanciae' and 'caritates' are extra allowances in the refectory: the manors from which these contributions come are all in Essex, except Comberton which is in Worcestershire.

The paragraph relating to the 'camera,' which supplied the monks' clothing, is illustrated by the following statement of Flete (p. 87) regarding Abbot Gilbert's anniversary:

Hic quoque pater venerabilis omnes redditus ad cameram pertinentes conventui assignavit...pro qua quidem assignatione camerae anniversarium ipsius principaliter est celebrandum septimo idus Decembris, ut patet libro Consuetudinarii, quarta parte, capitulo de anniversariis 57°.

It is unfortunate that the chapter of the Customary to which Flete here refers is no longer extant[4]: but in c. xv under the head of the

---

[1] The grant cannot be later than 1102 when Robert the prior went to St Edmund's. This charter and those which are subsequently referred to are found in D. f. 129.

[2] pp. 68 f. (Pitancer's roll for 1351—2).

[3] *The English Dialect Dictionary* shews that the 'hoop' varies in different localities from a quarter of a peck to four pecks: but most frequently it is the equivalent of a peck.

[4] The *Customary* edited by Sir H. Maunde Thompson contained no more than 48 chapters: c. xlvi contains a 'recapitulatio' only of anniversaries, and here there is a mere fragment about Abbot Gilbert, too imperfect to be of any use (p. 589 of the transcript in the Chapter Library). Flete must have been quoting from a copy which had supplementary chapters, one of which dealt with the anniversaries at full length.

'camerarius' we have this statement, which gives us some light on the matter:

Extenditur autem camera ex assignacione commendabilis memoriae abbatis Gilberti ad vesturam et calciamentum quater viginti monachorum, praeter domnum abbatem; ad quae plenarie exhibenda, una cum aliis subtitulatis rebus usui fratrum necessariis, recipit idem camerarius annuatim de pensionibus ac redditibus quater viginti et octo libras ad minus.

Our document speaks of £70 as the annual provision 'ad cameram et omnia quae necessaria sunt.' It is reasonable to regard that as the provision made by Abbot Gilbert. In the middle of the 13th century the sum had risen to £88 at the least.

The next paragraph is of interest for its references to the servants of the monastery and to the vineyards. The newly planted vines are, as we have seen, mentioned in the Domesday Survey: their memory survived till recently in the name of 'Vine Street.' The last paragraph refers to the Maundy.

It is worth while to compare this document as a whole with a somewhat parallel statement preserved in the *Liber Eliensis*, which refers to the troublous period when Ranulf Flambard was extorting the last penny from the Church for his master William Rufus[1].

Lib. 2, c. 136. *Quod Ranulfus quidam jussu regis annonam monachis, sed brevem, constituit.* Haec igitur sunt quae idem Ranulfus et Symeon abbas ex jussu regis Willelmi constituerunt uno quoque anno dari ad opus fratrum. ad vestimenta eorum septuaginta libras[2]. ad coquinam eorum sexaginta libras, et ad sagimen ducentos porcos, et porcos qui in curia pascuntur, et totum caseum et butirum, excepto hoc quod est in firma praepositorum; et unaquaque ebdomada septem treias frumenti et decem treias braisii. ad luminaria monasterii, praesentem ecclesiam cum sepultura villae, et totum quicquid pertinet ad sanctum Botulfum cum festivitate. et, si tantum fuerit de vino, semper habebunt in lectionibus [in] duodecim caritatem et in sabbato; sin autem, medietatem medonis habebunt.

This Ely reckoning was made about 1093, and no doubt it represents the maximum which was left to the monks when for the last seven years of his reign the abbey was in the king's hands.

I venture the conjecture that our Westminster document represents the allowance made to the monks when the abbey was in K. Henry's hands from the death of Gilbert in December 1117 till the appointment of Herbert in January 1121[3]. This, then, might be a copy written by

---

[1] *Liber Eliensis*, ed. Stewart, p. 278.

[2] This is the same sum as at Westminster: at Ely there were about this time 70 monks.

[3] In a charter of 1121 occurs the phrase 'dum abbatia fuit in mea manu,' D. f. 58 *b*.

a royal official, and left with the monks at the time when the composition was made.

Let us now glance at the estates which are mentioned under the various headings. And first let us take those which are assigned to the 'camera'; for here we have a remarkable example of monastic conservatism. In 1381 John Lakingheth, the treasurer, assessed all the offices of the abbey at their true value, and the *Liber Niger Quaternus* gives us the estates which furnished to each office its revenues[1]. After the mention of certain 'pensiones' from churches which the chamberlain received, we read as follows:

Bona ejusdem camerarii in civitate London' taxantur ad xxxix ħi. Item in Stebenhith, xx s. Item in Wokynton ad turm', xx s. Item in Estham lx s. Item in Dodinton, xii ħi. Item in Soleby, cii s. Item in Cippenham, 1 s. Item in Cholyngton, xliii s. iiii d. Item in Hamme apud Ospreng, xx s. Item in Hadleya, xl s.

These 'temporalia' amount to £68. 15. 4; and, when the 'spiritualia' above-mentioned are added in, the total comes to £74. 2. 0. We may compare this total with the £70 of our document, and with the '£88 at the least' of Abbot Ware's Customary (c. 1266). It is not unlikely that the estates had fallen considerably in value after the Black Death in 1349, and some of the additional properties in the above list may have been assigned to the chamberlain in consequence. His original assignment was, according to our document:

Omnes redditus Lundoniae, Dodintuna, et Cillentuna, et Sippeham, et Sulebi, et i molendinum apud Stretfort, et Perham.

Two items of this list are gone, and five others have come in to supply their place, in the course of two centuries and a half.

1. *The mill at Stratford* (co. Essex) was given to the abbey by Ailnod of London shortly after the Conquest[2]. This Ailnod was a nephew of Suain of Essex, who was a considerable benefactor of the abbey, and of whom we shall hear more presently[3]. In the chamberlain's roll for 1382–3, that is to say, just after the assessment made by John Lakingheth, we discover that the mill had been in some way alienated, and, though it had been recovered in the previous year, it had brought in nothing, because there was no tenant:

De xx s. (due from the mill at Stratford) nil hic, quia recuperatur per breve de Cessavit anno proximo preterito, et jacet vac'.

[1] *Lib. Nig. Quat.* f. 85 b, ff. 140 sqq.
[2] See the charter of Will. I (below, no. 2), which is of considerable interest.
[3] See below, pp. 49 f. and nos. 1, 2, 8.

The next extant roll of this office is for 1399—1400, and there we read:

Nil adhuc, quia est in manu ballivi, et respondet de firma ejusdem compoto suo.

It had thus passed from the chamberlain to the general account of the convent, and its rent was received by the principal treasurer, who was also styled the bailiff.

2. *Perham* (Parham, co. Sussex) is mentioned in the Telligraphus of St Edward (D. f. 47), but nothing is said about the way in which it came into the abbey. It occurs duly, however, in the Domesday Survey. We hear of it in the latter half of Henry I's reign, when Abbot Herbert made good his claim to it against an aggressor (D. f. 597 b):

Sciatis quod abbas Herbertus...diracionavit terram de Pereham et de Mapeleford erga Herbertum filium Herberti...T'. episcopo Sarum apud Odestocam [1].

In Henry II's time Peter fitz Herbert receives £100 from the abbot and convent for the surrender of his rights. Then Abbot William Postard assigns it to the kitchener, and presently Abbot Ralph confirms this assignment. As all these charters (D. ff. 597 seqq.) occur under the heading of the infirmarer, we must conclude that Parham ultimately came to his office.

3. We now come to the estates which remained with the chamberlain. Of the London property we need not speak. We begin with *Dodintuna* (Doddington, 6 m. west of Lincoln). It was given by Ailric, and confirmed by a charter of Will. I to Abbot Vitalis [2]: and it appears accordingly in the Domesday Survey. The next we hear of it is in a charter by which Hugo de Euremou restores 'Dotinton' to the abbey. Abbot Gilbert had given it to him in exchange for another manor, which K. Henry afterwards took away and gave back to count Eustace (i.e. Eustace the younger of Boulogne). Henry's charter which confirms the restoration of Doddington tells us that the other manor was Ducesworthe, and that the king gave Hugo an equivalent for its surrender [3].

4. *Cillentuna*, or Cholyngton, as it is called in the assessment of 1381, has proved very difficult to locate. Our first completely trustworthy notice of it is in a charter of William I (D. f. 168) addressed to

---

[1] Cf. *Hist. Abingd.* Rolls S. ii 5 : 'Herebertus filius Hereberti, i militem pro Lechamstede x hidarum'; in a list of Abingdon knights, *temp.* Hen. I.

[2] D. f. 524 b: 'manerium Dodinton', quod Alricus Merietisunæ dedit.' In William's 'First Charter' (D. f. 50 b): 'Dudintun...Aegelricus nomine filius Mergeati.'

[3] The texts of these charters are given below, nos. 25 and 26. For Hugo de Euremou, who enters into the legend of Hereward 'the Wake,' see Round, *Feud. Engl.* pp. 159—161.

Abp Lanfranc and Bp Odo, which gives to Abbot Vitalis the hunting in the wood at Battersea, and certain properties in London and elsewhere: 'et terram de Celintona, quam tenet Boselinus de Diva.' But there is nothing here to fix its locality[1]. We must therefore try back among our fictitious charters to see what the tradition about it was. In Will. I's First Charter (D. f. 52*b*) and in his Telligraphus (D. f. 49*b*) we find 'villam Cillinctune, quam prius Boselinus de Diva ei [sc. ecclesiae] per vim abstulerat': but this notice is obviously drawn from the charter to which we have just referred. In St Edward's First Charter (D. f. 39*b*) we have 'Colintuna,' which is immediately followed by 'Cillingtune' (cf. his Telligraphus, D. f. 47): this gives us no further light. But in the Telligraphus of Ethelred (D. f. 80*b*) we read[2]:

Item Aelfwine prefectus meus de Kent tres cassatas cenobio prefato pro animula sua conjugisque largitus est in loco qui vulgo Sillingtune dicitur.

Here we have at last a hint as to where we must look. If the king's prefect of Kent gives it for his 'poor soul,' it is probably somewhere in that county. But the Domesday Survey of Kent does not recognise it. Yet our next mention of it would be in harmony with such a locality: for about the year 1150 Abp Theobald requires two aggressors to give it back to the abbey on pain of excommunication, which shall be strictly enforced throughout the whole of England (D. f. 681, under the heading *Scripta vacua nunc*):

T. dei gratia Cant' archiepiscopus, Anglorum primas, apostolice sedis legatus, Gaufrido Batailla et Ricardo de Frachevilla, salutem. Ex parte G[ervasii] abbatis [we have learned that] ingressi estis manerium de Chelindona, quod a tempore Edwardi regis predicta ecclesia possedisse dicitur....

We shall see presently that, when Abp Theobald interposed on behalf of Sulby in Lincolnshire, he required the Bp of Lincoln to strike the aggressor with ecclesiastical censures, if need should be[3]. But in the case before us he acts directly, as he must of necessity do if the place be in his own diocese. Once more therefore we are inclined to look to Kent, though the indications are still but slight; and there is a Shillington and also a Chellington in Bedfordshire, and other counties offer similar names equally attractive[4].

---

[1] In the Domesday Survey for Sussex (f. 16) part of Mallinges is held by 'filius Boselin'.'

[2] Comp. St Dunstan's charter, D. f. 36, where it is called Schollingtune.

[3] Below, p. 48.

[4] E.g. *Kelituna* (now Kenningtons), the Essex part of Kelington, which is across the river in Suffolk.

The 'Valor Ecclesiasticus' of Henry VIII generally notes the county in which a property is situated; but here our estate is missing from the list of those held by the chamberlain; and indeed it does not appear anywhere in the list printed in the *Monasticon*. Our last hope is in the chamberlain's account roll, though it is most unusual to find there any notes of locality. Most fortunately this case is an exception. In the roll for 1382—3 we read:

Et de redditu de Cholyngtone in parochia de Burne, iii li.

In the next extant roll (1399—1400) there is a neat erasure at this point, but the extent of it exactly corresponds with the above words: so that it is plain that this property was lost to the chamberlain only a few years after the assessment of 1381.

Where then is the parish of Burne? There is no such parish, it seems, in Kent at the present day. But a few miles east of Canterbury we find Bekesbourne, and six miles south-east of that is the village of Chillenden, or Chillingden—for after a thousand years its spelling is still open to question. When now we turn back to the Domesday Survey, we find to our satisfaction that the neighbourhood of what is now called Bekesbourne is described simply as Burne.

5. *Sippenham* (Cippenham, co. Bucks) is mentioned in a charter of William Rufus as having come to the abbey by his father's gift. It is confirmed to Abbot Gilbert, who had established his claim before certain of the king's barons. Subsequently Abbot Gilbert in the last years of his life granted it to William de Bokeland for a yearly rent of fifty shillings, the sum which appears in the assessment of 1381. The two charters here referred to are printed below[1]; the second contains the interesting phrase, 'quando rex Angl' communiter accipiet xx solidos de milite.'

6. *Sulebi* (Sulby, co. Northampton) was connected with Westminster in K. Henry I's time, as we gather from later documents. A writ of Archbp Theobald, apparently between 1147 and 1154, requires Robert de Chesny, bp of Lincoln, to see that Robert Foliot restores Sulby which he has taken away (D. f. 680*b*); and a charter of Robert Foliot confirms to the abbey the perpetual tenure of the manor of Sulby, for the service of one knight, as in the time of his predecessors under K. Henry[2]. In the *Red Book of the Exchequer* (ed. Hall), p. 331, we read:

---

[1] Nos. 9 and 37.

[2] 'Sciatis me et Margaretam uxorem meam...eodem servicio quo faciebant predecessoribus meis tempore regis Henrici, videlicet servicium unius militis' (D. f. 523).

Carta Roberti Foliot.

De baronia Roberti Foliot de veteri feffamento:

...................................................

Abbas de Westmonasterio, i militem.

It is possible that further research may throw more light on the early history of this property[1]. In later days the manor was let to Sulby Abbey (40 Hen. III) for 102 shillings, the figure at which it stands a hundred years later still in John Lakingheth's assessment.

The other properties mentioned in our document must, with one exception, be briefly dismissed with a mere mention of their localities. Bienflet is Benfleet, and Fantone is Little Faunton[2] in North Benfleet: Pakelesam[3] and Winetona[4] are Paglesham and Wenington: all these are in co. Essex. Cumbritona[5] is Comberton, co. Worcester. Hanewrde and Coueley[6] are Hanworth and Cowley in co. Middlesex. Titebirste and Merdeleya are Titeburst in Wheathampstead and Mardley, both in co. Hertford. Elteneya[7] and Okkenduna[8] are Ilteney and Ockendon in co. Essex. Knichtebrigge is the familiar Knightsbridge. Of Wateleya (Whatley or Wheatley, co. Essex) it is worth while to speak more particularly.

*Watelea* occurs in the Domesday Survey as part of the land of Suain of Essex. A charter of Abbot Gilbert grants it to Robert son of Suain for sixty shillings a year, at which figure it stands in our document. Suain had given it for his soul's sake to St Peter, and Robert with his mother had made gift thereof on the altar of St Peter on the day of his father's burial[9].

---

[1] In a Northampton survey of the time of Hen. I, Richard Foliot is said by Dr Round to be the heir of Guy of Renbodcurt, or Raimbercurt, a Domesday owner, see *Feudal England*, 219 f. Was this Richard the father of the Robert Foliot of our charter? According to Dugdale (*Baronage*), Richard's father was Robert Foliot, who married Margery, daughter of Richard de Reincurt.

[2] For confirmations of Fanton by Hen. I see below, nos. 23, 24.

[3] Given by Ingulfus (Edw. Telligr. D. f. 47 *b*).

[4] This is the 'Winton' of a charter which speaks of the church having been broken into: see below, no. 31.

[5] See the charters printed below, nos. 27, 28.

[6] Cofenlea in St Dunstan's charter, D. f. 36. Under the cellarer in D. f. 469.

[7] Telligr. Will. I (D. f. 49 *b*): 'Deinde in Eastsex' prope burgum Maldune, in Elteneie xxx agellos arabilis terre,' given by Geoffrey de Mandeville.

[8] Under the cellarer in D. f. 469. Wokendune and Fering were held by Harold, and were given by the Conqueror to the abbey as part of the exchange for Windsor (D. f. 254). Henry's confirmation of this grant is printed below, no. 22.

[9] The charter is printed below, no. 8.

R. C.

4

Suain of Essex was the son of Robert fitz Wimarc[1]. This Robert was a staller under Edward the Confessor. He became sheriff of Essex, and was succeeded in that office by Suain[2]. Suain's son, Robert of Essex, was the father of Henry of Essex, who lost the royal standard in battle and forfeited his lands to K. Henry II. Wateleya, which was a manor in the Honor of Rayleigh, thus came to the king.

Henry II's daughter Matilda was married to Henry the Lion, duke of Saxony, in 1168. The duke was banished in 1180, and resided in England for some years after 1182: his daughter Matilda was married in 1189 to Geoffrey count of Perche. These facts will explain a charter by which Geoffrey count of Perche confirms the gift of sixty shillings annually, originally made by Suain of Essex, to be paid on Palm Sunday for the approaching Maundy (D. f. 520*b*):

...ego Gaufridus dei gracia comes de Pertico...confirmavi, consensu Matildis uxoris mee, donacionem illam quam Swanus de Essexa, avus videlicet Henrici de Essex' dedit...videlicet sexaginta solidatas redditus in villa de Wateleya...percipiendas...dominica scilicet in Ramis palmarum, ad mandatum pauperum faciendum proxima die Jovis.

The obligation recorded in our document thus remained attached to the property: 'ad servicium cenae domini lx sol' de Wateleya.'

---

[1] Wimarc was his mother: her name is Breton, according to Dr Round (Vict. Co. Hist. *Essex*, p. 345; and cf. *Dict. Nat. Biog.* 'Robert the Staller ').

[2] Then came Ralph Baynard, and after him, at the time of the Survey, Peter de Valognes.

## V. Abbot Gilbert's Literary Remains.

The esteem in which Gilbert Crispin was held as a theologian some thirty years after his death is strikingly illustrated by an incident which is recounted by John of Salisbury in the *Historia Pontificalis*[1]. After the formal proceedings of the Council held at Rheims in 1148 by Eugenius III were concluded, certain bishops and abbots were still retained to consider various errors imputed to Gilbert de la Porée, bishop of Poitiers. St Bernard gathered a private conference in his lodging, and tried to get the consent of some influential persons to certain positions in advance, in order to shew that Gilbert de la Porée had contravened them and so to secure his condemnation. At this conference there were present, as the writer could attest ('quod vidi loquor et scribo'), Theobald abp of Canterbury, Geoffrey of Bordeaux, Henry (Murdoc) of York, Suger abbot of St Denys, Baldwin abbot of Castellio (Châtillon)—all of whom were now dead; also Thomas of Canterbury, Roger of York and many others. St Bernard asked them, if he were wrong in opposing Gilbert de la Porée, to correct him: if not, to defend the Church. Then he made certain propositions, which one of his monks wrote down and read out, saying *Placet vobis?* The first was 'Quod deus est deitas, et e converso': they said *Placet*. The second was 'Quod tres personae sunt unus deus, et e converso': again they said *Placet*, but they did not like this method of procedure. The third was 'Quod essentia dei incarnata est, sive natura': once more they gave their assent.

Quarto loco subintulit quod quoniam deus simplex est et quicquid in deo est deus est, proprietates personarum sunt ipsae personae, et quod pater est paternitas, filius est filiatio, spiritus est processio, et e converso. quae cum similiter prioribus excepta essent et interrogata, surgens archidiaconus quidam Catalaunensis, scilicet Robertus de Bosco, et tam voce quam manu silentium impetrans petiit hujus responsionis dilationem. audierat enim, ut dicebat, in scolis clarissimorum doctorum fratrum Anselmi et Radulfi Laudunensium hoc fuisse quaesitum; sed ab eis minime receptum est, quia verebantur transgredi terminos quos posuerant patres. sed nec

---

[1] c. 8 (ed. Arndt, in Pertz's *Mon. Germ. Hist. SS.* xx, p. 523). I am indebted for my knowledge of this interesting incident to Mr C. C. J. Webb.

Gilbertus Universalis, qui post fuit episcopus Lundonensis, nec Albericus Remensis, qui post in archiepiscopum Bituris sublimatus est, hoc ob eandem causam admittere voluerunt: nam et ipsos audierat et super hoc interrogaverat. *item, ut aiebat, omnibus his sibi litteratior visus est Gillebertus abbas Westimonasterii prope Lundoniam, qui hoc nunquam concedere adquievit.* consuluit ergo ut in re tanta non praecipitarent sententiam, praesertim cum ab hac diffinitione tanti viri abstinuerint interrogati, et domnus papa praesens esset et ecclesia Romana, et ad illam convenerant qui praestantiores esse videbantur in orbe Latino. paritum est consilio ejus, conventu sic soluto.

St Bernard however got at the Pope himself, and dictated a form of words in which judgment was given: but Gilbert de la Porée consented to correct his commentary on Boethius *de trinitate* accordingly, and was acquitted.

The position which Robert du Bois assigns to Abbot Gilbert of Westminster is very remarkable in view of the eminence of the theologians to whom he prefers him. We have now to ask what were the writings which gained him so great a reputation.

We shall begin by considering the evidence of certain mediaeval lists in which his name occurs.

(1) *Catalogues of the library of Bec.* Although most of the manuscripts of Bec have perished, we fortunately possess two early lists which are of considerable interest[1]. They are both reprinted in Migne *P. L.* 150, col. 771 ff. from Ravaisson *Rapports sur les bibliothèques des départements de l'Ouest*, Paris, 1841; and a more recent edition is found in *Cat. des MSS. biblioth. publiques de France*, t. II pp. 385 f.

The first belongs to the early part of the twelfth century and is entitled 'Tituli librorum Beccensis almarii.' Here we find a volume containing works (a) of St Chrysostom and (b) of Gilbert Crispin. The entry is as follows:

*Libri beati Iohannis cognomine Chrisostomi.*
*In uno vol.* De reparatione lapsi, lib. I. Item ejusdem ad Demetrium de compunctione cordis, lib. I. Item de eadem re ad Stelechium, lib. I. Item omelia ejusdem de subscriptione I[1] Psalmi. Item omelia ejusdem de I° Psalmo. Item contra Judeum lib. Gisleberti Crispini abbatis Westimonasterii. Item ejusdem de Simoniacis, et de veritate corporis et sanguinis Domini. Item ejusdem sermo in dedicatione ecclesie. Item omelia ejusdem super *Cum ingressus Jesus.* Item ejusdem epistole III.

[1] For a full discussion of the subject see *Histoire de l'abbaye du Bec* par le Chanoine Porée, Curé de Bournainville (Evreux, 1901, 2 vols.), I 91—94. This scholarly work, to which I have already had occasion to refer, is written by a country parish priest in the neighbourhood of Bernay, and is of the first importance for the study of Norman monasticism. It deserves to be better known in England.

The second list was drawn up by Robert of Torigny, when the Bec library had received a legacy of books from Philippe d'Harcourt, bp of Bayeux, who died in 1164. Here in a composite codex we find: 'Gislebertus contra Judeum.'

If we add the 'Vita domni Herluini abbatis,' which occurs without the name of the author in the first list, we complete the tale of his writings to be found in his old home at Bec in the middle of the twelfth century.

(2) *Boston of Bury.* This learned librarian of St Edmund's monastery expanded in the fifteenth century a catalogue of books existing in English libraries, which had originally been drawn up by the Franciscans[1]. Here we have this entry:

Gilbertus Abbas Westm̄ floruit circa A. Ch.  et scripsit

De disputatione Judaei cum
 Christiano i. cum seipso
 tunc Abbate ad Anselmum

| Archiepiscopum | Lib. i. Reverendo | pronunciabatur 82. 165. 11. |
| De anima | Lib. i. Unde infanti | sub judice 168. |
| De casu diaboli | Lib. i. De angelo | honoret 168. |

The numbers refer to the various libraries: 82 = Bury, 165 = Brinkbourne, 11 = Westminster: 168 is a mistake for 165, the last number being 167: this is proved by another entry under 'Gilbert of Swyneshed' in Boston's own catalogue, where we have without 'incipit' or 'explicit,' and on the authority of 'Catalogus librorum Angliae,' the following:

| De anima | Lib. i | 165 |
| De casu diaboli | Lib. i | 163 |

But in the *Septem Custodiae* both have the number 165.

We see then that in England in the fifteenth century Gilbert was best known by his *Disputation with a Jew*; but that two other tracts were also supposed to be his, which were not in the Bec lists. It seems probable that at Brinkbourne the three were to be found in one volume.

(3) We may now supplement the information gained from these ancient lists by the evidence of existing manuscripts. The first which

---

[1] See note by Dr M. R. James in *Westminster Abbey MSS.* p. 22. Tanner's *Bibliotheca* gives the fullest printed information; but I quote from transcripts made for Dr James by Mr Rogers of the Cambridge University Library.

we shall notice shews us that the three works last mentioned were actually to be found in one volume in the twelfth century.

i. *Brit. Mus. Addit.* 8166: described in *Catal. of Romances*, II 352, as a tall quarto, vellum, twelfth century, which 'seems to have been intended to form a collection of the works of Gilbert Crispin, abbot of Westminster.'

f. 3 begins with a table of syllogistic forms: 'Si sit a cum sit b. ĕ. c': followed by interpretations of names, *inc.* 'Ephesus, voluntas vel consilium' (7 churches, 12 tribes, Hebrew alphabet), *expl.* 'Tau, signum.'

f. 3 *b.* *Disputacio Gisleberti abbatis Westmonasterii contra iudeos* (see below, pp. 60 ff.).

f. 17 *b.* *Sermo eiusdem in ramis palmarum:* Exigit solempnitas... *expl.* coheredes autem Christi, cui &c.

f. 18 *b.* De angelo perdito veritas dicit...*expl.* incircumscriptus est, cui honor et &c. (see below, p. 72).

f. 22 *b.* Quod de altaris sacramento fides catholica... *expl.* deus et homo, cui honor et imperium &c. (see below, p. 72).

f. 28. Poems (leonines) *De confessione* Crimina deploret...; *De corpore et sanguine domini* Mysterio magno....

f. 28 *b.* A Lyric (adonics) *Ad Anselmum archiepiscopum* Que modulando... (see below, p. 83): followed by Elegiacs *De creacione sex dierum* Unde dies inquam....

f. 29. *Disputacio x̄piani cō gentili de fide Christi edita a Gilleberto abbate West-monasterii* A duobus philosophis... (see below, pp. 73 ff.).

f. 37. *Disputacio Gisleberti abbatis de anima* Unde infanti anima... *expl.* sub iudice lis est (see below, p. 72).

f. 39 *b.* Proverbial sayings (from A to I): Alienum est....

f. 40. *Versus eiusdem de rege querenti uxorem.* The poem which follows seems to have nothing to do with this title: it is one of two Aesopic Fables in hexa-meters—(i) Kite in Hawk's nest, (ii) Ram in Dog's skin. These fables are fully described in the *Cat. of Romances* above mentioned.

We may note that the form of the *Disputation with a Jew* here found varies somewhat from the form in which the book ordinarily occurs: it looks like a first draft, made before Anselm became archbishop[1]. Possibly the compiler of this codex had access to various literary remains of Abbot Gilbert, and wished to make a single collection out of them; but some foreign matter has evidently crept in, and there is a great deal of confusion. Nevertheless we have here a valuable addition to our know-

---

[1] See the notes to the dedicatory letter, printed below, p. 82. After the ascription of praise which closes the book as hitherto known ('per omnia saecula saeculorum. amen.') this MS continues: 'Ex condicto item convenimus die altero, et considentes loqui cepimus. Rogasti ut cogitarem ac recogitarem....' New matter here follows (ff. 15—17 *b*) down to 'et scripture sacre auctoritatem esse probatur.'

ledge of Gilbert's writings; and we have certainly got the two treatises
' De anima' and 'De casu diaboli' of which Boston of Bury speaks.

ii. *Brit. Mus. Cotton.* Vesp. A. xiv: described in *Catal. of Romances*,
ii 529, as a small quarto, vellum, about A.D. 1200. Three MSS are here
bound up together; and the middle one, which concerns us, is badly cut
at the bottom in binding.

1. ff. 1—105. Kalendar, with saints mainly Welsh; followed by lives of some.
2. f. 106. Correspondence between Gregory the Great and Augustine: from Bede.
   f. 109. *G. abbot of Westminster to A. abp of Canterbury:* On the Holy Spirit
   (see below, p. 70).
   f. 111. Vision of Drihthelm, &c.: from Bede.
3. ff. 114—179. Epp. of Alcuin, &c.

Here we have another tract of Gilbert's, oddly preserved amid alien
matter[1].

iii. *St John's College, Oxford, no.* 149. This codex is described in
detail in Coxe's catalogue: I shall therefore state its contents sum-
marily, only calling attention to one or two new points of interest[2].
Coxe assigns it to the beginning of the thirteenth century: it may be
rather earlier: some leaves, as we shall see, are undoubtedly earlier.

f. 1. Ailred's Life of St Edward. [I have collated this with Twysden's edition: the
chapter-headings are throughout different; and it contains the story of the
devil and the money-bags, which is not in Twysden, but is to be read in
Richard of Cirencester, *Spec. Hist.* iv 9. Twysden got his MS from Ussher: it
is probably no. 172 in Trin. Coll. Dublin: it was a Westminster book.]
f. 59 b. Abbo's Life of St Edmund.
f. 72 b. Passion of St Kenelm.
f. 82. 　„　„ St Christina.
f. 91 b. 　„　„ SS. Faith, Hope and Charity.
f. 99. *Incipit liber domni Gisleberti de symoniacis* (see below, pp. 57 ff., 111—24).
f. 111. Virtues of St Gregory of Neo-Caesarea.
f. 114. Revelations of St Elizabeth.
f. 170. Poem on B.V.M.
f. 176. Passion of St Margaret.
f. 181 b. Passion of 11,000 virgins of Cologne. [The page, by means of enlarge-
ments of the letter *s*, is made to end with 'pregustaret': the next page (182 a)

---

[1] It was noticed by the learned authors of the *Histoire Littéraire de la France* in their
account of Gilbert Crispin (t. x. pp. 192—201). My attention was called to both the above-
mentioned MSS by Mr Herbert of the British Museum.

[2] I have to thank the President and Fellows for granting me special facilities for
consulting this MS, so that I was able to transcribe Gilbert's treatise in the abbey in which
he wrote it.

goes on 'ut inenarrabilem' in an earlier hand; and there is the remainder of a leaf which has been cut away before this. The Passion ends on f. 191 *a* (*ad fin.*) without an *explicit*: f. 191 *b* is blank.]

f. 192. 'Concilium remis habitum presidente papa calixto' (still the earlier hand).

f. 193. Proverbial verses (returning to the hand of the first portion of the codex).

f. 198. Lections for SS. Cyriacus, &c.

f. 205 *b*. Scraps of proverbs, &c. by various hands, but giving no guidance as to the provenance of the book.

It is a mystery how Abbot Gilbert's treatise *De Simoniacis* came to be embodied in a collection of this kind. Its recovery puts an end to an interesting speculation of H. Boehmer, in his valuable book on 'Church and State in England and Normandy in the eleventh and twelfth centuries.' He had suggested that a tract 'De sacramentis hereticorum,' which is the answer of a certain 'magister G.' to a question put by a 'discipulus G.', might be the work which the Bec catalogue ascribed to Abbot Gilbert under the title 'De simoniacis et de veritate corporis et sanguinis domini.' The fact that the judgment of a certain 'sacer senex,' presumed to be Anselm, is referred to, and the occurrence of Gilbert's *Disputation with a Jew* in the same codex, formed the grounds of the theory: but the highly rhetorical style of the writer made the identification very doubtful. It need not now be further considered[1].

We pass now to consider certain works which have been wrongly assigned to Gilbert Crispin.

(1) *Homil. 47 in Cantica Canticorum.* The only evidence for giving this to our Gilbert appears to be Leland, who found a copy of it at Wardon (*Collectan.* IV 12); but when he next mentions the book (as at Peterhouse, Cambridge) he assigns it simply to 'Gilbertus monachus.' Gerberon (Migne, *P. L.* 158, col. 1167) refers to these Homilies, 'quas apud Eberbacenses exstare monet additiuncula in Trithem.' Boston of Bury, however, attributes them to 'Gilbertus Albus monachus et abbas de Swyneshed.' This is Gilbert of Hoyland, who was a pupil of St Bernard and by him made a Cistercian (Tanner). There is no doubt that this is the true attribution: for St Bernard's 86 discourses on the Song of Songs[2] end at iii 1, where his exposition was cut short by death. Gilbert took it up at this point, but his own death cut it short again at v 10.

---

[1] See Boehmer, *Kirche u. Staat*, p. 172; and for the text of the tract *Monumenta Germaniae Historica*, Lib. de lite III 12—20 (from Wolfenbüttel MS 782).

[2] Migne, *P. L.* 184, col. II.

Besides the Peterhouse MS, there is one at Trin. Coll. Dublin, no. 117 [A. 5. 5]: 'Incipit tractatus Gisleberti abbatis super cantica canticorum, ab eo loco [iii 1]: In lectulo meo...Varii sunt amantium affectus...': 47 tractates, ending, 'qui approximant illi approximant igni. amen. Expliciunt cantica canticorum secundum magistrum Gilbertum.'

(2) *Commentary on Jerome's Prologues.* Cave, *Hist. Litt.* I 634 (Lond. 1688), assigns to Gilbert Crispin:

Item *in prologos S. Hieronymi super Biblia,* ibid. [i.e. Peterhouse].

*Contra peccata cogitationis, locutionis et operis,* in bibliotheca privata Gualteri Cope.

Of the second of these I know nothing. Of the first there is a MS at Turin (Pasini, cod. MCLX: f. II 21: saec. xiv), which on Cave's authority is assigned to Gilbert Crispin. I have examined the Peterhouse MS (Bernard's Catal., 1754: Dr James's, 259). On a fly-leaf in a seventeenth century hand is written, 'Com. Gilberti in prologos Hieronomi in Biblia.' On f. 77a we find a mention of Gilbert, which probably has led to the error: 'Incipit prologus vel potius introitus gilberti pictagavensis in apocalipsim.' Gilbert de la Porée, bishop of Poitiers, appears to be meant.

(3) *Commentaries on Isaiah and Jeremiah,* assigned to our Gilbert by Pits, and perhaps some other expository writings so assigned, may also with probability be given to Gilbert de la Porée.

(4) *Liber de statu Ecclesiae,* also assigned to our Gilbert by Pits, belongs to 'Gilbertus Lunicensis,' bp of Limerick: see Migne, *P. L.* 159, col. 995 and 1003.

Of the genuine writings of Gilbert Crispin there remain three items in the Bec list which still elude us[1]:

Sermo in dedicatione ecclesiae.
Omelia super *Cum ingressus Jesus.*
Epistolae III.

But we may feel satisfied that we have undoubtedly got nearly everything that is mentioned on good authority as having been

---

[1] The *De veritate corporis et sanguinis domini,* which follows the *De Simoniacis* in the Bec list, is doubtless meant for a separate title. In Brit. Mus. Addit. 8166 (described above) after the discussion 'de angelo perdito' (f. 18 b) follows a discussion 'de altaris sacramento' which perhaps is the tract in question. There is also in the same manuscript a poem entitled *De corpore et sanguine domini,* which begins: 'Mysterio magno legali vescimur agno.' But it consists of only about twenty-five lines, and is not at all likely to have been singled out for notice in a catalogue.

written by him. The following is a summary list of his extant works :

1. Life of Herluin: Corp. Chr. Camb., 318.
2. Disputation with a Jew: many MSS.
3. De Simoniacis: St John's, Oxf., 149.
4. De Spiritu Sancto: Vesp. A. xiv.
5. De casu diaboli: ⎫
6. De anima: ⎪
7. Sermo in ramis palmarum: ⎬ B. M. Addit. 8116.
8. Versus ad Anselmum: ⎪
9. Disputatio Christiani cum gentili: ⎭

## 1. *The Life of Herluin, first abbot of Bec.*

It is somewhat remarkable that this, which in course of time has come to be the most important of Gilbert Crispin's works, should never have been printed in a complete form. It is the foundation of all our knowledge of the great Norman abbey which gave Lanfranc and Anselm, and afterwards Theobald, to the archiepiscopal throne of Canterbury; and, as Gilbert lived at Bec for twenty-five years, and only left it a few years after Herluin's death, his narrative has a unique worth which careful historians have not failed to recognise. But in truth, paradoxical as it may sound, its very value as a historical document has involved its text in this unmerited neglect. For the writer of Lanfranc's Life[1] relied almost exclusively upon it for the earlier part of the archbishop's career, and embodied large sections of it in his biography. When Luc d'Achery edited Lanfranc's works in 1648, he prefixed to them the *Vita Lanfranci*, and he added in an appendix Gilbert's *Vita Herluini*. But in order to save repetition he did not print the latter work in full; and he puts us off again and again with a disappointing '&c.,' referring us for the omitted passages to the earlier pages of his volume. Unfortunately the changes and additions which the author of Lanfranc's Life had introduced make it impossible thus to reconstruct Gilbert's work with accuracy: we are in constant danger of ascribing to Gilbert words that he never wrote. The most striking instance of this is the story of Lanfranc's adventure with the robbers, which is commonly supposed to have decided him to adopt the monastic life. Of this adventure there are two somewhat different traditions.

[1] Milo Crispin, precentor of Bec († c. 1150): see above, p. 18.

One of them is given in the *Vita Lanfranci,* where it occurs in the middle of a passage borrowed from Gilbert's work: but as a matter of fact it is altogether absent from the *Vita Herluini,* and thus loses what has hitherto appeared to be its most important attestation.

It is only in this mutilated form that Gilbert's Life of Herluin has hitherto been known to scholars[1]. It exists in manuscript in the library of Corpus Christi College, Cambridge, in a codex (no. 318) given to Abp Parker by the Dean of Rochester. This is a Rochester book of the twelfth century, beginning with Ailred's Life of St Edward, and containing among other pieces Eadmer's Life of St Anselm.

It is also found in a codex of the Vatican (no. 399 fonds de la reine de Suède), which contains the lives of the early abbots and the *Chronicon Beccense.* This MS was written c. 1480: a copy of it made by André Duchesne is in the Bibliothèque Nationale at Paris (lat. 5427). See L. Delisle, *Notice sur vingt manuscrits du Vatican,* 1877 (extr. de la Bibliothèque de l'École des Chartes), and Porée, *Chronique du Bec* (1883), p. xiv.

D'Achery probably printed his text from one of the MSS described by Montfaucon (*Bibliotheca biblioth. MSS,* II 254) as existing at Bec at the end of the seventeenth century.

In the *Historia Normannorum* of William of Jumièges (l. vii, c. 22 : Duchesne, p. 279), after a brief mention of Abbot Herluin, we read :

Si quis vero conversionem et conversationem ipsius plenius nosse desiderat, librum qui de vita ejusdem patris venerandi eleganti sermone conscriptus est a viro religioso Gisleberto Crispino, postea abbate Westemonasterii, et tam nobilitate generis quam scientia saeculari et divina pollenti, perquirens relegat, in quo sufficienter reperiet unde suo desiderio satisfaciat.

In l. vi, c. 9 of the same work (Duchesne, pp. 261—265) large portions of Gilbert's book are actually embodied. M. Leopold Delisle, however, writing of two MSS of W. of Jumièges at Leyden (nos. 20 and 77) in *Mélanges de Pal.* p. 173, says that it is known that Orderic Vitalis, c. 1130, in the abbey of St Evroul revised and completed the work of W. of Jumièges, and that some ten years later this text was further developed by Robert of Torigny in the abbey of Bec. This particular chapter, commencing 'Circa haec tempora,' which concerns the history of Bec, has long been pointed out as an interpolation by

---

[1] It is reprinted in Mabillon, *Acta SS. Ord. Ben. s. vi,* in Migne *P. L.* 150, col. 697 ff., and by Giles (Lanfranc's Works, Oxf. 1844) : Giles knew of no MS of the *Vita* (*ibid.* I 406).

Robert. In one of the Leyden MSS it has been added subsequently, and a leaf has been inserted to make room for it.

Gilbert's work has been recast in the *Altera vita Herluini*, printed in the *Acta SS. ordinis S. Benedicti* (saec. vi, part ii, pp. 335—365) from an ancient Bec codex. After the prologue, 'Quoniam Christi militis Herluini,' &c., it begins: 'Felix in domino vir Herluinus, primus pater et fundator Beccensis ovilis,' &c. This is to be found in a Jumièges codex in the public library at Rouen, U. 102, saec. xii—xiii. The writer does not mention Gilbert's name: perhaps he did not know it, for the *Vita Herluini* probably circulated anonymously[1]. He says that some found the old Life tasteless and others found it tedious[2]. His new Life, however, extends to much the same length ; and two sentences will suffice to shew the style which he preferred: (p. 362) 'Coepit ergo deo dignus minister digna dignis altaribus digne ministrare': (p. 363) 'Dux siquidem immundorum in mundum immundum egressuro immundo per immunda loca immunditiae suae signaverat sero vestigia[3].' We may be thankful that Abbot Gilbert did not consult 'the urbanity of the moderns' after this fashion.

## 2.   *Disputation of a Christian and a Jew.*

If it is beyond all reasonable question that the Life of Abbot Herluin is now the most interesting and most valuable of Gilbert Crispin's works, it was otherwise in the twelfth and thirteenth centuries. Far more popular was the *Disputatio Judaei cum Christiano*, a controversial work of exceptional fairness, dedicated by Gilbert to his old master Archbishop Anselm, and in temper at any rate not unworthy of his school.

Two copies of this book were in the Bec library in the middle of the twelfth century, the second being part of the legacy of Philip Harcourt, bp of Bayeux. In England Boston of Bury vouches for copies at Westminster, Bury and Brinkbourne in the fifteenth century. The following

[1] In the xiith cent. list of the Bec library it occurs in the following entry without the name of the author: '*In uno*. Dicta beati Gregorii pape super cantica, et vita domni Herluini abbatis, et vita beati Anselmi archiepiscopi Cantuariensis' (cf. Migne *P. L.* 150 col. 771 f.).

[2] Prologue (p. 359) : '*Licet olim digesta sit a viro ut fertur erudito seu etiam lingua diserto, sterilem tamen in ea prolixitatem et incompositam dictaminis barbariem modernorum abhorret urbanitas : praesertim cum ex uno insipida ex altero taediosa non immerito judicetur.*'

[3] Cf. infra p. 95.

list of existing MSS, which makes no pretence of completeness, will shew at a glance how widely it was distributed in early times.

1. British Museum, Addit. 8166 [xii].
2.    „        „     Tit. D. xvi [xii]: from St Alban's.
3. Oxford, Bodl. 839 [xii].
4. Paris, Bibl. Nat. Lat. 12,311 [xii].
5.    „     „     „   Lat. 14,858 [xii].
6. Troyes, 423 [xii].
7. Valenciennes, 249 [xii]: from St Amand.
8. Rouen, 1174 (fragm.) [xii].
9. Evreux, 4 [xii]: from abbey of Lyre.
10. Munich, Lat. 14,509 (fragm. init.) [xii].
11.    „    Lat. 324 [xiii].
12. Wolfenbüttel, 782 [xii]: from Lampspring.

It was printed by Dom Gabriel Gerberon in his great edition of St Anselm in 1675 ('In ms. biblioth. Remig. B. 10, et ex ms. Victorino cc. 9, et ex ms. San-Germanensi'). It is reprinted in Migne, *P. L.* 159, col. 1005 ff.

In the *Bibliotheca Patrum*, Lugd. xx, p. 1884, there is printed under the name of William de Champeaux a treatise entitled *Altercatio Christiani cum Judaeo de fide Catholica*. This is preceded by an epistle dedicatory to Alexander, bp of Lincoln, which is closely parallel to Gilbert's letter of dedication to St Anselm[1]: and the opening sentences of the dialogue itself borrow thoughts and phrases from the beginning of Gilbert's work, though presently the writer takes an independent line of his own.

William de Champeaux (*de Campellis*) is a notable figure in the history of philosophy at the beginning of the twelfth century: he was for a time the teacher of Abelard, and he afterwards became bishop of Chalons-sur-Marne. It is exceedingly unlikely that he should have written such a treatise as that which we are considering. Indeed the only reason for referring it to him appears to be its occurrence in a 'codex Catalaunensis.' Now William of Champeaux is said to have died in Jan. 1121; and, even if this be Jan. 1122 of our reckoning, we cannot escape an anachronism: for Alexander was nominated to the bishopric of Lincoln at the Easter court of 1123, and was consecrated in the following July.

---

[1] This letter, which is anonymous, is printed at the end of Gilbert's *Disputatio* in Migne, *P. L.* 159, col. 1036.

We may with probability attribute the work to some English admirer of Gilbert's treatise, who wished to ingratiate himself with a powerful bishop. But it does not reflect Gilbert's modest and gentle spirit. It is worth while to read the two works together in order to see how much Gilbert rises above the ordinary controversialist of his day. The later writer is evidently dissatisfied with the leniency with which the earlier writer treats his opponent. He is determined to secure the victory for the Christian disputant: he substitutes threatenings for arguments, and overwhelms his opponent with New Testament quotations: it is obvious that he is writing a book rather to please Christians than to convert Jews.

As Gilbert's *Disputatio* is not here reprinted, it will be well to give some account of it in detail. It is not cast in the form of a conversational dialogue, but consists of seven set speeches on either side; those of the Jew, who raises the objections, being much shorter than those of the Christian, who has to make somewhat elaborate replies, and also to carry on a counter-attack. The whole treatment is eminently fair: the difficulties propounded by the Jew are genuine difficulties, and to some of them a fully satisfactory reply cannot easily be given. There is no loss of temper on either side, and at the end there is no token of surrender and no note of triumph.

That the Christian position was sufficiently maintained from the standpoint of the early middle ages is shewn by the wide and rapid circulation of the book, and by the fame which Gilbert acquired by means of it. And that his kindly reasonableness was not without immediate effect we may gather from the closing paragraph of his dedicatory letter to St Anselm. For, while he does not claim to have influenced his learned opponent, who had been educated at Mainz, he says that a London Jew by God's mercy had been converted at Westminster, had there made public profession of his faith and received baptism, and had enrolled himself in Christ's service as a monk of Gilbert's own abbey.

A few quotations will serve to shew how keen a disputant Gilbert had to deal with, and will also bring out some minor points of interest which lie buried in a treatise that not many people are likely to read.

(1) The Jew makes his own position clear: he believes Christ to have been a great prophet; he will even, he says, 'believe Christ'; but he will not 'believe in Christ,' but only in the One God:

Christum credo prophetam quidem omni virtutum praerogativa excellentissi-mum, et Christo credam; sed in Christum neque credo, neque credam; quia non credo nisi in deum, et unum. Audi, inquit, Israel, deus tuus deus unus est: unus, non triplex, sicut vos Christiani et negando dicitis et dicendo negatis[1].

(2)  Quoting Isa. ii. 3, he contrasts the invitation to 'go up to the house of the God of Jacob' with the Christian custom of calling churches by the names of saints:

Alii vestrum dicunt, Eamus ad domum Petri; alii, Ad domum Pauli; alii, Ad domum Martini: nulli vero dicunt, Eamus ad domum dei Iacob (col. 1012).

In his reply Gilbert says:

Quod autem dicere nos arguitis, Eamus ad domum Petri, eamus ad domum Pauli, ad domum Martini; nullus qui sane sapit hoc ita dictum esse intelligit. nullam quippe domum Petro seu Paulo facimus, sed in honorem atque memoriam Petri seu Pauli deo eam condimus. nec ulli pontificum fas est dicere in consecrationibus ecclesiarum, Tibi Petro, seu Paulo, hanc domum vel hoc altare consecramus: sed, Tibi deo in honorem Petri, seu Pauli, hanc domum vel hoc altare consecramus. propterea vero haec domus potissimum appellatur domus dei Jacob, ac specialius nominatur Jacob, quia primus omnium legitur Jacob deo instituisse hanc domum. Erexit, inquit, Jacob lapidem in titulum, fundens oleum desuper; et dixit, Vere locus iste sanctus est: et enumeratis quae viderat caelestibus mysteriis obstupefactus addidit, Quam terribilis est locus iste, non est hic aliud nisi domus dei et porta caeli. domus ergo dei nostri est domus dei Jacob, quia deum quem colimus coluit Abraham quoque Isaac et Jacob. in hac domo dei cotidie divinus sermo recitatur, populus fidelis quae bona appetat et quae mala fugiat edocetur, ac simul quae appetendorum sint praemia et quae mala quae aguntur poena comitetur (col. 1014).

(3)  Speaking of the prophecy of Emmanuel, the Jew says:

Animo libenti accipimus de Christo dictum, Et vocabitur nomen ejus Nobiscum deus: hoc est, tantae dignitatis et gratiae erit apud deum, ut in eo et per eum dominus, id est domini virtus, sit nobiscum. numquid quotiens ad vestrarum solemnia missarum dicitis, Dominus vobiscum, statim consequitur ut deus homo fiat, vel in turba homo factus consistat?

(4)  From the scheme of the Atonement which Gilbert sets out at length in col. 1021 ff. (beginning, 'Nosti quoniam Genesis...), one passage may here be given:

Quod si novus vel aliunde natus homo, seu angelus factus homo, hominem liberaret, non sic ad pristinum dignitatis ingenitae statum restitui posset. cum enim angelis homo par creatus, non natura sed rationis et concessae libertatis gratia, soli deo creatori ad serviendum obnoxius erat, ad eundem libertatis statum seu per hominem seu per angelum restitui non valebat: a quo enim quis a servitute redimitur, ei ad serviendum obnoxius esse judicatur. quia ergo per alium plena

---

[1] Migne, *P. L.* 150, col. 1011. In the following quotations I have corrected the text from Brit. Mus. Addit. 8166 and Titus D. xvi.

hominis restitutio fieri non valebat, necesse fuit ut creator creaturae subveniret, creaturam creator subiret, ut per ipsum creatorem homo restitutus soli creatori ad serviendum obnoxius remaneret, et hostis jure ditionem supra genus humanum habitam amitteret. nihil enim in Christo suum hostis invenerat, qui neque in iniquitatibus conceptus erat, neque in peccato partus fuerat, neque ullam prorsus peccati maculam vivendo contraxerat. quia igitur praesumptione injusta mors in eum feriendo deliquit, in quo nihil suum reppererat, nil omnino juris habebat : jure amisit eam jurisdictionem quam peccato primi hominis in hominem primum ejusque posteritatem obtinuerat (col. 1023).

The first half of this passage finds a close parallel in the fifth chapter of the first book of the *Cur Deus Homo* : but it may be questioned whether Gilbert would have written the latter part after the publication of that work, which Anselm finished during his exile at Capua in 1098. For Anselm had perceived the objection to admitting any 'claim' of the devil (*ibid.* II, c. 7), and had lifted the whole question into a higher region.

(5) The Jew has already complained of the violence done to the Scriptures by the determination of the Christians to find everywhere prophecies of Christ. In the following passage he recurs to this topic, and then proceeds to challenge the text of the Old Testament which Christians use.

Si fas est Christianis hoc modo scripturas de Christo legere et interpretari, multo plura invenietis quae ita quoquo modo poteritis interpretari. nos vestras litteras nescimus, et fortasse multa dicitis esse apud vos scripta quae apud nos scripta esse non credimus. sed si deus mihi et tibi vitam praestare voluerit, majori otio ad te revertar, librorum conferemus et apud nos et apud vos exemplaria, et ista requiremus exempla. ipse quidem fateor summae ineptiae, immo dementiae, esse seu me seu te contra evidentia scripturarum exempla et auctoritates resistere ; et idcirco ad praesens non est opus te ulterius disputando procedere. nam revera vos Christiani multa profertis de lege et prophetis, quae non sunt scripta in lege et prophetis. illud enim quod de Jeremia posuisti : Post haec in terris deus visus est, et cum hominibus conversatus est (*Baruch* iii 38), multaque huic versui superius annexa, Jeremias non dixit, non scripsit. quod si hoc in Jeremia scriptum esse inveneris, caetera veracissime dicta esse concedo; si autem in Jeremia non inveneris, depone tantam adversum nos animositatem ; erubesce adinventam contra nos falsitatem, et agnosce primam permanere apud nos in lege et prophetis veritatem (col. 1026).

This is a dignified rebuke. It is followed up by a challenge of the famous prophecy of Isaiah (vii 14), 'Ecce virgo concipiet,' where he says that the meaning is not 'virgo,' but 'abscondita': and he adds that, even if the rendering 'virgo' be admitted, he cannot allow the Christian gloss of the perpetual virginity.

Nam et illud quod universi vos Christiani ore tam securo adversum nos profertis: Ecce virgo concipiet et pariet filium, Isaias non dixit, non scripsit; sed. tantum, Ecce, inquit, abscondita concipiet et pariet filium. tamen si hoc ipsum dixisset Isaias quod dicitis, Ecce virgo concipiet et pariet filium, non tamen addidit quod vestra ex parte additis, quod virgo in conceptu mansit et post partum virgo permansit. hoc nec Isaias dixit, nec ullus alius propheta (col. 1027).

(6) Gilbert clearly knows no Hebrew, and he falls back on the Septuagint translators as unbiassed witnesses of the true text. But the Jew on his part knows nothing of any Seventy, except the elders whom Moses set to rule the people. The discussion (col. 1027 f.) is too long to quote; but it has an interest of its own, and it is noteworthy that Gilbert makes no reference to the work of St Jerome.

(7) The last objection raised by the Jew is interesting for its reference to the Christian art of the day: it may even have been suggested by a 'Majesty' in Gilbert's new refectory. The Christian has quoted the passage: 'Confundantur omnes qui adorant sculptilia et qui gloriantur in simulacris suis'; and the Jew replies:

Ex hac igitur tua illatione colligi potest, Confundantur et Christiani; quia et Christiani adorant sculptilia et gloriantur in simulacris suis. ipsum etenim deum effigiatis aliquando miserum pendentem in patibulo, cruci clavis affixum (quod ipso etiam visu horrendum est), idque adoratis; et circa crucem effigiatis semipuerum solem nescio unde exterritum et fugientem, lunam semipuellam lugubrem, semumque lucis suae cornu occultantem. aliquando autem deum effigiatis sublimi solio sedentem manuque porrecta signantem; et circa eum, quasi magno dignitatis praestigio[1], aquilam et hominem, vitulum et leonem. has effigies Christiani exsculpunt, fabricant et depingunt unde possunt et ubi possunt, et adorant et colunt: quod lex a deo data omnimodo fieri vetat (col. 1034).

Gilbert's defence is good. He reminds the Jew of the cherubim in the temple (1 Kings vi 29), and of the twelve oxen which supported the laver (1 Kings vii 23—25). He justifies the evangelic symbols from the Old Testament itself (Ezek. i 10); and he distinguishes carefully between the adoration of God and the adoration of the Cross.

Facimus deo picturas, facimus deo caelaturas, facimus et sculpturas; sed divino cultu nec adoramus nec colimus eas. nam ipsam crucem, quam crucem sanctam dicimus, utique lignum non deum esse dicimus, nullamque in se aut ex se virtutem habere eam dicimus: at postquam benedictione pontificali sanctificatur in memoriam dominicae passionis, jam crucem non divino sed debito venerationis cultu attollimus, adoramus et colimus; sicut in psalmo dicitur, Adorate scabellum pedum ejus, quoniam sanctum est (col. 1035).

As Gilbert's dedicatory letter, which speaks of the visits paid him on matters of business by the Jew who had been educated at Mainz,

---

[1] Addit. 8166 has 'presagio': but Ducange gives *praestigium = praetextum*.

and also of the conversion of a London Jew, gives us what is perhaps the earliest historical reference to Jews resident in England, we may quote here the passage in which William of Malmesbury informs us that the Conqueror had brought them from Rouen and settled them in London. Writing of William Rufus, he says:

Insolentiae vel potius inscientiae contra deum hoc fuit signum. Judaei qui Londoniae habitabant, quos pater a Rothomago illuc traduxerat, eum in quadam solempnitate adierunt xenia offerentes: quibus delinitus ausus est animare ad conflictum contra Christianos. Per vultum, ait, de Luca! pronuntians quod si vicissent in eorum sectam transiret.

Thus William of Malmesbury wrote in the first edition of his *Gesta Regum*, about the year 1125: but some ten years or more afterwards, when in a new recension he softened down many of his more piquant statements, he recast the passage as follows:

Insolentiae in deum Judaei suo tempore dedere indicium: semel apud Rothomagum, ut quosdam ab errore suo refugas ad Judaismum revocarent, muneribus inflectere conati; alia vice apud Londoniam, contra episcopos nostros in certamen animati, quia ille ludibundus, credo, dixisset quod si vicissent Christianos apertis argumentationibus confutatos in eorum sectam transiret. magno igitur timore episcoporum et clericorum res acta est, pia sollicitudine fidei Christianae timentium. et de hoc quidem certamine nihil Judaei praeter confusionem retulerunt, quamvis multotiens jactarint se non ratione sed factione superatos.

Here the 'insolence' of Rufus has become the 'insolence' of the Jews: Rouen is mentioned only as the scene of an attempt to recover converts by bribery; and the writer directs his sarcasm at the bishops who tremble at the possible issue of an open debate[1].

The kindly feeling of St Anselm towards converted Jews is shewn by a letter which he writes to Ernulf the prior of Christ Church, Canterbury [1096—1107], and William the archdeacon of Canterbury, bidding them see to the welfare of a convert named Robert:

Ut ea hilari pietate et pia hilaritate, qua omnes Christiani debent occurrere et subvenire de Judaismo ad Christianitatem fugienti, curam habeatis hujus Roberti, ne ulla indigentia vel occasione quam avertere possimus cogatur paenitere, qui propter Christum parentes suos et legem eorum reliquerit....Ordinate itaque vos, domne prior, de eleemosyna, non per servientes (qui plus quaerunt quae sua sunt quam quae dei sunt), sed per monachum eleemosynarium; et vos, domine Willelme, ex his quae mihi ex archidiaconatu servare debetis, quatenus ille cum familiola sua nullam duram patiatur indigentiam, sed gaudeat se de perfidia transiisse ad veram

---

[1] W. of Malmesb. *Gesta Regum*, Rolls S. II 371. The outrageous conduct of Rufus in taking the bribes and terrifying the converted Jews into renunciation of their new faith is passed over by this writer: but it is told at full length by Eadmer, *Hist. Nov.* Rolls S. 99 ff.

fidem, et probet ex ipsa nostra pietate quia fides nostra propinquior est deo quam Judaica[1].

Gilbert's book is written in the spirit of his master, and it is a book that was plainly called for by the circumstances of the time.

### 3. *De Simoniacis.*

Gilbert's treatise *De Simoniacis* deals with a burning question of the day, and administers a quiet rebuke to many angry and foolish words which were being spoken about it. Herbert Losinga, the otherwise excellent bishop of Norwich, had paid a large sum to William Rufus for his appointment: he had afterwards gone to Rome and with a deep sense of repentance resigned his office into the Pope's hands: he had been absolved and reinstated. Several English abbots were charged with simony at the Council of Westminster in 1102, and were deposed by Anselm. Moreover the struggle regarding Investitures was represented by the reforming party as a crusade against simony. Theological confusion had been introduced, and the minds of pious people had been upset, by some who taught that the sacraments administered by simoniacally ordained persons were no sacraments at all, and that the blessing of such persons was a curse.

The subject was mixed up with high politics as well as with common Christian duties. It needed to be dealt with on its merits: as a question of theology it called for a calm and even academic treatment. Gilbert wisely refuses to consider what is, so to say, only constructive simony: he limits himself to simony in its proper sense, that is, the giving of money in order to obtain holy orders[2]. We need not here trace his argument. It is enough to say that his method is absolutely fair: he sets out the severer view first, in terms which could hardly be improved on by its advocates; and then he confronts it with obvious facts, with the judgments of authority, and with delicate reasonings. He undertakes no more than to state the case on either side for Anselm's judgment. The tract ends abruptly without any peroration. It is as though he had asked a question, and then waited. But there

---

[1] Ans. *Epp.* iii 117.

[2] The curious phraseology 'munus a manu, munus ab officio' is explained by a passage of Gregory (*Hom. in Evang.* i 4. 4): 'Unde bene, cum justum virum describeret propheta, ait: *Qui excutit manus suas ab omni munere* (Isa. xxxiii 15). neque enim dicit, *Qui excutit manus suas a munere*; sed adjunxit *ab omni*: quia aliud est munus ab obsequio, aliud munus a manu, aliud munus a lingua. munus quippe ab obsequio est subjectio indebite impensa, munus a manu pecunia est, munus a lingua favor.'

can be no doubt as to his own position. The unworthiness of the minister, in his view as in ours, hinders not the effect of the sacraments, 'which be effectual, because of Christ's institution and promise, although they be ministered by evil men[1].'

Abbot Gilbert dwells much on the arguments urged against the validity of the sacramental ministrations of simoniacal persons in a book which he knew as the 'De observatione episcoporum' of Ambrose. It is clear from the way in which he quotes from it that he has not a copy before him as he writes; for he prefaces his quotation by saying, 'si non eisdem verbis, eodem omnino sensu ista dicit.' In the Bec library there were two copies of 'Ambrosius de observantia episcoporum'; and we may safely assume that Gilbert was relying on his recollection of one of these, and that he failed to reproduce the exact title of the work.

The book is printed in the appendix to the works of St Ambrose (Migne, *P.L.* xvii, col. 567: but in the reprint of Migne it is transferred to Gerbert's works) under the title *De dignitate sacerdotali.* Its editor remarks that, though almost every manuscript of it has a different title, they all with one single exception assign it to St Ambrose, to whom as internal evidence shews it cannot, in his opinion, possibly belong. The single exception seems to point to the true authorship : *Sermo Gilberti philosophi, papae urbis Romae, qui cognominatus est Silvester, de informatione episcoporum.* It is accordingly assigned to that remarkable personage, Gerbert, who as Pope Silvester occupied the Roman see from A.D. 999 to 1003.

Unfortunately for this theory a large quotation from the treatise is made by Abbo of Fleury in his *Apologeticus*, addressed to the kings Hugh and Robert, the former of whom died in 996: and Abbo gives as its author 'beatus Ambrosius in sermone pastorali[2].' Pfluck-Harttung, who has pointed this out, gives back the tract to St Ambrose[3]; and supposes that Gerbert may have worked it up for his own purposes in the considerably modified form in which it appears in the one exceptional MS which bears his name, and from which Mabillon edited the text in *Vetera Analecta*, II 103 ff. The reasons offered for the Ambrosian authorship are by no means strong: possibly they are capable of being reinforced. It should at any rate be noted that the biblical quotations point to a pre-Hieronymian text.

---

[1] See *Article* xxvi.  [2] Migne *P. L.* 139, col. 466.

[3] *Neues Archiv der Gesellschaft für die ältere deutsche Geschichtskunde*, I 587 ff.

The first half of the book is mainly an exposition of St Paul's description of a bishop's qualifications: the second half is a vigorous denunciation of the simony which was everywhere current in the author's day. How shamelessly the practice was defended appears from his statement that a bishop would say: It is true that I paid the archbishop so much for my consecration: but otherwise I should never have become a bishop at all. If I live, I shall ordain priests and deacons, and out of the proceeds I shall rectify my account, so that in the end I shall be able to say, See! my bishopric cost me nothing!

The words which Gilbert gives as conveying the author's arguments do not occur together in the treatise, but are scattered over a considerable passage which is of sufficient interest to be quoted in full[1].

Ita ut videas in ecclesia passim quos non merita sed pecuniae ad episcopatus ordinem provexerunt: nugacem populum et indoctum, qui talem sibi adsciverunt sacerdotem. quos si percunctari fideliter velis, quis eos praefecerit sacerdotes, respondent mox et dicunt: Ab archiepiscopo sum nuper episcopus ordinatus, centumque ei solidos dedi ut episcopalem gratiam consequi meruissem: quos si minime dedissem, hodie episcopus non essem: unde melius est mihi aurum de sacello invehere quam tantum sacerdotium perdere. aurum dedi et episcopatum comparavi: quos tamen solidos, si vivo, recepturum me ilico non diffido. ordino presbyteros, consecro diaconos, et accipio aurum: nam et de aliis nihilominus ordinibus pecuniae quaestum profligare confido. ecce et aurum quod dedi in meo sacello recepi: episcopatum igitur gratis accepi.

Nempe hoc est quod doleo, quia archiepiscopus carnaliter episcopum fecit. nam propter pecunias spiritaliter leprosum ordinavit. *Pecunia*, inquit, *tua tecum sit in perditionem; quia donum sancti spiritus gratiae pretio comparasti*, et commercium miserabile in animarum exitium peregisti. et nescii homines et indocti in ordinationibus eorum clamant et dicunt, Dignus es et justus es; et conscientia misera, Indignus es et injustus es, dicit. pronunciat enim episcopus hujusmodi ad populum dicens: Pax vobis. oculis quidem carnalibus videtur quasi episcopus magnus, et divinis obtutibus inspicitur leprosus magnus. per pecuniam acquisivit indebitum ordinem, et apud deum perdidit interiorem hominem. caro suscepit dignitatem, et anima perdidit honestatem. caro ancilla domina facta est animae, et anima quae erat domina facta est famula carnis. caro dominatur populis, et anima servit daemoni. carni sacerdotium comparavit, et animae detrimentum paravit. et *quid prodest* hujusmodi *homini, si totum mundum lucretur et animae suae detrimentum patietur? aut quam dabit homo commutationem pro anima sua?* quod dedit cum ordinaretur episcopus aurum fuit, et quod perdidit anima fuit. cum alium ordinaret, quod accepit pecunia fuit, et quod dedit lepra fuit. haec sunt mercimonia iniquorum in perniciem eorum.

Interrogo tamen fratrem et coepiscopum nostrum, quia et ego episcopus sum et

---

[1] The first portion is in fact that which Abbo quotes, introducing it with the words: 'Beatus Ambrosius in sermone pastorali, flendo potius quam ridendo, post multa subjungit.'

cum episcopo loquor. Dic ergo mihi paulisper, frater episcope: cum dares pecuniam, quid accepisti? Gratiam episcopalem accepi. Ergo interrogo te: Haec gratia cur tali vocabulo nuncupatur? respondet: Cur, inquis? ut reor, pro eo quod gratis datur, ideo gratia vocitatur. Ergo si gratia gratis datur, et auro non aestimatur, a te cur gratia pecuniis comparatur? respondet: Non, inquit, mihi daretur, si pecuniis non emeretur; nec episcopus fuissem ordinatus, si pecunias non dedissem. Ergo, ut apparet ex responsionibus tuis, gratiam cum ordinareris non suscepisti, quia gratuito eam non meruisti. et ideo, frater, si gratiam non accepisti, quomodo episcopus effici potuisti? nam et ad discipulos suos dominus dicit: *Gratis accepistis, gratis date.* cur ergo gratuitam aestimasti te pretio possidere gratiam? nam, ut video, aurum dans perdidisti, et gratiam sanctam non acquisisti.

Adhuc tamen semel adiciens fratrem perquiro episcopum, ne quid de approbamentis veridicis nos praetermisisse videamur: Quis dat, frater, episcopalem gratiam? deus an homo? respondes sine dubio: Deus. sed tamen per hominem dat deus: homo imponit manus, deus largitur gratiam: sacerdos imponit supplicem dexteram, et deus benedicit potenti dextera: episcopus initiat ordinem, et deus tribuit dignitatem. o justitia, o aequitas! si homini pecunia datur, qui nihil in ordine amplius operatur nisi solum servitium quod ei creditur, cur deo totum negatur, qui ipsum ordinem tibi largitur? justumne tibi videtur ut servus honoretur, et dominus injuriam patiatur; et injuste accipiat sacerdos pecuniam, et deus patiatur ab homine injuriam? sed quia pro concesso ordine deus a te nihil exspectat, cur a te sacerdos pecuniam impudenter exspectat? deus homini concedere voluit gratis, et episcopus rapax pecuniam ab homine expetit: deus homini, ut certe benignus, gratis donavit, et sacerdos malignus eum sine causa praedavit. *quid enim habes quod non accepisti? si autem accepisti, quid gloriaris, quasi non acceperis?*

It will be found that Abbot Gilbert recalls not only the arguments of this striking passage, but also nearly every one of its biblical quotations[1]. He puts its reasonings very succinctly, and they lose little by his abbreviation. He was prepared to give them full weight, but he was convinced that there was another side to the question, and that the ecclesiastical problem could not be settled by such arguments alone.

## 4. *De Spiritu Sancto.*

Our only knowledge of this treatise is derived from the Cottonian MS mentioned above (p. 55). That it is a genuine work of Gilbert Crispin will, I think, scarcely be questioned. The opening and closing paragraphs are strong evidence of his authorship, and incidental confirmation

---

[1] Gilbert frequently quotes scripture loosely. He has a wide knowledge of the Bible, and he obviously trusts his memory in many of his quotations. In citing the text 'Quod tetigerit immundus immundum erit,' he has reproduced the form in which Pope Innocent had quoted it in a passage immediately preceding that which is afterwards given in this book. The Vulgate has (Num. xix 22) 'Quidquid tetigerit immundus immundum faciet': but Aug. *Quaest.* xxxiii de Num. (*ad fin.*) has 'Omne quodcunque tetigerit illud inmundus inmundum erit' [LXX ἔσται].

of this view is furnished by several other passages within the brief compass of the tract. It begins with the following dedicatory letter to Archbishop Anselm:

Domino et patri reverendo ecclesiarum Angliae pastori A., frater G. abbas Westmonasterii, quicquid rectori subditus potest optare jocundius.

De sacris paginis undecunque apud nos sit quaestio, controversiae finis est ut determinationi vestrae nostra committatur altercatio. quaerunt aliqui de spiritu sancto, non id an deus sit : nam omnes Christiani credunt quia deus est pater, deus est filius, deus est spiritus sanctus : sed qua relatione seu habitudine sanctus spiritus dicatur patris et filii esse spiritus. quicquid enim id quod est alterius dicitur esse, aliqua specie habitudinis ab eo necesse est id quod est esse. sub persona igitur interrogantis magistri et respondentis discipuli tractetur, quaeso, haec nostra disceptatio.

M. Primo discutiamus an indubitanter dici et astrui possit, quod sanctus spiritus dicatur patris et filii esse spiritus : deinde inquiramus qua habitudine id esse dicatur.

D. Non fit quaestio inde, nec alicui fas est inde dubitare. audi ab ipso Christo dictum ad discipulos : *Non enim vos estis qui loquimini, sed spiritus patris vestri.*...

M. Pace tua dictum sit, non videtur id adhuc posse concludi. numquid enim quando ait apostolus : *An experimentum vultis ejus qui in me loquitur Christus?* intelligi voluit quod in eo personaliter loquebatur Christus ? sed loquitur in apostolo Christus, quando apostolus ea loquitur quae locutus est Christus....

Several other proof texts are alleged, but the master refuses to be satisfied, and forces his pupil to a more thoughtful consideration. Presently, after the pupil has come to the end of a long piece of reasoning, the master replies :

M. Ne taciturnitate mea aliquod mihi praejudicium fiat. unam harum consequentiarum concedo, alteram concedere non audeo ; sed induxisti nos in laqueum et in condensam silvam quaestionum....

A careful discussion follows, in which the master refuses to accept the loose argumentation of the pupil in reference to the Procession of the Holy Spirit; and the pupil in despair challenges him to remove the stumbling-blocks which he has placed in the way of his faith. More accurate definition follows, and at the end the pupil presses a new question as to why the Incarnation of the Son should not involve the Incarnation of the Father and the Spirit also. Here however the master checks him, and closes the discussion:

M. *Noli altum sapere sed time* ; et oportet te *ad sobrietatem sapere*[1].

D. Fateor me sapere ad sobrietatèm, quia indubitanter credo esse et trinitatem in unitate et unitatem in trinitate : et, si non intelligo id quomodo sit, credo tamen firmissime quia sit.

[1] Ro. xi. 20, xii. 3.

We shall presently see that the phrase 'Pace tua dictum sit' occurs in a somewhat similar context at the beginning of the tract *De casu diaboli*. The illustration of the Holy Trinity by the Nile (which is 'fons, rivus et lacus,' and yet not three Niles, but one Nile) is found both in this tract and in the *Disputation with a Gentile*.

Gilbert draws to a considerable extent upon St Augustine *De Trinitate*. The following references may be of use to a future student of his work: *De Trin.* v 10 [ed. Ben. VIII 838] 'Tamen cum quaeritur quid tres, magna prorsus inopia humanum laborat eloquium. dictum est tamen *tres personae,* non ut illud diceretur, sed ne taceretur': VI 12 [*ib.* 851] 'oportet igitur—apparet vestigium': VII 7 [*ib.* 858] 'et dum intelligatur saltem in aenigmate quod dicitur, placuit ita dici—verius enim cogitatur deus quam dicitur, et verius est quam cogitatur.'

## 5—8. *Minor pieces.*

The treatise *De casu diaboli* begins thus:

INTERROGATIO. De angelo perdito veritas dicit in evangelio: *In veritate non stetit....*

RESPONSIO. Pace tua dictum sit, res confuse et permixta ponis...

This topic is soon followed by questions on freewill, man's creation to supply the place of the fallen angels, and the use of 'unitas' and 'numerus' in respect to the godhead. Presently we pass without any clear break in the manuscript to a discussion of the Eucharist (see above, p. 57 note):

Quod de altaris sacramento fides catholica credit et tenet, teneo et credo : scilicet quod panis et vinum quae offeruntur sacerdoti ad consecrandum, per sacerdotalem consecrationem fiunt substantialiter corpus et sanguis Christi, manente priori forma et qualitate panis et vini. credo item et teneo quod ipsum corpus Christi, quod ab altari sumptum comeditur, resurgens a mortuis jam non moritur, et nulla comestionis lesione corrumpitur. credo item et teneo quod unum et idem numero est corpus hoc et illud....Quaero itaque utrum haec, quae fide indubitata ita credimus esse, aliqua ipsius naturae potentia ita posse esse possimus demonstrare....

The little tract *De anima* is a modest enquiry as to the origin of the soul of an infant. The creationist and traducianist hypotheses are discussed in simple language, and the preference is given to the latter, not on any grounds of philosophy, but for the reason that the theory of the atonement requires that the soul of Christ should have its ultimate derivation from the soul of the first man Adam. If the one stood in no relation to the other, it is inconceivable how the suffering of the one should atone for the sin of the other. The difficulty that original sin would have thus been transmitted to the soul of Christ is met in the following noteworthy sentences:

Sola consilii sui sapientia deus ex nichilo creavit omnia. qui ergo ex non existentibus fecit existentia, ex ipsa jam existenti materia potest assumere massam de massa sine assumptae alicujus infectionis macula. de carne peccati cum peccato sumpta est caro beatae Mariae matris Christi: tamen de ipsa carne matris Christi sumpta est sine peccato caro Christi. si hoc ipsum de anima vult facere omnipotentia dei, potest si vult ex anima de traduce peccati sumpta aliam sumere animam de eadem massa sine peccati culpa et fermenti macula.

These words shew that on a question which was to be much debated in the next generation Gilbert held the same view as his master Anselm.

The tract has interest also for its simple statements on the Atonement. As to the main question which he has proposed, Gilbert only professes to have answered it in a tentative manner: 'de hac quaestione multi multa dixerunt atque scripserunt; sed adhuc manet illud dictum antiquum: Grammatici certant, et adhuc sub judice lis est.'

The *Sermon for Palm Sunday* begins:

Exigit solempnitas hodierna...et processionis sacrae facies insolita, ut de sacramento hujus diei dicamus vobis prout deus dederit....

The *Versus ad Anselmum* are printed below, p. 83.

### 9. *Disputation of a Christian with a Gentile.*

The opening passage of this treatise represents so curious a scene, that it is worth while to transcribe it in full.

A duobus philosophis sumpta erat disputatio de unius dei cultu et verae fidei unitate. noveram locum, sed non praesumebam ire, quia multus erat et varius exitus viae. summonuit me quidam illuc ire et verae fidei assertiones audire. obtendi meam debilitatem totque viarum dubiam mihi varietatem. promisit ducatum, porrexit manum et amica me violentia coepit trahere post se. tandem venimus ad diversorium quod videbamus. intravit ille domum, quia erat de intraneis: extra remansi, quia eram de extraneis; circa ostium consedi, quia eram notus de ostiariis uni.

Considebant ibi plures litterati homines, et, ut mihi videbatur, logicae disciplinae studens. nam quaestio ista inter eos tunc erat: quomodo sit accipiendum quod Aristotiles ait: Non existentibus primis substantiis impossibile est aliquid aliorum esse. Porphirius enim et alii astruunt philosophi quod ea quae sunt individua non tollunt secum species ac genera, species vero ac genera tollunt secum individua. individua dicit Aristotiles esse primas substantias; et secundas substantias dicit esse species ac genera.

Altera inter duos alios juxta me habebatur quaestio, videlicet utrum grammatica sit logica. nam si grammatica non est logica, non erunt tres logicae artis species nec septem liberales artes. sed constitutivae partes cujusque generis sunt constitutivae partes speciei ejusdem generis. inventio et judicium sunt constitutivae partes logicae : erunt igitur et grammaticae, aut grammatica non erit species logicae. at de inventione et judicio in disciplinis grammaticae nusquam fit sermo. grammatica itaque non videtur ars esse naturalis, nec logica, nec ars liberalis.

Harum quaestionum expectabam solutionem ; sed mox melioris causae suscepimus actionem. ecce ab eis qui erant intus venit ad nos qui eramus foris persona dignae speciei. paucis et gravibus verbis silentium jussit fieri, et ut intenti (intendi *cod.*) ac debita reverentia quae intus dicebantur audierimus imperavit. propius accessi, intro aspexi, et introivi. sermo erat inter duos magnae famae sed diversae sectae philosophos. unus erat gentilis et Christianae fidei sub rationis executione callidus impugnator : alter erat e contra veris assertionibus ejusdem fidei expugnator. sic itaque gentilis ille intulit....

If this philosophers' club with its inner and outer circles be not altogether a fiction of the imagination, it shews us an unsuspected side of the London life of Abbot Gilbert's day. No doubt there is an imaginary element in the dialogue, and perhaps the 'Gentile philosopher' is an anachronism : yet we can imagine that he might have found toleration under Rufus, who is said to have encouraged public disputations between Christians and Jews, and to have sworn with his usual oath that he would join the latter if they got the better of the argument. The abbot's weak health and his unwillingness to venture himself in the perilous maze of the streets seem realistic touches. If the picture is a fancy one, it is at any rate an evidence of learning and literary skill.

The opponent of Christianity begins by asserting that the ancient poets while they offered pleasant fables to the vulgar taught deep truths to those who could understand them. Man must act under the guidance of reason and justice, and ever remember what is due to God his Creator.

The Christian philosopher at once quotes scripture on ' the whole duty of man.' But his opponent objects to arguments from sacred writings, and demands reason rather than authority. Christians profess, he says, that the author of their scriptures and the Jewish scriptures is one and the same ; and yet neither will Christians keep the Jewish law, nor Jews the Christian. He will have no arguments based on the authority of the scriptures.

The Christian accepts his terms, and proceeds to argue, on grounds of reason only, for the unity and against the plurality of deity. In his reply the opponent with a naïve inconsistency objects that the Christian speaks of the immutability of the deity, but his scriptures speak of changes in the divine intentions: 'Haec est mutatio dexterae excelsi'; and he instances in particular the Deluge. The Christian replies with the illustration of the gentler and severer methods of the same physician, who is not cruel when his treatment causes pain. The objector is satisfied on this point, but proceeds to attack the doctrines of the Incarnation and the Trinity.

After much interesting discussion, in which he has made many admissions, the objector declares that no argument can ever convince him of the doctrine of the Trinity; and he sadly and respectfully takes his leave. Thereupon the rest of the audience, who are Christians, beg that so great a master will not leave them uninstructed in those deeper reasons for the Catholic Faith which could not properly be proposed to an unbeliever.

One of their number having agreed to state the difficulties as an enquiring disciple, the master proceeds. A discussion follows in which among other points the gradual revelation of the Faith through the teachers of the Old Covenant, through our Lord Himself, and through the apostles and the later doctors of the Church, is skilfully drawn out, and the necessity of belief in accordance with available knowledge in each period is emphasized.

The closing sentences may be quoted, as illustrating the temper of Anselm's pupil.

Qui ergo deitatis unitatem et in deitatis unitate personarum intelligit esse trinitatem, agat deo gratias : et qui capere non potest, ita esse indubitanter credat. in parvulis vero baptizatis, quorum aetas et sensus ad haec capienda minime potest assurgere, et in laicis qui sunt idiotae catholici, fides et baptismus salutem operatur ; sicut promittit ipse dominus: Qui crediderit et baptizatus fuerit, salvus erit. gratias deo, qui omnibus nobis dedit hoc refugium vitae et salutis.

So this Disputation ends. But in the manuscript it is followed at once by a short exposition [1] of the meaning of *Septuagesima*, the period of seventy days which comes to a close on the Saturday in Easter week, on which day a *duplex Alleluia* is sung. Whether Gilbert is its author or not, the exposition is worth transcribing for its liturgical interest.

Legitur quod filii Israel septuaginta annis peregrinati sub rege Babiloniae : septuagesimo vero anno data est eis licentia revertendi, et reversi sunt ab exilio in patriam, a Babilone in Jerusalem. in memoriam cujus peregrinationis et reversionis nos

---

[1] It is preceded by *Gentilis* (rubricated) as if it were a continuation of the Disputation: but this is due to the ignorance of the scribe, who has already used *Gentilis* for the Christian disciple who takes up the discussion after the Gentile philosopher has departed.

etiam in praesenti ecclesia septuagesimam celebramus, partim in dolore in signum peregrinationis, partim in gaudio in signum reversionis.

Habet autem haec septuagesima initium a *Circumdederunt me*, et peragitur cum luctu et maerore usque ad sexagesimum tertium diem, qui est sabatum paschale. deinde in gaudio procedit usque ad octavum diem, id est, ad sabatum quod est in ebdomada paschae, ubi est terminus septuagesimae. hoc autem totum fit in figuram peregrinationis quam in praesenti vita habemus, in qua peregrinamur a domino, longe a patria in regionem dissimilitudinis recedentes, civibus Babiloniae admixti corpore etsi non mente. tota enim praesens vita non patria sed exilium est.

In figuram cujus peregrinationis pars septuagesimae in jejunio et luctu cele-bratur, usque ad sabatum paschale, ubi per baptismum datur repatriandi licentia, quando veterem hominem deponimus et novum induimus : et ideo dies ille baptismo est consecratus. et quia post acceptam licentiam jam laeti sumus spe redeundi, ideo statim cantamus canticum domino, scilicet *Alleluia: Confitemini domino.* sed quoniam nondum Babiloniam exivimus, sed exilio tenemur, mente tamen suspirantes ad patriam, et interim quia grandis restat via difficultatem itineris abhorrentes ; quia, inquam, hoc est, post canticum tractum, post *Alleluia Laudate* subjungimus. deinde vero in sequenti dominica, quae pascha dicitur, incipimus proficisci et cum filiis Israel ab exilio transire in patriam, et quia illis sex diebus a die paschae in itinere gradimur, ideo per totam septimanam illam graduale cantatur, *Haec dies quam fecit dominus.* sed quoniam, licet nondum pervenerimus, tamen quodammodo gaudeamus spe futuri, ideo post graduale sequitur *Alleluia.* septimo autem die, quae est octava a sabato paschali, jam laeti re praesenti, jam potiti patria, et tractum †q...† graduale omnino deponimus, et in signum perfectae laetitiae duplex *Alleluia* decantamus.

Vel possimus dicere quod tota volubilitas hujus saeculi, quod per sex dies vel per sex aetates discurrit, sit quasi una septuagesima, in quam per peccatum primi parentis ejecti a patria exulamus. sed in morte cujusque, cum anima a carcere corporis solvitur, datur licentia repatriandi, tum anima exuta a corpore in aeternam beatitudinem resurgit ; et ideo psalmus ille, qui dicitur canticum pro verbo trans-migrationis[1], scilicet *Te decet ymnus, deus, in Sion* praecipue cantatur in exequiis mortuorum. sed quia quandoque per purgatorium ignem transeundum est, et quia corpus in sua foeditate permanens corrumpitur, ideo nondum est perfecta laetitia usque ad octavam quae erit in finem, revolutis vii diebus vel vii aetatibus praesentis saeculi ; scilicet, cum corruptibile hoc induerit incorruptionem, et mortale corpus fiet immortale ; et sic duplicem stolam habebimus. et ideo in sabato quod est in octavis paschae cantatur duplex *Alleluia*, cum in praecedenti sabato simplex cantaretur.

---

[1] In the heading of Ps. lxiv (Vulg.) we have ' populo transmigrationis '; but ' de verbo peregrinationis ' is found in MSS of the ' Gallican Psalter.'

## VI. Correspondence.

### 1. *Lanfranc to Gilbert.*

Dilectissimo suo G. dilectissimus suus Lanfrancus dilectionis coeptae felicem perseverantiam.

Fratres quos, carissime frater, litteris edocendos bonisque moribus instruendos praecipue transmisi, honeste et secundum voluntatem meam tractari quorundam relatione cognovi: pro qua re gratias benignitati tuae refero, et ut coeptis insistas, si tamen admonitione indiges, admonere te cupio. carissimum mihi fratris mei filium, fratrem videlicet tuum, caritati tuae commendo, rogans sicut rogari oportet a me jocundissimum filium fratremque meum, quatenus cum magna jocunditate animi tui eum diligas et ad vitam laudabilem pro viribus tuis informare non desinas. fratrem tuum propterea dixi illum, quoniam revera sic [1] esse volo multumque rogo: nam et revera venerabilis mater tua, sicut mihi relatum est, filium suum eundem vocare dignatur, cum illa de excellentissimo genere, iste humili loco sit natus, proculdubio receptura ab eo mercedem suam qui dixit: Qui se humiliat exaltabitur. crucem cum reliquiis fraternitatis tuae oculis dum missam celebras conspiciendam tibi transmitto, quam perpetuae amicitiae monumentum inter te et ipsum esse desidero.

Magno gaudio me replesti quia promissionem in pueritia factam in juventute adhuc per divinam misericordiam te servare scripsisti: quam si ad finem illaesam perduxeris, terribilem aliis judicem proculdubio cum magna securitate videbis. omnipotens deus cordi tuo per sancti spiritus sui inspirationem inserere dignetur quatenus in omni aetate tua sic me diligas, sicut in pueritia et adolescentia tua quondam diligere me solebas: et ipse te benedicat atque ab omnibus peccatis propitiatus absolvat.

Lanfranc, *Ep.* 45. Written while Gilbert was at Bec, c. 1074. See above, p. 9.

[1] D'Achery (*Lanfranci Opp.* p. 323) has : 'quem (*al.* quoniam) revera sibi.'

## 2. *Anselm to Lanfranc.*

Domino et patri reverendo archiepiscopo Lanfranco frater Anselmus servus servorum dei Becci remanentium, cum eisdem dominis suis, quod domino fideles servi, quod reverendo patri reverentes filii.

De domno Gisleberto, ut eum vobis mitteremus, vestrae satisfecimus jussioni: quod autem tardius quam jussistis, verum est quod non est factum negligentia, sed ob multa quae nunc enarrare longum est impedimenta. sed scitote quia, si quis fecerit ut ipse in Anglorum terra remaneat, nimis grave et majus quam breviter dici possit damnum in praesenti et in futuro interius et exterius ecclesiae nostrae et tristitiam faciet. quapropter precamur et obsecramus quantum salva justitia et vestrae sanctitatis reverentia nobis licet, per pietatem et per caritatem quam erga nos vestram semper habere paternitatem cognovimus, ut si absque dei voluntatis obviatione fieri posse videritis, potius fratribus et amicis desiderantibus ad certam suam salutem et aliorum utilitatem per vestram instantiam reddatur, quam quibuslibet alienis ad periculum sui damni et illorum utilitatem dubiam ingeratur. breviter quod multum volumus et expedire credimus obsecramus; quia sapientiae vestrae pauca verba sufficere non ignoramus. quod si divinam dispositionem nostrae sic resistere petitioni vestra cognoverit prudentia, ut aliter fieri necesse sit, quod mihi si praesens essem vestra prudentia de re ipsa concedere aut facere consuleret, vestrae committo potestati.

Anselm, *Epp.* II 13. Probably written at the end of 1079, soon after Anselm's return from his first visit to England. See above, p. 9.

## 3. *Anselm to Gilbert.*

Domno, fratri, amico, dilecto dilectori Gilberto frater Anselmus, quod scribere non valet.

Dulcia mihi sunt, amice dulcissime, munera dulcedinis tuae; sed nequaquam consolari possunt desolatum de te cor meum a desiderio dilectionis tuae. certe si mittas omnem aromatum odorem, omnem metallorum nitorem, omnem lapidum pretiositatem, omnem texturae varietatem, renuet, immo non poterit, consolari a scissura sua, nisi recepta altera parte sua scissa anima mea. testis est angor cordis mei hoc ipsum cogitantis, testes lacrimae obtenebrantes oculos et rigantes faciem et digitos id ipsum scribentes. et quidem tu sciebas sicut ego ipse erga te dilectionem meam. sed utique ego ipse nesciebam eam: qui nos scidit ab invicem, ille me docuit quantum te diligerem. vere non habet homo scientiam boni vel mali, qui non experitur utrumque. nesciebam enim, non expertus absentiam tuam, quam dulce mihi erat esse tecum, quam amarum sine te esse. sed tu habes ex ipsa nostra disjunctione praesentem alterum quem non minus aut certe plus amas: mihi vero tu, tu inquam, es ablatus et nullus pro te oblatus. te igitur in consolatione tua gaudente, solum mihi vulnus remansit in mente. forsitan gaudentes de te offenduntur a me ista tibi dicente. sed si ipsi gaudent quod desiderant tenentes, cur prohibent vel dolere quod semper amat perdentem? ex se excusent me, si me vident in se. alioqüin vel tu intellige quam compatienter, quam consolanter ipsi haec faciant; et unde mitescat dolor meus, quem nemo vult consolari qui potest, nemo potest qui vult. sed ille qui omnia quae vult potest sic consoletur me, ut nullum contristet; sic nullum contristet, ut amorem tui integrum ubique conservet. amen.

Anselm, *Epp.* i 75. Written when Gilbert was with Lanfranc, c. 1080.

#### 4. *Anselm to Gilbert.*

Suo dilectissimo, olim divina dispositione filio, nunc dei gratia coabbati, Gisleberto frater Anselmus, in hac vita diu sancte vivere cum prosperitate, in futura feliciter cum aeternitate.

Etsi tarde propter aegritudinem impedientem dilecto dilectori meo pro nova sibi divinitus data gratia scribo, non tamen tepide quantum ad voluntatis benevolentiam pertinet, dico: Gloria in altissimis deo, et in terra gaudium hominibus bonae voluntatis; qui judicium suum de te manifestavit, quod hactenus apud se occultum, licet semper de te pro humana aestimatione bona crederemus, servavit. in eo namque vitae proposito, in quo te custodiendo semper ejus gratia sapientia erudivit et in sanctitate nutrivit, patrem et doctorem pastoremque animarum te constituit. multo enim melius de te sperandum est et de similibus tuis quorum vita est in sancta conversatione nutrita, quam de me et de similibus meis quorum vita olim est saeculari conversatione detrita. de vobis enim sperandum est, cum ad aliorum curam promovemini, quod dum et alios ad vestri similitudinem instruitis justitia vestra perficiatur: de nobis vero timendum est, cum tanto pondere gravamur, ne injustitia nostra occulto dei judicio augeatur. quanto igitur melius est de tua sanctitate in suscepto officio sperandum, tanto magis est et securius de tibi concessa gratia gaudendum. omnipotens deus, qui te custodem aliorum constituit, ipse te sua gratia sic adjuvet et custodiat ut pro tua et illorum justitia aeternam tibi beatitudinem retribuat.

Anselm, *Epp.* ii 16. Shortly after Gilbert's appointment to Westminster, 1085.

### 5.　*Anselm to Gilbert.*

Amico fratri, domino patri, dilecto dilectori, reverendo abbati Gisleberto frater Anselmus, perseverantem in longa vita cum prosperitate sanctitatem, et indeficientem in aeternitate felicitatem.

Si velim scribere mutuae nostrae dilectionis affectum, timeo ne aut videar ab ignorantibus veritatem excedere, aut necesse sit aliquid veritati subtrahere.　qui affectus quantus et quam verus sit, cum multum cognoscerem quando sese oculo ad oculum, osculo ad osculum, amplexu ad amplexum ostenderet, nunc multo magis experior cum abesse illum irrecuperabiliter in quo tanta jocunditate delectabar intueor.　sicut enim abundans nescit quid sit indigenti, ut qui deliciis affluit ignorat quid sit esurienti, ita qui amico fruitur non sentit languorem animae carentis.　quoniam ergo nec scribi sufficienter potest quid nobis invicem sit, nec ignoranti loquor, his interim omissis oro vobiscum ut aliquando nos invicem videntes oculo ad oculum, osculo ad osculum, amplexu ad amplexum, non oblitum amorem recolamus.

De his autem quae de vitae suae conversatione caritas vestra mihi dignata est exponere, gratias ago deo quia nihil ibi videre possum quod non sit laudabile.　de fratre illo quem in claustrum reduxistis, quod vultis donec vobis aut nobis aliter videatur concedo; sed occulta ejus vestra discutiens prudentia prout judicaverit illi consulat.　de damno vestro quod mandastis miror et condoleo.　quod dignatur vestra caritas excusare se, quia non potest modo facere quod vellet, gratias ago vestrae dignationi et bonae voluntati.　de domno Lanfranco nihil melius scivi aut potui, quam quod in Anglia feci et dixi.　valete.

Anselm, *Epp.* ii 36.　The younger Lanfranc is here referred to.

### 6.　*Anselm to Gilbert.*

Domino servus, amico amicus, dilecto dilectus, domno abbati Gisleberto frater Anselmus, sempiternum gaudere.

Si sane, si bene, si prospere cuncta sunt erga domnum abbatem Gislebertum dilectum dilectorem meum, vere inde gaudet cor meum, quia certe sic est desiderium meum.　si dilectionem et beneficia quae nobis et nostris rebus impenditis alienus alienis impenderet, utique gratiarum magnam actionem in scriptis et voce exhiberemus ne deficeret.　sed quoniam hoc ille facit de quo nunquam possumus desperare, sufficere credimus majores gratias cum semper prompta voluntate, praesertim cum hoc ipsum non ignoretis, indesinenter in cordis arca servare. scio quia vestra dilectio quomodo se habeat status noster desiderat cognoscere: qui deo protegente, secundum modum nostrum et secundum temporis hujus varietatem, in cunctis bene esset et prospere, nisi quia cum nuper in Francia essem aliis quibusdam affectum laboribus levis quaedam febris subito irruens plus me terruit quam laesit. sed cum videret mentem meam intentissime conversam ut ad amicos nostros pro auxilio mitterem orationum, exterrita bis tactum fugit exterritum. unde aliquamdiu post passus sum cum edendi fastidio dormiendi difficultatem et membrorum majorem imbecillitatem.

Dominos et fratres nostros, dilectissimos filios vestros, quanta possum devotione saluto; de quorum erga me dulci dilectione re mihi cognita quoties recogito exulto. de Ricardo serviente vestro, qui vos in Angliam secundum jussionem vestram secutus est, vellem vestram si vobis non displiceret benignitatem rogare; quoniam quem deus suo judicio ab impacto crimine excusavit, si ipse ab incepto fideli servitio non deficit, jam nihil est quod bonae vestrae voluntati quam de eo incepistis debeat obviare. justus [*fors.* justum] enim est, et plus decet honestatis vestrae auctoritatem, ut vestra constantia cujuslibet perversitatis impetus circa illum repellat, quam ut aliena non laudabilis pertinacia laudabilem intentionem benevolentiae vestrae reflectat. valeat semper dulcis mihi vestra dilectio.

Anselm, *Epp.* II 47. Anselm writes a similar letter to Gilbert, abbot of Caen (II 44): from which we learn that he was returning from Caen and hoping to reach Bec before the feast of St Benedict (21 March, or the Translation 11 July), but was delayed by business in France.

### 7. *Gilbert to Anselm.*

Reverendo patri et domino Anselmo sanctae Cantuariensis ecclesiae archiepiscopo suus servus et filius, frater Gislebertus, Westmonasterii coenobii procurator et servus, prosperam in hac vita diuturnitatem et beatam in futura aeternitatem.

Paternitati et prudentiae tuae discutiendum mitto libellum quem nuper scripsi, paginae commendans quae Judaeus quidam olim mecum disputans contra fidem nostram de lege sua proferebat, et quae ego ad objecta illius pro fide nostra respondebam. nescio unde ortus, sed apud Maguntiam litteris educatus, legis et litterarum etiam nostrarum bene sciens erat et exercitum in scripturis atque disputationibus contra nos ingenium habebat. plurimum mihi familiaris saepe ad me veniebat, tum negotii sui causa, tum me videndi gratia, quoniam in aliquibus illi multum necessarius eram; et quotiens conveniebamus mox de scripturis ac de fide nostra sermonem amico animo habebamus.

Quadam ergo die solito majus mihi et illi deus otium concessit, et mox unde solebamus inter nos quaestionari coepimus. et quoniam quae opponebat convenienter satis et consequenter opponebat, et ea quae opposuerat non minus convenienter prosequendo explicabat; nostra vero responsio vicino satis pede ad proposita illius respondebat et scripturarum aeque testimonio nitens eidem ipsi concessu facilis esse videbatur et approbanda; rogaverunt qui aderant ut memoriae darem hanc nostram disceptatiunculam, fortasse aliquibus profuturam. scripsi ergo: et, tacito mei et ipsius nomine, scripsi sub persona Judaei cum Christiano de fide nostra disceptantis; scriptumque et exaratum hoc opus tuae transmitto examinandum censurae.

Si res approbanda est, tuo placebit approbata judicio; si vero respuenda est, seu tota seu pars ejus aliqua, quidquid respuendum erit accipite amico dictum in aure, et quia soli amico innotuit silentio supprimatur nec alicui haec ad legendum pagina communicetur: salvo quidem amore mutuo et integra prorsus pace mutua deleatur quidquid delendum esse tibi placuerit, aut corrigatur si quid est quod corrigi posse tibi visum fuerit. fateor quamlibet protuleris sententiam animo libenti excipiam et aure obtemperanti audiam.

Tamen quidam ex Judaeis qui tunc Londoniae erant, opitulante misericordia dei, ad fidem Christianam se convertit apud Westmonasterium, coram omnibus fidem Christi professus baptismum petiit, accepit, et baptizatus deo se inibi serviturum devovit, et monachus factus nobiscum remansit.

Sic ergo Judaeus ille disputator, aliis pluribus interpositis, me provocando adorsus est.

This is the dedicatory epistle prefixed to the famous *Disputation of a Jew with a Christian*. Where the text differs from that printed in Migne *P. L.* 159, col. 1005, I have followed the readings of *Titus* D xvi. There are two notable omissions in Brit. Mus. Add. 8166: it omits the words 'sanctae Cantuariensis ecclesiae archiepiscopo,' and also the account of the conversion of the London Jew ('tamen quidam ex Judaeis...nobiscum remansit'). These omissions suggest that we have in this MS an earlier form of the work, written before Anselm became archbishop. See further, p. 54 above.

## 8.  *Gilbert to Anselm.*

Quae modulando
clara solebat
dicere laudes
fistula vestras,
5 murmure rauco
nunc canit, atque
lugubris extat:
dicit et Unde
vos ab ovili,
10 pastor, abestis?
grex duce nullo
devius errat:
nemo reducit:
pascua quaerit;
15 et, quia quae sunt
commoda nescit,
noxia sumit;
morbidus ergo
et moribundus
20 omnis habetur.

Insidiosus
circuit hostis;
spectat ovilis
septa relicti:
25 undique liber
intrat et exit,
exit et intrat:
nemo repellit.
ille lupinas
30 intus agendo
exerit iras:
nemo resistit.

Omnia sternit;
cuncta necantur,
35 debile, pingue,
agnus ovisque.
quippe luporum
nil satis extat
ingluviei:

40 non satis esse
aestimat unus
milia mille.
accipe plures
intus adesse,
45 atque videto
quanta relicti
undique strages
fiat ovilis.

Creditor, inquam,
50 illa requiret:
nam sua quaerit
credita quisque.
vos, ut opinor,
restituetis;
55 quippe fuerunt
credita vobis.
debita reddi
nemo refellit:
ergo timendum.

60 Milia quippe
multa requirit,
quae sub ovili
credita vestro
perdita fiunt.
65 Anglia tota,
gens populosa:
Scotia tota:
insula longe
longior illis,
70 gens numerosa,
sunt et Hiberni:
quando revisa
regna perampla
ista fuere?
75 nemo revisit:
annus et anni
praeteriere:
ergo timendum.

6—2

For this epistolary poem, which is entitled in the manuscript *Ad Anselmum archiepiscopum*, see above pp. 22 and 54.   I subjoin the following variants:

2   solebat] sedebat MS.
18   morbidus] moribus MS.
23   ovilis] ovile MS.
65—72   The MS has these lines thus (reading across the page):

| | |
|---|---|
| Anglia tota | Gens populosa .a. |
| Scotia tota | Insula longe |
| Sunt et hiberni | Quando revisa |
| Longior illis | Gens numerosa .b. |

The scribe has attempted to rectify the disorder: but plainly it is the last two lines that require transposition.

77   praeteriere] preterire MS.

VITA DOMNI HERLUINI ABBATIS BECCENSIS

LIBER DOMNI GISLEBERTI ABBATIS DE SIMONIACIS

SELECTED CHARTERS WITH NOTES

# VITA DOMNI HERLUINI ABBATIS BECCENSIS.

Herluin re-
nounced the
world, when
it was most
attractive.

QUONIAM in re militari quae quis memoratu digna egit scripto
eduntur ad posteritatis exhortationem, et laudibus attolluntur
prout ingenium scriptoris et facundia praestat, silentio supersederi
non debet ad divinae virtutis gloriam et magnae in deum fidei
formam, quae in satellitio Christi nostra memoria praeclare egit
abbas venerabilis Herluinus Beccensis; cujus virtutis hoc ad
quendam titulum praescribatur, quia mundum sibi jocundissime
ad votum arridentem ea aetate penitus recusavit qua vehementius
alii se ingerunt recusanti, et in qua patria tunc incolumem armis
militem abrogatis monachum fieri portentum habebatur.

His noble
origin.

A Danis qui Normanniam primi obtinuere pater ejus originem
duxit; mater proximam ducum Flandriae consanguinitatem attigit;
Ansgotus ille, ista Helois nomen habebat. Gilebertus Brionnensis

He is trained
under Gilbert
count of
Brionne.

comes, primi Ricardi Normanniae ducis nepos ex filio consule
Godefrido, illum enutritum penes se inter omnes curiae suae
primates habuit acceptissime. habilis ille ad arma plurimum
erat, nec minori ea animositate gestabat. omnes omnium totius
Normanniae majorum familiae in electis illum habebant, in armis
omnique rei militaris usu et cultu corporis sui attollebant. ab
inhonestis avertebat animum, honestis quae curiae magni faciunt

His prowess,

impendebat omne studium. domi ac militiae commilitonum
suorum praestantissimus non esse impatiens erat. quibus de
rebus non solum singularem domini sui obtinuerat favorem,
verum et apud Robertum totius patriae ducem et apud exterarum
dominos regionum pepererat sibi nomen plurimum accessumque
familiarem. alia, quae ad captandum nomen in saeculo plurima[1]

and mag-
nanimity.

fecit, omittamus: hoc ad fortitudinem[2] animi illius ac fidei con-
stantiam et in armis confidentiam non sileamus. indigne passus

*The variants of the MS are given, where the edited text has been preferred.*
[1] *om.* plurima.          [2] fortitudinis.

# 88 *Gilbert Crispin*

aliquando factam sibi a domino iniuriam famulatus sui commodum
ei subtrahendo contulit se eo inviso longe aliorsum.  eo itaque
sub tempore comes ipse Gilebertus quorumdam potentissimorum
Normanniae lacessitus injuriis multam militum manum contraxit,
injurias suas effere volens ultum iri: homo ferocis animi, magni
potentatus, nominisque supremi avidus, utpote ducum tantorum
propinquus, ad potentiae suae ostentatum per nuntios eis non
prope diem belli sed per plures ante dies id se facturum et
quando transmisit.  ita condicto tempore bellum utrimque ap-
paratur, quod exequi non posset sine multa partium utrarumque
strage, nec amplius evitari salva eorum dignitate.  quod vir

but comes to
his aid in a
moment of
danger:
animosus[1], quem scribendum accepimus, ubi compertum habuit,
ilico injuriarum oblitus viginti secum delectos milites assumens
pergit ad diem certaminis, minime cum domino verum seorsum
procul ab agmine illo; suae etenim suorumque salutis objectu fidei
suae sponsionem asserebat, mortis periculo appetebat, nullius
emolumenti vicem ab illo exquirens.  dictum satis est, et iis
lucide agnosci potest, quis fuerit.  non desertores pugnae quos
in aliorum perniciem metus absolvit, sed quos in dominorum
necem et patriae excidium cupiditas inducit, hoc exemplo allo-
quimur, nec tam militaris gloriae obtentu quam servandae causa
fidei proferimus.  dux per excelsi montis latus agmen cum
deduceret, videt a tergo viginti armatos eminus in plano subsequi,
ac hostile aliquid verens imperat confestim qui essent scitum ire.

accedunt suos et causam agnoscunt: approbant plurimum mag-
nanimitatem, ac duci renuntiant.  admiratus pro injuriis tanti sibi
servitii vicem restitui, ilico remittit accessum, cum ampliori gratia
reddens omnia quae sua fuerant.  bellum quod instabat crastinae
lucis sub exortu nuntii praedicti provinciae ducis Roberti noctu
ante venientes dirimunt, jus fidemque sacram obtestati, ut ab
armis discedant, et judicium belli curiae suae expectent definitioni.
itaque pars utraque ac neutra superior altera discessit ab armorum
excisione.  divina sibi providentia lignum illud ad omne opus
bonum utile conservabat.  nolebat summus artifex violentia saecularis aurae jam plus illud distorqueri aut infructuosis affectationibus
exhumectari.

Vitae hujus jocundissimo statu annos ille jam excesserat triginta
septem, cum tandem divino [metu] succendi amore mens illius coepit,

---

[1] animos.

his soul was
kindled with
divine love: et ab amore mundi tepescere sensimque in dies frigescere, ab exterioribus oculum cordis convertens ad se ipsum. ibat frequentius ad ecclesiam, orabat devote, ac saepe prorumpebatur in lacrimas. ludicra re omni omissa, jam minus frequens erat in curia, qua hoc solo retinebatur, quod praedia sua deo secum lucrari satagebat. quod et obtinuit, extorquens ea sibi a domino suo multa instantia servitii. saepe sub diem pernoctabat orans in ecclesiis, et mane in curia primus coram aderat ad mensam domini. quia inter sodales parsimoniam exercere nolebat, multis quae adinveniebat impedimentis absens, saepe totum jejuniis transigebat diem. in armis in cultu corporis non idem studium quod prius satis indicabat altercationem animi illius, quam adhuc seria dissimulatione celabat. angebatur mens et in plura cogitationum deliberatione distrahebatur. militiae ac ceterae saecularis rei usum relinquere summa

but there was
no man to
guide him.
The Norman
clergy were
secularised. erat voti. verum quo se conferret, quod vivendi genus assumeret, ignorabat. rarus in Normannia tunc recti tramitis index aut praevius erat; sacerdotes ac summi pontifices libere conjugati et arma portantes ut laici erant; veterum ritu Danorum universi adhuc vivebant. sed sicut spiritus ubi vult spirat, ita quem

His rigorous
life, while still
at Gilbert's
court. aspirat unctio ejus docet de omnibus. abrenuntians ergo militiae, vili tegumento indutus, barba et crine intonsus inter aulicos ea quidem diu servivit quam diximus intentione, exiturus ab Egypto ille Hebraeus, ea videlicet transiliens quae transeunt ac omni conamine se extendens in ea quae aeterna existunt, ab eis qui remanebant mutuatum in opus dei asportare[1] conabatur quicquid pretiosum poterat, jam domini sui laetus assidens ad mensam inter multimodas epulas et comessantes pane asperiori vescebatur et aqua: ridebatur ab universis, amentiae quicquid agebat reputabatur. minis, promissis, injuriis, dominus et universi satellites nil poterant a proposito suo eum avertere conantes. mittebatur homo olim universis acceptissimus saepenumero ad curias sedens asinum, moeror ac risus diversis quo adveniebat, servitiorum quidem gratiositate, quia metuebat saeculo irretiri nec equitare jam volebat, asinando serviens domino sine cujus permissu discedere nolebat[2]. et quia pro deo abjectus esse nequaquam erubuit, nec deus illum erubescens super terram quoque amplissimam illi restituit vicem.

A crisis comes Comes Gilebertus de cujusdam compatriotae sui damno agens

---

[1] absportare (adsportare *ed.*).        [2] volebat.

when he declines an unjust mission.

quod in illius vergebat perniciem, ad principem Normanniae Robertum, cujus quicquid super hoc agebatur intererat, praedicto viro hac de re imposuit allegationem. at vir pacis ferre damnosa alicui machinamenta penitus recusavit. perstat dominus in sententia hortans et comminans, ut homo sibi intimus verbum consilii sui ad dominum suum perferendo referat. agitur ut jam ostendat miles ad utrumlibet positus, cui servire, superno an terreno domino, malit. sed mox ut superni causa domini exegit, ilico funem, quo sub terreni servitio domini retinebatur, abrupit: abdicata[1] omnino legatione discedit a curia. quin tamen iret comes Gilebertus nullo modo discredens post paucos dies curiam ivit, rescire volens quid dux responderet. verum ut cognovit ad eum non fuisse perlatum, efferatus in illum cui imposuerat, mandat abduci quicquid habebant

His lands are wasted.

ipse et sui. continuo abripiuntur omnia sua, nec curat; vastantur quoque pauperes sui, unde non parva sollicitatur cura. pauperum

He returns to plead for his poor dependents.

ergo transmissus questu et lacrimis post parva dierum intervalla rediit ad dominum, nullamque sui curam gerens egit suppliciter causam innoxiorum. accersitur negotium totius curiae, et acerrime in causam deducitur. intenduntur crimina, quae humili et sufficienti ratione cuncta purgando removebat; qui in eo judici respondebat spiritus dei, tacitis unde judex potius erat infestus, alia quaedam admissa intendebat, sciens iste quid lateret in fundo. Quae mea sunt, inquit, hinc accepta universa distrahantur, dum pauperibus, qui vestram nullo crimine iram meruerunt, sua restituantur. motus ad pietatem dominus, quem mundanae celsitudinis fastus plurimum obtinebat, abducto in partem viro perquisivit animi commutationem et finem consilii. cui paucis ille verbis cum multis lacrimis respondit: Saeculum amando et tibi obsequendo nimium deum ac me ipsum hactenus neglexi. quae corporis erant cultui omnino intentus nullam animae meae eruditionem accepi. quapropter precor, si quid unquam bene merui a te, liceat vitae quod superest in monasterio transigi salvo circa me amore tuo, et

The count is melted:

da mecum deo quae habui. habitae diu deliberationi finis iste consedit: corde in lacrimis concitato sustinere nequit ille ulterius loquentem: abripit se in cameram. pietas humana multa in eo

and grants him his release,

erat circa illum militem suum, multa et illi circa dominum; ac vix ab eo missionem requirere valebat, sed praevalebat fortis ut mors dilectio. tandem gratissimo clienti expetitam concedit, tam sui

---

[1] abdi dicata.

quam suorum omnium facultatem. quem eatenus ut bene obse-
quentem sibi amaverat, jam coepit amare ut dominum, ac libens
obsequebatur illi. plures dies multo cum honore detentum apud

with all his
patrimony.
se debita honorificentia remisit, ditioni illius ac servitio tradens
quidquid paterni juris habebant fratres sui, qui eadem dignitate
geniti pares extiterant sibi: quia dignior et vera nobilitate
generosior germanis efficiebatur, jure ab eis illi subici nec indignum aut injuriosum aestimabatur.

He retreats to
Bonneville,
and builds a
chapel :
Protinus in villa quae dicitur Burnenvilla extruendum servitio
dei opus arripuit non parvum brevi peractum. ipse non solum
operi praesidebat, sed opus ipsum efficiebat, terram fodiens,
fossam efferens, lapides sabulum calcemque humeris comportans
ac ea in parietem ipsemet componens. quibus alii horis aberant,
ipse congerebat quae ad opus exigebantur, excludens otium ab
omni parte diei, quanto vanitate tumida olim delicatior, tanto
vera humilitate nunc ad omnem laboris tolerantiam propter deum
patientior. cibum praeter quibus non licet diebus semel accipiebat,
nec exquisitum et parce satis, expleto cum die opere suo. et quia

and learns at
night to read
his psalter.
interdiu nequibat, ediscendo psalterio noctem paene totam impendebat. his exercitiis multa jocunditate exercebatur novus tiro
Christi.

His great
proficiency
due to divine
grace.
Prima litterarum elementa didicit cum jam existeret annorum
prope quadraginta; et divina opitulante gratia eo usque processit,
ut etiam ipsis apprime eruditis grammatica in exponendis ac
intelligendis divinarum scripturarum sententiis merito haberetur
admirabilis. quod ut solius divinae gratia efficientiae actum
credatur, nocturnis tantum horis huic studio vacabat, quia propter
lectionem nunquam divini operis intermisit executionem. non
solum in cithara confiteri domino, verum et in psalterio decem
chordarum psallere gestiebat, congrua temporum distributione,
nunc attentus bonae actioni, nunc intentus lectioni atque orationi.

He goes to see
how monks
live :
Nova rursus molimina contra eum hostis antiquus invenit.
quod summum in humana vita ille excogitaverat, monasterialis
videlicet ordinis fastigium, paene dissuasit his occasionibus. coenobium quoddam adiit gratia inquirendi de vita monachorum. habita
oratione accessit omni cum reverentia multo cum timore ad ostium
claustri, velut ad ostium paradisi, desiderantissimus scire qui
monachorum habitus, qui mores, quae in claustro sedendi sit
religio. vidit longe ab ea quam coenobialis ordo exposcit gravitate morum omnes haberi. turbatus est, jam omnino incertus

but is ejected as a thief. quod vivendi genus approbaret. ad haec qui monasterii custos erat, ut illum sic introrsus accedentem conspexit, furem suspicatus immisso quanta vi potuit collo illius pugno per capillos foris usque ad ostium extrusit. at vir patientissimus pro illata sibi injuria nullum monacho laicus verbum impatientiae respondit. talibus quidem accedere plurimum extimuit: sed palmes propagatus ab ea quae vera vitis existit nullo adversitatum aestu arescere potest, alte radicatus in illius caritate quae omnia suffert.

He visits other monks, but finds them vain     Hoc de illo aedificationis referens solatium, aliud ea de re proximo natali dominico adiit majoris nominis coenobium. festiva processione cum fratres in die solemnitatis exissent, vidit indecenti benevolentia monachos passim arridere laicis, aggaudere in para- tioribus[1] ornamentis ostentando[2] ea aliis, ad introitum contentioso and barbar- ous. tumultu anticipare aditum. ad haec insistentem sibi nimium fratrem quidam monachus monachum pugno repercussum avertit, ac impulsum supinis dentibus demisit ad solum: adhuc enim, ut dictum est, omnes omnium per Normanniam mores barbari erant. hac rerum insolentia ne bonum damnaret inceptum, tantam actuum levitatem, tantam morum improbitatem contuens in illis ad quorum normam vitam suam corrigere volebat, dei manus One praying brother re- stores his hope. effecit subveniens labanti. sequenti nocte expleto matutinorum officio diu ante lucem aliis emissis oraturus ipse remansit occultatus in quodam angulo oratorii. mox quidam monachus eo non viso prope constitit ad orandum, qui nunc toto corpore prostratus nunc tantum genibus flexis cum lacrimis orans usque mane clarum perstitit. ejus igitur exemplo omnino redintegratus est.

These victories of faith are true miracles.     Referimus miracula, sed eis unde vulgus fert sententiam multum potiora; quanquam non defuerunt et ipsa. quid enim glori- osius⟨quam⟩ quod victus ab eo ubique hostis deo vincente succubuit? robur constantiae illius duris hactenus adversitatum ictibus per- fringere conabatur, sed conamen ejus omne frustrabatur: nunc malis pravorum exemplis suffodere molitur. verum ut in canticis Cant. iii 8. legimus canticorum: Uniuscujusque viri ensis super femur suum propter timores nocturnos; seu diurna oppugnatione seu nocturna subdole rationis alicujus suggestione accedat, invenit eum excu- bantem in propugnaculis. gerit in manu gladium, qui universas hostis compages ac medullas exequitur, dinoscens ac exterminans quae ab illo cogitationes atque intentiones suggeruntur: ad

---

[1] imparatioribus.          [2] ostendando (ostendendo *ed.*).

excipiendos ictus longanimitatis et patientiae forti clypeo munitur. positus infra divinae custodiae murum ad omnia illius molimina vigilis sui commonitione sollicitatur, quia non dormitabit, neque dormiet qui custodit Israel. igitur non exploratis ad votum quae volebat castrorum domini, redit firmaturus suum quod contra spirituales incursus[1] extruebat. avulsit ilico paternas domos, unde servorum dei habitacula construxit.

Sacrata vero quam construxit ecclesia ab episcopo Lexovii nomine Hereberto, comam totondit, ac saecularem habitum deponens ab eodem pontifice sacrae habitum religionis accepit, miles Christi per tot pericula fortis ante expertus. ejusdem ordinis cum eo jugum subierunt duo sui. postmodum a praefato praesule sacerdos consecratus, pluribus ducatui illius jam adscitis[2] fratribus abbas praeficitur. tuto imitandus aliis praeponitur, qui per annos tres improperium vitae spiritualis patientissime tulit coram saecularibus alienatus spectaculis, quibus innutritus cotidie alios videbat oblectari, rigorem abstinentiae non relaxans inter affluentissimas dominorum mensas, omni denique abjectioni corpus suum subiciens in curia. quos ergo regendos acceperat, arctissime sed more patrum priorum regebat. videres peracto in ecclesia officio abbatem collo sementem, manu rastrum vel sarculum gestantem ad agriculturam praeire monachos omnes, ruris operi sub diei terminum insistere. sentibus et spinis alii agrum emundabant, alii fimum scapulis comportantes spargebant, hi sarriebant, illi serebant, nemo panem absumebat in otio, ad horam agendi officium in ecclesia omnes ad unamquamque horam[3] conveniebant. victus quotidianus panis siligineus et herbae cum aqua et sale, aqua non nisi lutulenta, quia fons nusquam praeter[4] ad duo miliaria habebatur. caeleste aiebant beneficium, cum panis melior et caseus vel aliquod aliud edulium undecumque habebatur. exemplum magistri et conatus omnem murmurandi excludebat aditum. abbas prior ad opus, ab opere discedebat ultimus, operator ipse continuus. simili se inibi propter deum servituti nobilis mater ejus addixit, et concessis deo praediis quae habebat, ancillae fungebatur officio, servientium deo pannos abluens et quicquid injungebatur extremi operis accuratissime agens.

Ad opus servorum dei quadam die cum annonam torreret, nescio quo casu domus undique succensa est. cucurrit quidam

---

[1] incurias.    [2] additis.    [3] *om.* horam.    [4] *om.* praeter.

ejulando nuntians abbati domos ambustas et matrem ejus inibi esse combustam. at ille licet lacrimis suffusus ad deum manus levavit; Gratias tibi, deus, inquiens, quod in officio servientium tibi matrem meam ignis absumpsit. fortis in amore dei constantia, quae tot diaboli arietibus impulsa labare non poterat: malleos ac ignes inimicus nesciens suggerebat, quibus vir patiens minime fundebatur, sed purgatus ad coronam gloriae formabatur. nil tamen mali in illa conflagratione praedicta domina passa fuit.

He moves to a more habitable spot near the Bec.

Dein post aliquantum temporis per visum divinitus commonitus est, ut dimissa solitudine campestri, quae competenti oportunitate omnino carebat, eum ad locum sui juris mansionem transferret, qui a rivo illic mananti Beccus appellatur, ad miliarium a castro quod vocatur Brionnium. est hic locus in ipso saltu Brionnensi, valle ima montibus saltuosis hinc inde occlusa, omni oportunitate humano usui commodus: propter densitatem ac rivi recreationem ferarum illuc multus erat accursus. trium tantum molendinorum tres domus illic erant, et solum habitabile permodicum. quid ergo faceret? molendinorum in uno pars sibi nulla, aliorum duorum sua pars erat tertia; nec tantum soli liberum quantum oportuna domuum capacitas exigebat. comes Gilebertus nil usquam eo saltu pretiosius possidebat. quid plura? spe in deo firmata coepit operari, ac deus evidentissime cooperari; nam consortes et conter- mini quas habebant partes seu venditione seu gratuita donatione omnes sibi suas dedere, ac brevi sub tempore silvam Brionnii quae circum erat totam obtinuit.

He builds a church, and a wooden cloister which collapses in the night.

Consecrata paucis extructa annis non parva ecclesia, columnis ex ligneis claustrum construxit, in quo ad morem patriae fratres jam nusquam progressuros considere instituit. nocte vero subse- cuta, orationi eo intento in stratu suo, diabolus futuri illic bonorum operum incrementi primordia cernens impatientissime tulit. tectum dormitorii multa vi conscendit, unde quasi conamine multo colli- gens se supra novam novorum parietum insiluit cooperturam, ac in unum ad terram universa dejecit. verum his non erat semen quod in petrosis ortum areat, quia non habet humorem; sed pingui terra exceptum attulit fructum in patientia. mane quia inimicus hoc fecerat indicavit fratribus, et dejectos eorum animos redintegrans claustrum ex lapidibus reaedificare coepit.

A godless neighbour's fate

Juxta vicinus degebat nomine Rodulfus cognomine Pinellus, homo saeculi plurimum addictus concupiscentiis; qui ab ipso abbate cum saepenumero ad bene vivendum moneretur spernebat, irridebat:

irridendo, cum ab armis defessus ac mundi voluptate satiatus esset, monachum se futurum respondebat. quadam ergo die dominica pro quibusdam altercationum controversiis praedictum abbatem adiit, penes quem demoratus in vesperum, nocte jam ingruente more solito admonitus, rogatus et irridens, domum rediit, et circa ejusdem noctis **is revealed to** medium morte subita praeventus hominem exuit. quod abbas ipse **the abbot.** eadem hora agnovit, animam illius raptam a daemonibus audiens miserabili planctu ejulantem, et ita per longum temporis et loci intervallum abduci. mittit sub acceleratione quid de illo ageretur inquisitum iri. legatus illuc pervolans pulsatas fores irrupit, irrumpens ad cubile pervenit, in cubile jam gelidum ac membris omnibus rigidum ad latus nesciae uxoris invenit. hujus miraculi unum fratribus testem habuit, qui cum eo ejusdem ejulatus audivit.

**A ghostly** Quadam die circa vespertinas horas cum foris ad opus resideret, **visitor bears** vidit daemonem sub habitu clerici prope locum transire et eam **away a sinful** **monk.** dormitorii officinam, in quam fratrum ad necessaria secessus est, adire. re vera suspicatus clericum et quod ad oratorium ire voluisset, fecit a compluribus inclamari qua ibat non esse viam oratorii. nequaquam exaudientem prosequitur missus qui revocaret, sed elapsi nulla prorsus vestigia invenit. intellexit tandem inimici praestigium, ac rei eventum expectavit. nocte proxima quidam monachus de monasterio fugiens per eadem loca egressus discessit, ut e vestigio subsecutus prodidit. quod mane ille cum comperisset dixit, cui militabat et qui eum abducere sategit, a vespertinis horis praestolabatur ibi immundus immundum dominus satellitem per immunda jure abducturus.

**The abbot** Variis ergo simultatibus quae saepe introrsus oriebantur coepit **prays for help** dolere multum et anxiari. ad ea enim componenda qui in claustro **in ruling his** **monks.** praesideret minime erat, sumptuum congerendorum necessitas illum extra immorari compellabat. hac de re multotiens deum cum jam exorasset, divina sibi miseratio accommodavit auxilium, sufficiens ad universa quae agenda forent suffragium.

**Lanfranc, a** Ortus Italia quidam vir erat, quem Latinitas, in antiquum ab **great scholar,** eo restituta scientiae statum, tota supremum debito cum amore et honore agnoscit magistrum, nomine Lanfrancus[1]: ipsa quoque in liberalibus studiis magistra gentium[2] Graecia discipulos illius libenter audiebat et admirabatur. is patria egressus, quamplures multi nominis scholares secum habens, in Normanniam devenit.

---

[1] Lanfrancum.      [2] *om.* gentium.

considerans vero scientissimus vir quod captare auram mortalium
vanitas est, et quia ad non esse prona sunt universa, praeter eum
qui semper est et qui ei intendunt, ad obtinendum ejus amorem
animum convertit et studium.  quod igitur in litteris perfectius
invenit consilium placendi deo arripuit, ut relictis omnibus, abdicato
etiam sui ipsius jure, illum sequeretur qui dixit: Si quis vult post
me venire, abneget semetipsum, et tollat crucem suam et sequatur
me.  et quia, quanto magnus fuerat, tanto fieri optabat humilior,
locum adire disposuit ubi litterati aliqui non essent qui eum honori
ac reverentiae haberent.  Beccum itaque adiit, quo nullum usquam
pauperius aestimabatur vel abjectius coenobium.  forte tunc abbas
extruendae fornaci occupatus ipsemet operabatur manibus suis:
cujus humilitatem animi sermonisque dignitatem ille plurimum
veneratus et amans, monachus ibi efficitur.

Videres ergo inter eos pium certamen.  abbas quondam cleri-
catus ex grandaevo laico verebatur sibi subditam tanti doctoris
celsitudinem.  ille nullam pro eminenti scientia gerens insolentiam,
humillime ad omnia parebat, attendebat, admirabatur, et praedicabat quam ipsi in intelligendis scripturis gratiam deus concesserat.
abbas erga illum debita veneratione, ille erga eum omnimoda con-
tendebat submissione: forma gregi uterque vivendi, unus active,
alter contemplative.  abbas peritus erat in dirimendis causarum
saecularium controversiis, prudens in iis quae ad exteriora pertinent;
in aedificando et procurando quae necessaria forent neque prudentior
neque efficacior salva religione poterat esse.  praesentia corporalis
foris inter curas mundi cum residebat, animus ad sui curam et
amorem dei praecipue intendebat ; nullam saecularis pompae curam
gerens, soli deo in actibus suis gratificari gestiebat.  humillimus,
summae patientiae, in exequendo carnis appetitu modesto rigore
continentissimus, semper ad orationem primus exsurgebat, nec
diurni laboris multa defatigatio illum in lecto post alios retinebat[1].
quo jure, qua tranquillitate subditos sibi regebat: legum patriae
scientissimus praesidium suis erat contra iniquos exactores; et si
quid inter eos controversiae nascebatur, aequissimo confestim statu
componebat.  undecumque vel quibuscumque loquebatur, sermo
ejus dignitatem in se maximam gerens obaudiebatur.

At doctor ille maximus in claustro omnem operam impendebat
quieti et silentio, cordis sui novalia verbi sacri excolens assidua

---

[1] requiebat.

*Marginal notes:*

turns from
the world,

Mt. xvi 24.

and comes to
Bec to live
unknown.

The abbot and
his scholarly
recruit.

The abbot's
practical gifts
and strenuous
life.

The scholar's
life of
solitude

lasts for three years.

He is found out, and crowds of pupils flock to Bec.

lectione, irrigans ea dulci quam saepe obtinebat lacrimarum compunctione. sic per tres annos vixit solitarius infrequentia hominum, gaudens quod ibi nesciebatur, praeter paucissimos quibus aliquando loquebatur omnibus ignotus. rumor ut hoc factum prodidit[1] longe lateque protulit, et fama viri praeclarissima Beccum et abbatem Herluinum brevi per orbem terrarum extulit. accurrunt clerici, ducum filii, nominatissimi scholarum Latinitatis magistri; laici potentes, alta nobilitate viri multi pro ipsius amore multas eidem ecclesiae terras contulere. ditatur ilico Beccensis locus ornamentis, possessionibus, personis nobilibus et honestis : interius religio atque eruditio multum accrescere, exterius rerum omnium necessariarum subministratio coepit ad plenum abundare. adimpletur visio quae in eodem monasterio visa est paucos ante dies quam vir ille tantus ad ordinem coenobialem venisset : fons videbatur ortus in valle monasterii, cujus aqua ad montium cacumina excrescens, hinc inde effusa, per campestrium diffundebatur amplitudinem. abbas fons erat in convalle scilicet humilitatis exortus : ⌐aquae exundantes et hinc inde latissime effluentes, monachi qui ab illo incrementum acceperunt religionis⌐[2], divinae videlicet eruditionis disciplinam, qua multi ab eodem loco longe lateque postea sunt meliorati.

Lanfranc becomes duke William's counsellor:

but is accused, and banished.

Lam. iii 26.

He meets the duke,

Ad administranda[3] quoque totius regni negotia summus ab ipso Normanniae duce Willelmo consiliarius assumitur. cujus gratiae nimiam quae una die irruit repente obnubilationem, insperato deus confestim laetificavit sereno, dignoque relatu. quorundam accusationibus delatorum dux in eum vehementer amaricatus mandat ut monasterio exturbatus patria discedat : nec motus animi sui hac vindicta sedare valens mandavit juris ejusdem monasterii villam, quae Parcus[4] dicitur, flammis excidi : paretur tam efferae jussioni. eo discedente, qui gaudium omne fratribus erat et consolatio, dolor altus remanet. quia melior non habebatur, tripes quarto pede inutili equus illi tribuitur, et unus famulus. instant itaque fratres orationi, juxta illud Jeremiae, praestolantes cum silentio salutare domini. protinus quam ille discedebat, duci obvius venienti appropinquans, equo per singulos passus caput ad terram submittente, dominum salutat. innocentiae quidem conscius, si locus dicendi daretur, non diffidebat causae. majestas illa humana primo vultum avertit, sed divina agente[5] clementia mox miserando respectat, et nutu benivolentiae loquendi[5]

---

[1] prodiit.  [2] *sic ed.: codex habet* qui ab illo incrementi aque exundantes hinc illinc latissime effluerent accepit.  [3] ministranda.  [4] parens.  [5] loquenti.

R. C.  7

98     *Gilbert Crispin*

**jests with him,** aditum concedit. tunc ille decenti joco ait: Tuo jussu tua provincia discedo pedes, hoc inutili occupatus quadrupede: vel ut jussioni tuae parere queam, da equum mihi meliorem. cui dux subridendo, Quis, inquit, ab offenso judice, infecto criminis illati negotio[1], munera exposcit?

**clears himself,** tandem disertissimus orator petiit audientiam et accepit: causaeque finem in eo constituens qui linguas infantium fecit disertas, dicendi opem subministrantibus eis qui pro illo ad deum orabant, causam exorsus brevi ad optatum finem peroravit.

**and is restored to full favour.** in amplissimam confestim gratiam receptus accipit promissum quod nulla deinceps accusatione subiret purgandi se praejudicium. gratissimi mox succedunt amplexus et oscula, quibus argumentis omnino subsedit adversariae partis omne firmamentum. multo etiam cum augmento restituenda promittuntur quae dux depopulari nuperrime jusserat. alacerrime quidam praecurrens nuntiat fratribus illum redire. commutantur lacrimae:

**The monks sing *Te Deum* all day long.** personat non semel, ut fieri solet in ecclesia, sed ubique et per totum diem ab universis altius corde quam ore pium Te deum laudamus. abbas rei inopinae fidem adhibere non poterat, donec desideratus advenit, quem per diem metus per annos reddiderat absentem. accumulatur gaudium, quia incensorum fit integerrima restitutio, terrarum quoque plurium[2] concessarum eidem ecclesiae ab eodem domino obtinetur[3] confirmatio.

**Great growth of the abbey.** Qui ergo in ipsius monasterii inchoatione domibus necessariis solum sufficiens non habuit, ejus paucos infra annos ad miliaria protenditur dominium. quid referam illic servorum dei usui extructas commoditates, stagna, virgulta, culturas, vineta? nulla est abbatia quae omni hominum commoditati magis commodificata existat.

Non multo post propter inhabitantium multitudinem contigit **Isa. xlix 20.** in ea illud dictum[4] a domino per Isaiam prophetam: Angustus mihi est locus, fac spatium mihi ut inhabitem. adunatam etenim **Lanfranc urges larger buildings on a new site.** illic fratrum multitudinem quia domorum spatiositas iam capere non valebat, et quia situs loci degentium incolumitati contrarius existebat, venerabilis Lanfrancus abbatem Herluinum de majoris monasterii et officinarum aedificatione compellare coepit. tanti **Herluin refuses,** operis solam commonitionem[5] ille extimuit, aetatis jam deficientis viribus plurimum diffidens. confortari, adhortari, ac saepe id ipsum ingerere, qui coeperat non omisit. nolente ille ullatenus

[1] *om.* negotio.   [2] plurimum: *om. ed.*   [3] obtinet.   [4] *om.* dictum.
[5] commotionem *ed.*

till the presbytery of the church falls down.
adquiescere, divino nutu monasterii presbyterium corruit. anxianti super hoc et multum conturbato abbati suus in omni sua desolatione consolator accessit, obsecrans ut vel nunc adquiescens ampliora inchoaret aedificia. tandem victus, spem in deo certissimam gerens et plurimum in consiliarii sui ope confidens, cujus opera sibi bona

A healthier site is chosen, and large buildings are begun.
omnia proveniebant, in salubriori multum situ nova inchoavit monasterium et officinas, opus pergrande, dignum, cuius dignitati ditiores multae non accedunt abbatiae. ad initiandum hoc opus tantum non res suae, quia permodicae erant, sed maxima in deum

The abbot's faith brings unfailing supplies.
fides animum firmavit, quae universa conferendo sic accumulavit quod a die qua primo fundamenta posita sunt usque ad extremi lapidis impositionem nec materia defuit nec sumptus. testantur per quorum manus expensae agebantur, quod septimana exacta multotiens ante horam quod daretur operariis minime habebatur, et ad horam undecumque ad sufficientiam deus largiebatur.

Lanfranc is made abbot of Caen.
Post triennii vero completionem, sola necdum completa basilica, venerabilis Lanfrancus coepti operis institutor, tam domini quam Normanniae primatum supplicatione coactus, ecclesiae Cadomensi

The work, retarded for a moment, goes forward rapidly again.
abbas praeficitur. remoratur coepta aedificatio aliquantisper, verum illius consilium ac beneficientia, prout opus fuit, praesto semper extitit. denique tot et tanta Beccensis ecclesia jam habebat, tanta vigebat sollertia praesidentis, quod cessare opus nulla indigentia coegit : illam vero ad tempus expletionis moram subsecuta[1] iterum prosperitas nimia acceleratione compensavit.

Lanfranc goes to Canterbury.
Interea saepedictus Normannorum dux Willelmus, haereditarium sibi Angliae regnum pervadens, imperium rebelle armis ad quae voluit jura composuit. deinde ad meliorandos ecclesiarum status animum intendit. totius igitur Christianitatis summi pontificis Alexandri, viri vita et scientia excellentissimi, consulto et rogatu, omnium quoque Anglici et Normanni imperii magnatum libentissimo assensu, rex Willelmus, quod potissimum solumque acceptabat consilium, doctorem supra memoratum ad hoc elegit negotium. victus multiplici ratione in Angliam traducitur, et, quae insularum transmarinarum primatum obtinet, Cantuariensis ecclesiae suscepit praesulatum. qui multarum ditatus amplitudine terrarum, auro argentoque locupletatus, executus mandatum quod
Ex. xx 12.
in Exodo mandatur, Honora patrem tuum et matrem, ut sis longaevus super terram, omnibus modis benignus extitit circa

---

[1] subsecutam (*hunc locum non habet ed.*).

patrem suum spiritualem et matrem ecclesiam. cujus ad eas partes transmigratio, paucos ante dies quam inde allegatio veniret, venerabili abbati Herluino per visum ostensa est hoc modo. videbatur quod in virgulto arborem malum habebat, cujus ramorum spatiositas multa erat et magna fructuum ubertas, pomorum vero species delectabilis et sapor optimus. hanc rex supradictus exposcebat, volens ad quoddam suum eam ⌐transferre hortum⌐1. reluctante isto et quod sola ea sustentaretur opponente, quia dominus erat evicit et arborem asportavit. verum radices penitus avelli non potuerunt; ex quibus pullulantes virgulae confestim in arbores magnas excreverunt. post parvum denique sub eo visu intervallum memoratus rex de arboris ipsius nimia fructificatione coram illo gaudebat, et ille se ex ea laetissimas habere propagines aggaudendo respondebat. invitabatur a rege ut ipsum arboris translatae incrementum iret videre, sed parantem proficisci nescio quae alia impediebant. haec autem omnia sicut visio digessit rerum eventus explicuit, ⌐praeterquam quod⌐2 revera ivit et quod audierat vidit.

Virgultum abbatis erat Beccensis ecclesia, cujus arbor maxima, ille doctor, non solum eam verum alias omnes per patriam suo exemplo et doctrina sustentabat ecclesias. qui ob religionis sacrae institutionem tradendam Anglis a praedicto rege ad transmarina migrare per abbatem suum, cui tanquam deo ipsi parebat, postulatus, multum invitus salva obedientia atque ab invito abbate jussus paruit. cujus quantus inibi postea extiterit fructus, latissime attestatur innovatus usquequaque institutionis ecclesiasticae status; coenobialis ordo, qui omnino ad laicalem prolapsus fuerat dissolutionem, ad probatissimorum reformatur disciplinam monasteriorum; clerici sub canonicali coercentur regula; populus, rituum barbarorum interdicta vanitate, ad rectam credendi atque vivendi formam eruditur.

Hanc fructuum deo suavissimorum fragrantiam, cujus ex odore domus dei per orbem impleta est, quam et ipse abbas absens jocundissime senserat, postea praesens quanto vicinius tanto jocundius sensit, profectus ad eum in Angliam. quo in itinere

evidentibus miraculorum signis multa circa illum gratia divina innotuit. cum enim Boloniam venisset, volens egredi ad portum qui plus sex leugis ab urbe non distat, tentavit qui cum eo ibat

---

¹ virgultum **transferre** *ed.*     ² praeter quia (quia *super ras.*)

comitatus, comitissa quoque comitis Eustachii conjunx, femina
deo amabilis, persuadere plurimum sategit, ut in urbe remaneret,
quoniam in portu navis nulla erat, et ventus, qui de transmarinis
eas referret, jam per quadraginta fere dies nullus omnino extiterat.
at ille certissima in deo spe ait: Ibimus ad navalia, naves sine
mora habituri; fratres qui domi remanserunt oraturi pro nobis
sine cunctatione eas nobis praesto habebunt. dixit, et ventus
statim convertitur. itur sub omni acceleratione ad portum, quo
tamen prius sedecim naves appulit ventus quam pervenissent.
noctis erat tunc primordium, cujus ante medium rursus aspirante
vento qui transferret, circa aurorae exortum puppes omnes in
fluctus retrahuntur. ingressurus navim, aliis ad alia quae tam
tumultuosae rei conveniunt intentis, abbas cum monachis haud
A strange<br>shipmate. procul letaniam dicebat. repente juxta quidam, nescitur unde,
astitit homo grandaevae aetatis et modestissimae alacritatis.
frater qui letaniam pronunciabat illum vidit, et ab universis
putabat conspici, aestimans pauperem esse qui praestolaretur,
ut finitis letaniis postularet aliquid sibi dari. verum intrantibus
eis vidit eundem jam in navi loco eminenti consedisse. suspicatus
igitur magni alicujus meriti illum existere, qui pauper habebat
se tam imperiose, assidens prope circa illum attentius manebat.
navis cum in altum mare evecta fuisset, territi sunt nautae quibusdam monstris quae in salo videbant. hac tumultuatione
prospectantibus aliis ille gravi quadam dignitate subridens metum
eorum reprehendebat, tunc primo, ut aiebant, visus ab eis.
exigentibus confestim nauticis, quis foret, quis induxisset, vel
quo pretio navem locaret, eo auctoritate multa se habente et nil
omnino respondente, dixit frater qui jam diu eum viderat: Ex quo
letaniam diximus in portu nobiscum manet, et ut credo plus eo
navigium quam ipse navi indiget. coeperunt ergo mirari, et
mirando illum omnes contueri. viderat abbas quendam cui valde
conformis erat, et quaesivit nominatim an is esset. ille paululum
vultu exhilarato hoc solum respondit, Non sum. hoc unum in tota
ea navigatione protulit verbum. navi prosperrimo cursu apud
Doffrensem[1] portum appulsa, per comitatus hominum qui in
navibus erant multum requisitus ille comes navigii nusquam
reperiri vel qui eum exiisse vidisset potuit. dein omnium rerum
cum incolumitate quinto die ad archiepiscopum abbas pervenit.

He visits<br>Lanfranc: Quae tunc inter eos submittendi sese ad invicem pia contentio?

[1] Dorobernensem.

who receives him with the deepest humility. summus antistes et in ecclesiis transmarinis vices apostolicas gerens submittebat se suo quondam abbati, ut alius quivis monachus; secundus ab eo ubique nisi ad missarum sollemnia residendo, et manum illius cum ab eo aliquid accipiebat, nisi raptim ille avertisset manum, osculando. illi sedes eminentior ac imperandi jus omne tribuebatur. donabat famulorum delinquentium reatus, ac caetera in domo quae libebat. domini nomen alius, sed ille auctoritatem gerebat. quanto curia sua frequentior, quanto utriusque ordinis personarum totius regni excellentium conventus fiebat numerosior, tanto majori obsequio coram omnibus illum archiepiscopus praeferebat. multum mirabantur universi, maxime Angli, archiepiscopum Cantuariensem sic submitti ulli mortalium. sumant itaque oboediendi formam, qui subditi contumaces existunt praepositis, cum vir tantus in ipsa tot gentibus praelatione humilitatis adhuc spontaneus sustineat jugum atque oboedientiae.

The honours of the humble. Abbas vero quam debebat dignitati tantae submissionem conabatur exsolvere, sed nullatenus permittebatur. ecce quid in hac etiam vita servientibus sibi opulentissima dei manus retribuit. qui pauperiem Christi assumens ab universis olim contemptui habebatur, habet nunc qui morem sibi gerebat primatem totius regni Angliae cum omnibus sibi commissis pontificem. eam benignitatis dei vicem et ille acceperat, qui, abnegans semetipsum sibi cui olim pro deo sui tradiderat libertatem, videt ecclesiastici juris censura nunc ad vestigia sua provolvi, ut omittam consulares multos, immo maxime totum sibi acclive regnum.

His prosperous return. Praedicto abbati rursus mirabili rerum successu ad votum omnia cesserunt, mox ut redire disposuit. nam die qua voluit, circa sextam diei horam venientibus quos ad mare archiepiscopus praemiserat ac renuntiantibus ventum omnino esse contrarium et pelagus infestum, assueta in deo ille confidentia discessit ad mare obluctantibus universis et nocte jam ingruente; quo multa parte noctis exacta perveniens, ventum quem volebat, et qui commodior erat ad transferendum, eadem hora praesto habuit. interim somnum capiens, dum naves ad mare impelluntur, primo lucis sub exortu navem ingressus tam ipse quam omnes sui confestim transvecti sunt prosperrimo omni navigii eventu. non amplificamus rem gestam, sed simplici narratione scribentes relinquimus eam aliis considerandam dignaque amplificatione attollendam.

The notable
fruits of Bec: De arboris illius magnae radicibus quae in horto suo remanserunt, ut per somnium viderat, vidit postea praedicandus vir
pullulantes quasdam virgulas in arbores magnas excrevisse, multos
videlicet ad magna bonorum operum incrementa per illius institutionem accessisse: illius etenim sementis existit quicquid
unquam boni fructus in Beccensi coenobio vel ab eo extiterit.
Anselm, arbor fructibus opima fuit venerabilis Anselmus ecclesiae Au-
gustensis clericus, qui illum doctorem maximum ad ordinem
monachorum subsecutus ad · prioratum quoque ejusdem coenobii
Beccensis post eum accessit, et defuncto beatae memoriae supra-
dicto Herluino abbati successit; quique . postea successit in
episcopatum venerandae recordationis saepedicto Lanfranco Can-
tuariensi archiepiscopo: vir ingenio admirabilis, facundia non
impari, et quod ad humanum spectat iudicium morum omnium
probitate insignis. quod de approbanda actuum ejus honestate
dicimus, vicinitas universa testatur, longe lateque Normannia
William, attestatur, et Gallia amplissime contestatur. arbor fructuum
jocunditate plurimum acceptabilis fuit ecclesiae Cormeliensis
abbas Willelmus, apprime nutritus et eruditus. arbor alta atque
Henry, fructuosa extitit Henricus Cantuariensis ecclesiae decanus, qui
postmodum abbas fuit de Bello, vir ecclesiasticis omnibus disciplinis optime instructus. arbores bonorum operum fertilitate
Hernost, multum gravidae in domo domini extiterunt venerabilis Hernostus
and Gundulf. ecclesiae Rofensis episcopus, et qui ei ad idem officium ibidem
successit, vir morum sanctitate admodum reverendus, Gundulfus
episcopus. hos ecclesiae suae filios vidit grandaevus pater aliis
ecclesiis patres constitutos. hi sunt filii de quibus in psalmo
Ps. cxxviii 4. dicitur, Filii tui sicut novellae olivarum; qui ab inferioribus
extenuati, ad superiora roborati, caritatis dei adipe et pinguedine
repleti aliorum animas verbis ac bonis exemplis reficiendo roborant,
roborando sustentant, sustentando ad summa virtutum incrementa
educunt. multam quoque educaverat sobolem spe certissima
posteritatis spiritualiter in domino jam juvenescentem; nobilissi-
morum etenim atque optimorum tam clericorum quam laicorum
ex multis partibus orbis illic adunatus numerus ad centenariam
pertingebat summam. vidit filios filiorum, ex sancto videlicet
Cadomensi coenobio fratres ad idem opus assumptos, in extremis
nationibus multos gignere in domino.
Herluin grows
infirm, Corporeae eum vires jam deserebant, quas per tot annos
laboris vehementia, vigiliarum et inediae continuatio plurimum

and weak of sight:

attriverat.  visus maxime destituebatur officio, et ab horis vespertinis indigebat ducamine.  quamobrem non in dormitorio cum fratribus, neque ad psallendum choro interesse jam valebat;

but will not relax his strictness of life.

sed tamen ad nocturnale officium primus surgebat, nec ulla diurni laboris defatigatio in lecto illum post alios retinebat.  cibi ac potus parcimonia, quae in juventute, eadem servabatur in senectute; praeter quod ab omni fratrum conventu coactus, exceptis legalium jejuniorum diebus, bis comedebat in die: quod quidem ipsum non tam refocillandi lassi corporis cura concesserat, quam ut escam sumens eis sumentibus, quibus ad opus praesidebat, insistere posset.  operi usque in vesperam, ac persaepe etiam usque in noctem consistebat.  otium aut voluptas nullum in eo sibi locum sortita est.  non aetas eum annorum numerum jam excedens de

Ps. xc 10.

quo dicitur in psalmo, Et amplius eorum labor et dolor, non vehemens qua multum saepe in internis angebatur infirmitas illum ab actionibus necessariis retinebat.  paterno affectu omni modo circa monachos suos intentus, districta eos disciplina regebat

His hatred of negligence and of ignorance.

et affectuosissimo amore diligebat.  si quem inter fratres segnem, si quem sui ordinis ac studii litterarum negligentem, si quem in ecclesia somnolentum deprehendebat, hunc omnino invisum habebat.  semper inquibat, Homo litterarum et mandatorum dei nescius quid praestat?  quem considerabat vigilantiorem, studiosiorem, ad virtutum exercitia promptiorem, hujus non abbas sed servus exstabat, plerosque plus ad studium incitabat illius favor quam scientiae ipsius amor.  sedulus enim perquirebat quis omnium eorum qui erudiebantur acutioris ingenii esset, quis tenacioris memoriae existeret, quis vehementius instare cuivis studio valeret, denique ex omnibus quis ad singulas virtutes et amorem dei plus intenderet: nec minus quam in se amabat et enutrire satagebat quidquid amandum videbat in singulis.  litteratus aliquis volens monachus fieri, quando ad illum veniebat, qua exultatione suscipiebatur, quae suscepto benignitas et veneratio exhibebatur.  laicos qua instantia ut ad discendum psalmos intenderent agebat, quibus modis ut quod inchoaverant amando tenerent instabat.  omnibus omnia se conformans omnes ut filios et illi ut patrem eum amabant.

He desires that Lanfranc may consecrate the new church.

Nova necdum sacrata erat ecclesia, quam ab ipso, cujus eam consilium inchoavit et auxilium consummavit, expectabat consecrari, instanter hoc a deo exposcens: cujus petitioni, qui ad caetera sibi benignus exstiterat, optatum deus concessit effectum, adimplens per omnia super hac re illius affectum. multo enim ampliori quam praesumere poterat honorificentia consecrata est, et a quo exoptabat. nam pro quibusdam negotiis tam saecularibus quam ecclesiasticis saepe supramemoratus gentium transmarinarum apostolicus ad curiam venit eminentissimi regis Anglorum Willelmi in sua terra Normannorum tunc commorantis.

Lanfranc comes to Bec: Sed primo veniens ad ipsum monasterium qua non potuit majori humilitate cum fratribus se habuit, juxta quod scriptum Ecclus. iii 20. est: Quanto magnus es, humilia te in omnibus. ad abbatis jam senio incurvati osculum accedens, tantae eminentiae archiepiscopus ad pedes ejus advolvi conatur; verum illo e contra id ipsum conante, longo uterque luctamine dum alterum sustentat, neuter explevit quod satagebat. post multum[1] diuque optatos amplexus cum fratribus in claustro sedit archiepiscopus ut quivis alius ipsorum; senes, juvenes ac infantes, unumquemque compellans his kindly familiarity, singulatim et debita confortatione adhortans. ad mensam dextrorsum et sinistrorsum fratres cum archiepiscopo sedere, ac communi calice et scutella una cum eo coguntur cibum sumere. pontificali amota celsitudine ipsis etiam puerulis affandum se exhibebat, benignitatis exhibitione ad amorem dei aetatem invitans, quae sermonis sui capere nequibat altitudinem. quem enim summi in saeculo viri admodum verebantur, nec solum a consessu verum ab accessu procul arcebantur, illis ob sacrae professionis habitum communis habebatur. neque sola aedificationum[2] solatia fratribus impendit; quia, exceptis quae pretiosa and generous gifts. multum ecclesiae concessit ornamenta, tanto hospite digna hospitium locavit munificentia, ut[3] ex reliquiis festive geminari potuerint[4] octavae.

He obtains the king's leave to consecrate. Compellatus ab universis de consecratione ejusdem ecclesiae, paratus eorum morem gerere voluntati, ad curiam inducias respondendi postulavit ab eis et accepit. tantam quippe rem noverat pendere ab edicto regis et consilio. dein affectuosissimis fratrum omnium votis et lacrimis commendatus ad regem pervenit. locutus cum eo unde rogatus discesserat diem dedicationis accepit, et confestim nuntium remisit non modo qui diceret, verum et unde fieret.

Preparations. Dies ergo a multis per multos annos multum exoptatus longe

---

[1] multos *ed.*     [2] aedificatione *ed.*     [3] *om.* ut.     [4] potuerunt.

lateque insinuatur. ex longinquis regionibus viri consulares, ecclesiasticorum graduum summae personae, hominum genus infinitum adventurum praenuntiatur, libentissime accipitur. congeruntur maximi sumptus ad suscipiendum omne genus hominum;

**Ps. lxviii 9.** ubi adimpletur, Pluviam voluntariam segregabit deus hereditati suae. nil ab aliquo exactum, nil expetitum; se ipso sufficiens

**Ps. cxiii 7.** quod coeperat perfecit deus, qui de stercore erigit ac in sublimi ponere pauperem consuevit; solo suae manus gestamine, cujus in consummatione hujus operis sui manus adeo larga exstitit. quod res sumptuosissime acta universis ad votum et sufficientiam fuit, nec ullam in posterum contraxit indigentiam. ad tantum solemnitatis tantae gaudium languor, qui per octo ante dies vehementissimus tenuerat, mortis imminentis metu ipsum monasterii patrem deesse minitabatur. porro, ne quod moeroris nubilum diei illius lucem offunderet, deo miserante ad diem plenissime convaluit.

**23 Oct. 1077.** Igitur decimo kalendas novembris, anno ab incarnatione domini millesimo septuagesimo septimo, sanctae omni ecclesiae reverendus gentium transmarinarum summus pontifex Lanfrancus advenit consecrando consummaturus ecclesiam, quam inspirante deo inchoavit, et in cujus extruendis fundamentis lapidem secundum

**A great assemblage.** ipse manu sua imposuit. convenerunt universi Normanniae episcopi, abbates, et alii quique viri religiosi; affuerunt proceres regni; rex aliis detentus negotiis adesse non potuit. regina Mathildis libens affuisset, nisi regiis detenta occupationibus fuisset; affuit tamen per condecentem beneficientiae suae largitionem. noluit rex supernus operi gratiae suae regem terrenum supremam manum imponere, sibi totum reservans operis consummati gaudium, quod infra sedecim annos solis pauperum expensis complevit monasterium cum omnibus officinis, opus pulchrum et maximum. affuerunt et regni Franciae clarissimi consules, et ex aliis ejusdem regni primatibus complures; clerici, monachi ex universis adjacentibus provinciis. confluxit innumerum genus hominum. agitur dedicatio laetissima solemnitate et solemnissima omnium alacritate, alacritati hominum aer ipse purissimus diesque lucidissimus arridebat. prae tumultu circum-

**Scenes of enthusiasm.** euntium populorum vix exaudiuntur chori canentium. in tanta compilatione nullus laesionis alicujus sensit molestiam, nulla in agendis turbatio obvenit. peracta processione vix pontificibus intrare licet sine collisione. irrupit sequens populus avulsis omnibus januis, universis tamen illaesis, quantum ecclesiae[1] spatiositas potuit adstringere. distribuuntur altaria consecranda pontificibus, ipsum principale sacrandum archiepiscopo remansit. fit per totam ecclesiam summa celebritas, et in agenda celebritate pia quaedam contentiositas. vix semet ipsum quisque cantantium exaudit prae multitudine vociferantium. multi jubilantes quid dicebatur nescientes, aut quibus concinerent minime attendebant.

The older monks are crowded out. graves ejusdem monasterii personae, quae propter nimiam aliorum multitudinem paucae aderant, solis lacrimis et devotione cordis solemnitatem explebant. personabat in aliis vox laetitiae et jocundationis, in illis modulabatur domino cum lacrimis sola sibi

The service is followed by a feast. soli[2] tota intenta affectio mentis. quid plura? finitur majori quam coepta fuerat jocunditate solemnitas: itur ad refectionem. paschales nulli defuerunt epulae, a mane usque ad profundam noctem succedentibus fratrum turmis qui ad festum venerant, quantum refectorii tabulae continere valebant. universis tam notis quam ignotis, nec solum in domibus circumpositis, verum in villis etiam remotis, quae ad usus necessarios petierunt, sponsata deo regi ecclesia libens ministravit affluentia nuptiali: majoribus quibusque sic ad placitum et sufficientissime, ut qui accipiebant dicerent modum excessisse: neque solum ea die, sed multis per

The aged abbot's thankfulness. aliquot ante dies dum operiebantur, ita servitum est. venerabilis abbas requirens a ministris, qui ibant ac redibant nec momento uno loco stare poterant, quid agerent, quid dicerent, an sumptus adhuc deficerent, cum potius abundare audiebat ab eis, quoties

Ps. cxvi 12. illa die dixit, Quid retribuam domino pro omnibus quae retribuit mihi? et dicendo ista solas retribuebat domino lacrimas agentes gratias pro concessis sibi tot beneficiis. ac merito, quia, exclusa omni penuria, omni a deo sumministrata serviebatur sufficientia.

Lanfranc's departure, Tertio die saeculis memorandus jam saepe dictus Cantuariorum archiepiscopus ab universis fratribus eundi missionem poposcit. quis tantum tantae inter eos benignitatis virum recedentem siccis oculis aspicere potuit? omnes eruperunt in lacrimas; parvuli non valebant consolari. consulto maturavit recessum, quatenus a fletu se continerent vel post ejus discessum. abbas Herluinus, eum supra omnes mortales amans et ab eo amatus, discedentem per duo miliaria prosecutus est amicum ad suos visus nunquam in hac vita ulterius rediturum. quae cordis amaritudo, qui fletus,

---

[1] *om.* ecclesiae.     [2] sibi soli] solis.

quamvis comprimerentur, in ipso ultimo Vale et ultimo ab invicem discessu. postquam reversus est, sedens in camera solus cum solo, qui sibi ex omnibus erat familiarissimus, concitatis permittens lacrimis habenas ad caelum manus levavit, et his verbis ait: Nunc dimittis, domine, servum tuum in pace, quia viderunt oculi mei, quod ut viderem antequam morerer summopere optabam et indesinenter a te orabam. adimplesti quae volui. nunc servus tuus laetus ad te ibit quacumque hora tibi placuerit. sic verba compressit, sed lacrimarum affluentiam cohibere non potuit, donec frater qui cum eo loquebatur diutius nequiens sustinere aliunde sermonem induxit.

Ex tunc omni membrorum officio destitui penitus coepit, et longe ante diei ipsius annuam revolutionem quod oraverat obtinuit. nam proxime subsecuto mense Augusto, decimo †tertio† kalendas Septembris, die dominico, ex toto lecto decubuit. sensit pater longaevus certis indiciis jam adesse mortem. quod ubi amantissimae congregationi innotuit, mors quaedam universos pervasit. anguor et ex anguore quidam stupor animos cunctorum obsedit. cibus percipi non poterat: somnus recessit ab oculis. tertio die absolvi se et caetera quae morientibus exhibentur officia sibi exhiberi rogavit. adsunt filii valefacturi amatissimo patri eo primo orbandi; lacrimis et singultibus psalmos et caeteras orationes interrumpentibus, tandem ventum ad agendam confessionem. confiteri coepit, verum remanentium pietate filiorum superatus et ipse in lacrimas effusus dicere nil potuit. vix tamen eluctatus in vocem absolvit filios, dansque benedictionem et pacem omnibus, tam absentes quam praesentes immortali eos patri omnes commendavit, ac discedentes, quia plus non poterat, ut pro se orarent postulavit. dolor et lacrimae orationes fiebant, quoniam vix ab eis psalmus continuari valebat. dum quisque in alterum respiciebat, quasi jam cerneret fratrem patre orbatum, erumpebat in lacrimas. coram illo plangere nequaquam audebant, quia spe bona laetabundus non lacrimantes sed laetantes eos omnes videre volebat. si cujus in lacrimas concitati singultum sentiebat, confestim solita gravitate compescebat. profunda jam noctis parte transacta, quae in sabbatum illucescebat, cujus ad vesperum obiit, reverendissimus vir ejusdem ecclesiae prior Anselmus, de proximo illius fine non tam suspectus quam certus, collocavit se longiuscule ab eo, et clanculo, nolens ut ille agnosceret, quia moleste ferebat aliquem circa se. verum mox ut primum ad matutinas sonuit signum, ilico

*Marginal notes:*

and the abbot's *Nunc dimittis.*

Lc. ii 29 f.

His mortal sickness, 19 Aug. 1078. (*leg.* quarto)

excitavit domnum abbatem Rogerium, qui secus caput ejus ac-
cumbebat, et ait: Excitate priorem, ut dicat nobiscum matutinas.
plurimum miratus est ille quomodo id agnovisset, quia nec coram
eo venerat, nec aliquis ei dixerat, et post accubuerat. summo
vero mane omnes diei horas coram se dici rogavit. denique jam

**The holy viaticum.** ingruentem mortis horam sentiens communicari se expostulavit,
et animam sibi commendari. festinato ivit abbas Rogerius, sed
nullam in eucharistia hostiam invenit. turbati sunt fratres
universi. mors instabat, et tutamen salutare dominici corporis,
quod ille acciperet, non erat. verum circa morientem minime
defuit, quae circa viventem miserationis divinae gratia praesto
semper fuit. forte tunc quidam sacerdos pro eo missam celebrans
sumendum adhuc in manibus tenebat corpus dominicum. ejus
itaque oblationis, quae pro commendando illius exitu oblata deo
fuerat, praedictus abbas portionem unam suscepit, et ei ad
viaticum tulit. commendaturi exitum ilico fratres omnes accurrunt, quorum lacrimationem nec tunc sustinere praevalens,
peracta ex more Christiano commendatione, quo valuit nutu
verboque monuit ut in claustrum redeant, tanto instantius ei
subvenientes, quanto ad exitum propinquare videbant.

**The last moments.** Jam sola exitus hora expectabatur, ac precum et lacrimarum
armis communitur. quotiens camerae in qua decumbebat ostium
aperiebatur, verens quisque ne jam migrasse nuntiaretur, attonitus
prosiliebat, et quod verebatur audire expectabat. transegit diem
sic usque ad vesperam, ac saepe quasi aliunde reversus dicebat
abbati Rogerio, qui proximus astabat: Quid faciunt domini nostri?
cur morantur? quid esse putatis? cur non accedunt? ille quanquam de aliis eum crederet loqui personis, respondebat ac si
loqueretur de fratribus monasterii, Quid, inquiens, jubetis? sunt
in claustro, orant pro vobis, aderunt mox ut voletis. tacebat, et
parvum post intervallum eadem commotius iterabat. laborabat
ille addiscere quorum moram causabatur et accessum praestolabatur, verum nil plus ab eo audiebat. vespertina a fratribus
peracta sinaxi, cum diei ac diurni officii fine, vitae humanae
stadium felici cursu peregit, nocte jam proxima, quae in dominicum

**26 Aug. 1078.** illucescebat, septimo kalendas Septembris.

**The funeral.** Irruunt universi, nec jam solum monachi, verum ex familia
servientes, et qui ex villis confluxerant, fores et claustra effringere
conati. quos abbas Rogerius, qui sancto viro in ultima aegritudine
obsequentissimus fuerat, prudenti confortatione adhortans detinuit,

donec corpus decentissime funeratum solemni processione in ecclesiam est perlatum. in communi igitur posito jam licet omnibus communem lamentari desolationem. quae vivum semper assequebatur, in funere quoque illum gloria comitatur. ad persolvendum ultimum obsequium fratri, qui apud omnes maximi amoris atque reverentiae ob eximiam religionem fuit, animo libenti convenerunt plurimi abbates multaeque personae venerabiles. advenit et totum exequiale officium celeberrime egit[1] Ebroicensis episcopus, honestae vitae magnaeque litterarum scientiae vir venerandus Gislebertus.

The abbot's monument in the chapter house. Factum est in capitulo illi monumentum bonorum actuum, aeternum filiis monumentum. jure quo de spiritualibus locuturi studiis conveniunt illius praesentatur memoria, qui ex tyranno religiosus, ex multum saeculari omnino spiritualis, loci illius atque ordinis primus exstitit fundator et abbas. maximos patre amatissimo orbatorum filiorum questus referre supersedeo, ne dolorem legenti inferam, neu lectorem referendo moveam in lacrimationem. illo decenti honorificentia tumulato, largissimis expensis recreantur pauperes qui ex tota vicinitate confluxerunt. aeternam animae illius recreationem praestet, si votis opus est, qui vivit et regnat per omnia saecula saeculorum. amen.

---

[1] *om.* egit.

# GISLEBERTI ABBATIS DE SIMONIACIS[1].

Gilbert seeks
Anselm's
judgment as
to simoniacal
persons.

DILIGENDO patri et domino, sanctae Cantuariensis ecclesiae f. 99. summo pontifici, Anselmo frater Gilbertus abbas Westmonasterii: quae praeparavit deus diligentibus se.

Quia vobis multam deus concessit gratiam in scripturarum sensibus, precor ut audiatis quid me ac plures alios mecum moveat de simoniacis, et quid super hoc tenendum sit ecclesiasticis assertionibus edoceatis. utque minori taedio ad quaesita respondeatis, et quae hinc atque inde dicuntur coram posita liberius atque subtilius discutiatis, utramque partem quaestionis ad quem potui finem vestigando perduxi, et quae ex utraque parte dici possunt aeque scripta posui, quid conveniant, et unde controversia existat.

He will set
out the case
on both sides.

All agree that
simony is
heresy ;

Id equidem apud omnes convenit et constat de simoniacis, quia sunt haeretici. simoniacos dicimus qui munus dant pro sacris ordinibus. excludo[2] munus a lingua, munus ab officio, et si qua alia nobis sunt occulta exhibitionum genera. vereor comminantem apostolum : *Nolite*, inquit, *ante tempus judicare donec veniet dominus, qui et illuminabit abscondita tenebrarum et manifestabit consilia cordium.* tamen audiant nobiscum quod idem ait apostolus: *Nolite errare; deus non irridetur.* audiant et unde justum hominem propheta commendat: *Qui excutit manus suas ab omni munere.*

1 Cor. iv 5.

Gal. vi 7.

Isa. xxxiii 15.

Sed haec omitto. communi sensu accipio simoniacos, qui datione auri et argenti fiunt, verbi gratia, episcopi, et nisi id eis emeret datio auri et argenti non fierent episcopi. qua, inquam, auctoritate istis communicamus ? sancit lex divina, sanciunt canones et decreta, ut cum haereticis nullam prorsus communionem habeamus. quod approbari opus non est : quia ita esse nulli in ecclesia dei dubium est. deus[3] in evangelio nihil medium ponit: *Qui non est*, inquit, *mecum, adversum me est.* si quis ergo

and communion with
heretics is
forbidden.

Matt. xii 30.

---

[1] Incipit liber domni Gisleberti abbatis de Symoniacis MS.     [2] excluso MS (vide supra p. 37 n.).     [3] *fors.* dominus.

## 112 Gilbert Crispin

adversariis dei communicando dicit cum deo se esse, circa idem duo contraria statuit esse, quod non potest esse. inde ait et

2 Cor. vi 15. apostolus: *Quae participatio fideli cum infideli?* infideles vero dicimus et credimus esse omnes haereticos.

These err from the truth that grace comes *gratis.* At si quis obicit infideles dici eos tantum qui errando a veritate fidei animo pertinaci contemnunt redire ad veritatem fidei, concedimus. quia dicimus simoniacos omnino errare a veritate fidei, quia credunt id quod dei est pecunia emi posse:

Matt. x 8. cum veritas ipsa in evangelio dicit[1]: *Gratis,* inquit, *accepistis, gratis date.* unde et ipsum donum dei, quia gratis accipitur, gratis datur, gratia dei vocatur. neque enim dicimus eos tantum haereticos qui errant a veritate fidei seu in discretione trinitatis seu in unitate deitatis, sed etiam omnes eos qui animo pertinaci nolunt esse in omni ea | unitate fidei quam credit et tenet uni- f. 100. versalis ecclesia Christi.

What is bought comes not *gratis,* and is not grace. The bishop confers the outward signs: God gives the grace; Quod itaque comparatur, gratis non datur: si gratis non datur, gratiae nomen jam ibi prorsus evacuatur. igitur gratia dei non emitur: alioquin gratia non diceretur. ad haec: quae sua sunt episcopus operatur, exteriora videlicet officiorum signa, et ea seu vendere seu gratis conferre potest si vult. qui ergo ab episcopis ordines emunt, id emunt quod episcopi vendere possunt: sola videlicet exteriora officiorum signa. donum et gratiam dei, quae sua non sunt, nullo modo episcopi vendere possunt. alioquin aut deus omnipotens non esset, si violentia sibi ulla inferretur; aut justus non esset, si ab eo pravitati assensio ulla praeberetur. si autem non credunt simoniaci donum dei pecunia posse emi, emunt tamen, aut decipi deum posse putant, qui furtiva comparatione donum ejus sibi vindicant, aut injuriae tantae debitum ultorem

and this they cannot buy. esse deum non aestimant, qui injusta pervasione donum ejus rapiunt, tenent atque usurpant. quia vero nihil horum de deo dici fas est, et gratia dei nullo modo pecunia emitur, quicquid aliud confertur infructuose omnino exhibetur.

What then is their absolution worth? Joh. xx 22 f. Quid ergo juvat indulta ab illis peccatorum remissio? prius[2] enim ait dominus in evangelio: *Accipite spiritum sanctum;* et postea subintulit: *Quorum remiseritis peccata, remissa erunt, et quorum retinueritis, retenta erunt.* peccata ergo neque remittere neque retinere possunt qui spiritum sanctum prius non acceperunt.

or their benediction? quid denique confert illorum benedictio? benedictionis gratiam

---

[1] dicat MS.                    [2] primus MS.

dare non possunt qui benedicendi gratiam non acceperunt: immo
maledictionem pro benedictione inducunt.

O. T. proofs:
The unclean
makes
unclean.
Num. xix 22.

Ut de veteri testamento aliqua supersumamus exempla, in
lege scriptum est: *Quod tetigerit immundus, immundum erit.* quod
ad litteram accipi potest, et spiritualiter intelligi oportet. immundus enim erit quisquis immunditiam atque haeresim alicujus
agnoscens ab eo tactus atque tractus ad sui communionem fuerit.

None with a
blemish may
approach the
altar.
Levit. xxi 16,
21—23.

et alibi: *Locutus est dominus ad Moysen dicens, Omnis qui habuerit
maculam de semine Aaron sacerdotis, non accedet offerre hostias
domino, nec panes deo suo: vescetur tamen panibus qui offeruntur
in sanctuario, ita dumtaxat ut intra velum non ingrediatur, nec
accedat ad altare; ⟨quia maculam habet⟩ et contaminare non debet
sanctuarium meum.* per quamvis maculam peccatum signatur,
per leprae maculam haeresis designatur: qui ergo ab ipso altaris,
immo veli, accessu arcetur, ab omni altaris officio omnimodo
inhibetur. si itaque is qui maculam gerit, quamvis existat de
semine Aaron sacerdotis, cujus solam stirpem deus assumpserat
ad officium altaris, omnimodo prohibetur ab altaris accessu, nulla
prorsus quaestio restat de eo qui leprae macula infectus erit
| et qui de semine Aaron non fuerit. nulla igitur simoniacus f. 101.
ratione potest accedere ad altare; quia si accedit non sacrat sed
contaminat sanctuarium dei, utpote immundus atque haeresis, hoc
est leprae, macula infectus, et a semine Aaron sacerdotis omnino
alienus: *sumit* enim ipse *sibi honorem*, et non [et] *vocatur a deo
tanquam Aaron.*

Hebr. v 4.

Authorities:
Ambrose (see
above, p. 68).

Beatus quoque Ambrosius, in libro de observatione episcoporum inde disputans, inter alia si non eisdem verbis eodem
omnino sensu ista dicit: Quid accipit episcopus? aurum. aurum,
inquit, est quod accipit episcopus, ponit in sacello; sed accipiendo
pecuniam perdit animam suam: *quid* vero *prodest homini si totum
mundum lucretur, animae vero suae detrimentum patiatur?* qui
autem dat pecuniam pro ordinibus episcopo, quid sumit ab
episcopo? lepram, inquit, non gratiam: maledictionem, inquit,
non benedictionem. Item, Quando simoniacus dicit ad populum,
Pax vobis, quod habet dare potest, hoc est damnationem quam
habet: benedictionem et gratiam dei dare eis non potest, quia non
habet. qui enim dat pecuniam pro ordinibus episcopo, quia pro
gratia dei nihil dat deo, utique nil sumit vel accipit a deo. utique
his verbis beatus Ambrosius plane ostendit quia simoniacus nil
accipit, nil tradit.

Matt. xvi 26.

Leprosy, not
grace, he
receives: a
curse, not a
blessing, he
gives.

Or, again,
he receives
nought, gives
nought.

R. C.

8

Leo, Ep. clxvii (*ad Rusticum*) inq. 1.

Leo papa in decretis suis inter alia sic ait: Unde cum saepe quaestio de male accepto honore nascatur, quis ambigat nequaquam ab istis esse tribuendum, quod non eis docetur fuisse collatum? his quoque verbis ostenditur quia nihil confertur simoniaco, nihil tribuitur a simoniaco. uterque enim appellatur simoniacus, et qui dat pecuniam et qui accipit pecuniam pro sacris ordinibus.

Innocent, Ep. xvii (*ad Rufum*) §§ 7, 12.

Innocentius papa haec ita dicit: Adquiescimus et verum est certe, quia quod non habuit simoniacus dare non potuit (et nihil in dante erat quod posset accipere qui emebat)[1]: damnationem utique quam habuit per pravam manus impositionem dedit: et qui particeps factus est damnato quomodo debeat honorem accipere invenire non possum. ad summam: certe qui nihil a Bonoso acceperunt, rei sunt usurpatae dignitatis, qui conficiendorum sacramentorum sibi vindicaverunt auctoritatem, atque id se putaverunt esse quod nulla eis fuerat regulari ratione concessum.

How then does he differ from a layman?

Id attestari et contestando astipulari videntur quamplurimae aliorum quoque patrum in canonibus et in decretis sententiae. si igitur nil tradit qui sacros ordines vendit, nil accipit qui sacros ordines emit, quid refert inter simoniacum et aliquem sine ordinibus laicum, quantum ad altaris officium? nec ille nec iste quicquam habet, quia non accipit. unde apostolus Paulus ait:

1 Cor. iv 7.

*Quid enim habes quod non accepisti?* ut ergo per partes | dicam, f. 102. aut missa non erit quam simoniacus celebrabit, sacrata ecclesia non erit quam simoniacus sacrabit, cum sacros ordines non habeat quia nihil ab ordinante accepit; aut missa erit quam laicus celebrabit, sacrata ecclesia erit quam laicus sacrabit, qui item nullos ordines habet quia non accepit: de similibus enim idem judicium.

Scriptural warnings: Korah, Num. xvi 35.

In libro Numeri sic legitur: Chore et multitudo quae cum illo erat temerario ausu posuerunt incensum et thymiama coram domino, *et ignis egressus a domino interfecit ducentos quinquaginta viros qui offerebant incensum* coram domino. debitam igitur isti exceperunt temeritatis suae vindictam, quia non acceperunt officium a domino ut adolerent incensum atque thymiama coram domino, neque pro sacrificio sacrificium hoc habitum est a domino. item in libro Regum legimus quod David et universus populus

Uzzah, 2 Regg. vi 3, 6, 7.

Israel ducebant archam dei: *Oza,* inquit, *et Aio filii Aminadab minabant plaustrum novum. postquam autem venerunt ad aream Nachor, extendit manum Oza ad archam dei et tenuit eam, quoniam*

---

[1] *Verba uncinis inclusa superius scripserat Innocentius.*

*calcitraverunt boves et declinaverunt eam. irutusque est dominus indignatione contra Ozam, et percussit eum dominus super temeritate; qui mortuus est ibi juxta archam dei.* nihil ergo huic contulit accedere ad archam dei, qui mortuus est juxta archam dei. officium eis impositum erat minare[1] plaustrum: justa fortasse videbatur occasio et vicina necessitati ratio; calciaverunt boves, inclinaverunt archam; extimuit Oza pro archa dei, et extendit manum ad archam dei: et tamen percussit eum dominus super temeritate, et mortuus est ibi; quia officium illi impositum non erat extendere manum ad archam dei. lignea erat archa, et quamvis sancta tamen lignea. in archa erat manna, tabulae testamenti, et virga Aaron quae fronduerat. et quantum distat inter haec sancta et sancta sanctorum, corporis et sanguinis Christi mysteria. illa idcirco erant sancta, quia horum sacrorum erant umbra et figura; haec ipsius sanctimoniae sunt veritas et causa. si ergo percussit dominus Oza super temeritate sua, non quidem prorsus excogitata atque deliberata, sed ad tempus fortuito[2] casu illata; qua poena percutietur qui deliberatione continua fur et malitiosus cotidie extendit manum ad illa terrifica sacri altaris mysteria? non obtinuit ille pro temerario accessu gratiam, sed debitam excepit ultionis sententiam. non obtinebit et iste pro temerario accessu gratiam, sed meritam excipiet temeritatis suae[3] vindictam.

In libro Machabeorum primo legimus, quod Judas Machabeus et populus qui cum eo erat *mundaverunt*[4] *sancta* quae prius ritu lege instituto sanctificata et a gentibus contaminata erant: illud vero altare quod gentes construxerant atque sanctificaverant non emundaverunt, | sed a solo penitus destruxerunt et lapides ejus in loco immundo reposuerunt. quantum vero attinet ad rei istius mysterium, quid refert inter gentilem et simoniacum? sacrat gentilis altare qui non accepit a deo id facere, atque idcirco peccat, quia illud consecrare praesumit et usurpat. sacrat et simoniacus altare, cui omnino fas non est id facere, atque idcirco peccat, quia illud sacrilega praesumptione et, ut ita dicam, velit nolit deus, consecrare attemptat. denique si verum est avaritiam esse idolatriam, sicut ait apostolus, quis avarus dicetur idolatra, si idolatra non dicitur simoniacus, qui etiam dei bonitatem pecunia[5] venalem putat? quibusdam itaque nostrum

The Gentile altar not cleansed, but destroyed. 1 Mach. iv 43 ff.

f. 103.

Cf. Col. iii 5.

---

[1] minari MS.  [2] fortitudo MS.  [3] suam MS.  [4] manducaverunt MS.
[5] pecuniam MS.

videtur quia altare quod simoniacus sacrat nulla emundari sancti-
ficatione potest, sed prorsus a solo destrui ex auctoritate debet.
quod de altari dicimus, hoc ipsum de aliis sacratis rebus sentimus.

Conclusion:
simoniacal
ministrations
are invalid, Ut igitur quaestionis nostrae partem unde agimus summatim
colligamus, attende et paucis.   multis de causis, auctoritatibus
atque exemplis dicimus quia simoniacus nihil ab ordinante
accipit, nihil ipse ordinando aliquem illi tradit.   gratiam enim
dei seu emi seu vendi non potest.   ipsa vero officiorum signa
quae suscipit, quia furatur et rapit, nihil ei conferunt nisi male-
Jer. xlviii 10. dictionem, sicut scriptum est : *Maledictus qui facit opus domini
fraudulenter.*   ad nullum denique sacramenti effectum ea ab eo
and worse
than invalid. alii accipere possunt : immo damnato fit particeps quisquis ab eo
id scienter accipere conatur, unde ille fur et damnationis reus esse
notatur.   haec igitur ita se habent.

*E contra:*
everywhere
things con-
secrated by
such men are
simply recon-
ciled;
and persons
also, after
due penance. At vero ex alia parte per totum fere orbem terrarum videmus
loca sacra, sicut aiunt, a simoniacis sacrata sic manere; neque,
cognita hujus benedictionis sacrilega usurpatione, more sueto illa
sacrari, sed solummodo per debitum reconciliationis ordinem ab
episcopo reconciliari.   item vidimus a simoniacis ordinatos post
peractum paenitentiae tempus ecclesiastico more non sacrari, sed
solummodo per manus episcopi impositionem reconciliari: et id
quorundam auctoritas canonum, sicut aiunt, concedit posse fieri.

Canons of
Toledo, etc.
Bruns I 313
(§ 9). In Toletano concilio xi° sic legitur: Unde si digna simoniacos
satisfactio paenitentiae tempore invenerit, non tantum com-
munioni[1], sed et loco et totius ordinis officiis a quibus separati
fuerant restituendi sunt.   in pluribus aliis canonibus atque
decretis has permissorias restitutiones circa simoniacos fieri posse
This implies
that the
consecration
was real. legimus.   quod vero restituitur, in eo statu quem prius habuit
atque amisit iterum statuitur.   habuit itaque simoniacus sacrorum
ordinum dignitatem, cui restitui potest per paenitentiae satisfac-
tionem.   si ergo haec ita fieri licet et | veritas ita se habet, dicimus f. 104.
quia simoniacus benedicendi quoque gratiam accepit et habet,
quam aliis ex officio suo conferre potest.   si locus enim sacratus
non esset, aliquando eum more debito sacrari necesse esset.   si
episcopi ordinem non accepisset episcopus simoniace ordinatus,
aliquando eum canonico ritu ordinari oporteret.   at quia haec
non fiunt, nec fieri necesse esse dicunt, concedi oportet quia haec
eis aliquando exhibita [haec] fuerunt.   id equidem nos perturbat,

----

[1] communionis MS.

et inde controversia existit, quia haec fieri posse ratio et auctoritas contradicit et item fieri posse permittit.

The parallel of an evil-living bishop,

Ad ea quae proposuimus respondet fortasse aliquis: Ea, inquit, auctoritate communicare possumus simoniacis, qua auctoritate licet communicare raptoribus, ebriosis et non continentibus episcopis. haec enim non sunt opera lucis, sed opera tenebrarum; et *quae,*

2 Cor. vi 14.

sicut ait apostolus Paulus, *societas luci ad tenebras?* verum quam-

who must be obeyed till deposed by a synod.

diu seu hos seu illos ecclesia dei tolerat, donec synodalis censura eos canonice discussos judicet ac deponat, tolerandi sunt ab subditis, atque sine periculo exhiberi eis potest obedientia ab subditis. in his quae dei sunt obedientia illis exhiberi potest, assensio vero pravitatis ulla eis adhiberi non debet. quid enim nostra interest

Cf. Phil. 1 18.

seu ex occasione seu ex veritate Christus annuncietur, dum populus vocem dei audiat, et quae agenda sunt undecumque summonitus agat? quid nostra refert qua intentione episcopus super cathe-

Cf. Matt. xxiii 3.

dram Moysi sedeat? audi commonitionem[1] evangelii: *Quae,* inquit, *dicunt facite, quae autem faciunt facere nolite.*

Cf. Matth. xxi 2.

Obicis vero mihi illud ex evangelio: Ingressus in templum dominus cathedras vendentium columbas, et mensas nummulariorum evertit, et illos procul a templo exturbavit. super cathedram eversam quis, inquies, sedere potest? qui in templo dei remanere

Obj.: he has a legitimate place: the others have not.

non sinitur, quae, inquies, dicit in domo dei unde audiatur? super cathedram itaque Moysi simoniacus sedere non potest, quia eum nullam cathedram in domo dei habere fas est, nec istud exemplum referri potest ad simoniacum. ad illos referri debet qui legitime inthronizati super cathedram Moysi sedent in domo dei.

Yet they are in Moses' seat, however they got there.

Sed, rogo, attende. verum est, dicitur, quia indubitanter coram deo cathedra simoniaci evertitur, et ipse a conspectu dei damnatione perpetua eliminatur. si tamen violenter cathedram obtineat, velis nolis super cathedram Moysi sedeat, quamdiu deus id patiatur, quae dicit audi et fac, quae facit facere noli. accipe testem

Eccles. x 4.

inde et commonitionem sacrae scripturae auctoritatem: *Si ascenderit spiritus super te potestatem habens, non dimittas locum tuum[2].* ascendit super te, quando tu illi non potes resistere. tu tamen non dimittas locum tuum, etiam si ille super te arripit locum; quamdiu te quidem | sinit tenere locum tuum. unde et apostolus f. 105.

Rom. xiii 1 f. Paulus ait: *Non est,* inquit, *potestas nisi a deo: quae autem a deo*

---

[1] commotionem MS.    [2] *Apud Eccles. legitur*: si spiritus potestatem habentis ascenderit super te, locum tuum ne dimiseris.

*sunt, ordinata sunt*[1]: *itaque qui potestati resistit, ordinationi dei resistit.* ac si diceret: Judicem hunc seu illum deus constituit super te, et te constituit subditum illi esse: noli ordinationi dei resistere; sed age quod alibi ipse ait: *Bonum fac, et habebis laudem ex illa.* cum enim de potestatibus ordinatis a deo tractaret, hoc tandem in finem consilium dedit: *Vis non timere potestatem? bonum fac, et habebis laudem ex illa.* item: *Tu quis es qui judicas alienum servum? suo domino stat aut cadit.* ac si diceret: Si ille quod male accepit usurpando thesaurizat sibi iram in die irae justi judicii dei, tu sub eo positus exercendo patientiam in patientia tua possidebis animam tuam.

Rom. xiii 3.

Rom. xiv 4.
Cf. Rom. ii 5.

Cf. Luc. xxi 19.

Dicis vero mihi: Scio evidenter quia simoniacus est, quia a deo alienus est: quomodo illi communicare audebo? accipe. sciebat evidenter et dominus quia Judas fur erat, quia proditor erat, quia et diabolus erat: dominus, inquam, qui Judae subditus non erat, immo magister et dominus Judae erat: et tamen cum illo edebat, bibebat, et in nullo a communione sua eum amovebat, donec aperte malitia illius detecta in semet judicando se ipsum indignum et exsortem exivit a consortio aliorum. de illis quidem qui faciunt et consentiunt debitum jamdudum controversia finem accepit: facientes, inquit, et consentientes pari vindicta plectentur. agimus tantummodo de illis quos, velint nolint, necesse est esse sub illis.

The Lord did not refuse communion with Judas.

It need not imply consent.
Cf. Rom. i 32.

Quaeris: Quid juvat indulta ab illis peccatorum remissio? nil quidem obest, immo juvat et prodest, si animo fideli quaeritur, debito paenitendi ordine expetitur et quasi a vicario dei excipitur. in Ysaia scriptum est: *Narra si quid habes, ut justificeris.* dominus vero dicit in evangelio leprosis: *Ite, ostendite vos sacerdotibus: et dum irent mundati sunt.* quamdiu ergo in ecclesia dei sacerdotis officium simoniacus gerit, et id eum gerere sinit, tu qui sub ipso sacerdote vivis, vade, ostende te sacerdoti: narra si quid habes, ut justificeris: quia ab homine non obtinetur justificatio, sed a deo. si sacerdos justus est, juvant quidem preces ejus, juvant merita ejus; sed gratia dei te justificat. si sacerdos justus non est, juvat quidem cordis tui mansuetudo, juvat exhibita illi propter deum debita summissio; sed gratia dei te justificat. sicut enim de baptismo evangelium dicit: *Hic est qui baptizat,* deus videlicet, quisquis baptismi minister existat; ita de omni sacramento seu gratiae dei dono apostolus ait: *Haec,* inquit, *omnia operatur unus atque idem spiritus, dividens singulis prout vult.*

'What is their absolution worth?'

Isa. xliii 26.
Luc. xvii 14.

Look not to the minister, but to God, as giver of sacramental grace.

Joh. i 33.

1 Cor. xii 11.

---

[1] *Sic apud* Aug. contra Gaud. I. 20 (tom. ix col. 643 d).

ac si diceret: Quisquis sacramentorum | executor sit in quolibet f. 106. genere sacramenti, semper unus atque idem spiritus operatur gratiam et virtutem sacramenti.  non enim quicquam excepit, qui omnia unum atque eundem spiritum operari asserit.

If a man by black arts restores health, is the health not a gift of God?

Saepe quoque executor gratiae dei id ad mortem suam exequitur, quod a deo per eum salus ad vitam confertur.  inter dona spiritus domini gratiam curationum apostolus ponit: si ergo praestigiosus aliquis aliqua maleficii sui arte infirmum aliquem sanat, numquid sanitas ipsa non est sanitas, aut sanitas ipsa non est donum dei sicut alia quaelibet sanitas?  et tamen unde iste salvatur, ille damnatur.  *Si,* inquit apostolus, *distribuero in cibos*

1 Cor. xiii 3.

If alms profit not the loveless giver, may not the receiver be profited?

*pauperum omnes facultates meas, et si tradidero corpus meum ita ut ardeam, caritatem autem non habeam, nihil mihi prodest.*  si ergo elemosina nihil illi prodest a quo sine caritate confertur, numquid illi non prodest cui confertur, et beneficium hoc gratiae dei donum esse ⟨non⟩ dicetur?

The promise of Christ stands fast for the worthy receiver. Joh. vi 56. 1 Cor. xi 29.

De sacramento corporis Christi dominus dicit in evangelio: *Qui manducat carnem meam et bibit sanguinem meum, in me manet et ego in eo.* apostolus vero dicit ad Corinthios: *Qui manducat et bibit indigne, judicium sibi manducat et bibit, non dijudicans corpus domini.* unum et idem ergo sacramentum aliis est ad vitam, aliis est ad mortem.  qui manducat et bibit digne, vitam sibi manducat et bibit: *qui vero manducat et bibit indigne, judicium sibi manducat et bibit, non dijudicans corpus domini.*

Eccles. vii 20.

quia vero hominis est peccare, sicut scriptum est: *Non est homo qui faciat bonum et non peccet;* dei vero est justificare, de quo scriptum est: *Qui propitiatur omnibus iniquitatibus tuis, qui sanat omnes infirmitates tuas*; spiritus sanctus remittit etiam per simoniacos peccata, ubi pura confessione peccatum paenitendo narratur, atque dignus paenitentiae fructus sequitur.

Ps. ciii 3.

The Spirit of God absolves the penitent.

'What is their blessing worth?'

Quaeris: Quid confert illorum benedictio?  si, inquam, benedictio est, plurimum confert.  benedictionem vero esse quis prohibet?  Judas enim proditor cum caeteris apostolis praedicabat, miracula faciebat, benedictiones super populum dabat. numquid propter malitiam Judae sacramentorum virtus atque benedictio irrita fiebat?  qui verbum fidei ab ore illius percipiebat, credebat, numquid salvus non fiebat?  absit.  dicit enim scriptura: *Omnis qui crediderit in eum non confundetur.*  per malos autem ministros potens est bonitas dei benedictionis et gratiae suae dona operari.  Isaac volens atque omnino credens se

Judas was used to preach and heal and bless.

Rom. x 11.

Isaac's involuntary blessing was a true blessing.

Gen. xxvii 33.

benedicere filium suum primogenitum Esau, Jacob alterum filium suum benedixit. quia ergo ille non volens, immo deceptus, alterum benedixit, iste patri veritatem celando[1] furtivam ab eo benedictionem surripuit, numquid illa benedictio idcirco benedictio non fuit? fuit plane: nam postea scriptum est: *Expavit Isaac stupore vehementi, et ultra quam credi potest admirans ait: Quis igitur ille est qui dudum captam venatio|nem attulit mihi, et comedi ex* f. 107. *omnibus priusquam tu venires? benedixique ei et erit benedictus.* quoquo itaque modo illum benedixit, benedictum illum esse asseruit.

Former arguments allowed, with reserves. To the clean all is clean. Tit. i 15.

Exempla scripturarum quae posuisti debito sensu accipimus, atque per omnia tecum sentimus. illud enim in lege scriptum: *Quod tetigerit immundus immundum erit,* eo sensu dictum accipimus quo apostolus Paulus etiam abundantius ait: *Omnia munda mundis; coinquinatis autem nihil mundum,* neque mens eorum neque conscientia. si ergo immundus aliquid tangit, siquidem immundum est, immundum manet, et eo immundius jure computatur. si vero sacrum et mundum pro temerario suo tactu immundum illi et perniciosum reputatur; sicut de sacramento

1 Cor. xi 29.

corporis Christi apostolus testatur: *Qui manducat et bibit indigne, judicium sibi manducat et bibit, non dijudicans corpus domini.* sicut enim radius solis aeque mundus per munda et immunda loca transit; et sicut aeque commodus in se ipso semper manet, quando etiam lippo oculo in eum intuenti noxius existit: ita et

The sacrament does not lose its power.

sacramentum corporis Christi aeque mundum et sacrum, immo sanctimoniae causa, in se ipso semper subsistit, sive vitam sive judicium sibi manducat et bibit, qui ad illud percipiendum accedit.

If he cannot give a blessing, God can through him;

Quod autem beatus Ambrosius dicit: Quando simoniacus dicit ad populum, Pax vobis, maledictionem dare eis potest quam habet, benedictionem et gratiam dei dare eis non potest, quia non habet: concedimus, et per omnia viri tanti auctoritatem sequimur. benedictionem et gratiam dei ex merito suo dare non potest, quia non habet. sed per eum dominus benedictionem et gratiam suam dare eis potest, quia habet, potens cuicumque vult exhibere divitias bonitatis suae: qui per malignos quoque spiritus saepe gratiae suae dona operatur. quando vero simoniacus dicit ad

if a son of peace be there to receive it.

populum, Pax vobis, non dicit, Pax mea vobis; sed pacem dei orat a deo eis concedi[2]: et si quis fuerit inter eos filius pacis,

---

[1] zelando MS.          [2] concedit MS.

utique requiescet super eum pax dei; si autem non fuerit inter eos filius pacis, et infructuose dicitur, hoc minime fit culpa illius a quo caritative oratur, sed culpa illius super quem imprecatur.

'Leprosy, not grace': but yet a holy thing may be given, which, though death to one, is life to others.

Item beatus Ambrosius dicit: Qui dat pecuniam pro ordinibus episcopo, quid sumit ab episcopo? lepram, inquit, non gratiam. plane id ita esse credimus. qui enim quae sancta sunt datione auri et argenti tradit, datione auri et argenti sumit, indigne ille tradit, indigne iste sumit; ad perniciem et judicium sibi ille tradit, ad perniciem et judicium sibi iste sumit: tamen sacra sunt et quae ille tradit, et quae iste sumit. sicut de corpore Christi constat: qui indigne tradit, judicium sibi tradit; qui indigne sumit, judicium sibi sumit: tamen corpus Christi et ille tradit, et iste sumit. nisi enim aliquid sacri usurpando vel ille tra-|deret vel iste sumeret, unde vel ille tradendo vel iste sumendo f. 108. puniretur?

The outward signs are holy things.

Quae, inquies, sacra? ipsa, ut tu ipse dicere soles, exteriora sacrorum officiorum signa, quae tunc ceperant, gratia dei fructuose traduntur, fructuose sumuntur quando in neutra parte quicquam aliud consideratur, nisi ut serviendo deo amor ejus et gratia inde

Matt. vi 22 f. obtineatur. unde dominus in evangelio: *Si oculus tuus fuerit simplex, totum corpus tuum lucidum erit: si autem nequam fuerit, totum corpus tuum tenebrosum erit.* quia vero sic male traditus ordo injuste traditur, injuste sumitur, et ad perniciem usurpando tenetur, exigente justitia necesse est ut amittatur[1] donec digno

Their use may be forbidden, but afterwards restored. paenitentiae fructu gratia dei obtineatur, et tandem debito jure exequendi officii gradus restituatur. quod ubi restituitur, alia reiteratione consecrationis res non indiget, sed sola per manus episcopi impositionem reconciliatione opus est. sicut enim quando deponitur ipsa singulorum ordinum signa sibi tolluntur, ita quando restituitur eadem singulorum ordinum signa sibi redduntur, et sic per debitae benedictionis gratiam deo reconciliatur.

The vessels of Korah's company were treated as holy. Num. xvi 5–7.

Precor, attende. praecepit dominus Moysi ut omnia utensilia templi debito ritu sacrarentur: aliter vero deo indigna atque profana haberentur. legimus tamen in libro Numeri: *Locutus est Moyses ad Chore et ad omnem multitudinem: Hoc igitur facite; tollat unusquisque thuribula sua, tu Chore et omne concilium tuum, et hausto cras igne ponite desuper thymiama coram*

Num. xvi 31. *domino; et quemcunque elegerit, ipse erit sanctus.* sequitur: *Confestim igitur ut cessavit loqui, dirupta est terra sub pedibus eorum*

---

[1] admittatur MS.

## 122 *Gilbert Crispin*

*et aperiens os suum devoravit illos cum tabernaculis suis et universa substantia. sed et ignis egressus a domino interfecit ducentos quinquaginta viros qui offerebant incensum. locutusque est dominus ad Moysen, dicens: Praecipe Eleazaro filio Aaron sacerdotis, ut tollat thuribula quae jacent in incendio, et ignem huc illucque dispergat, quoniam sanctificata sunt in mortibus peccatorum; producatque ea in laminas et affigat altari, eo quod oblatum sit in eis incensum domino et sanctificata sint.* qui ergo contra legis statuta incensum et thymiama obtulerunt domino, pro temeritate sua debita ultionis vindicta percussi sunt: thuribula vero, quae temerario tactu profanata erant, in mortibus peccatorum dicit esse sanctificata. non dicit ea iterum sacrari oportere, sed in mortibus peccatorum expiata digno expiationis atque paenitentiae fructu dicit esse sanctificata.*

*Num. xvi 35-37.*

Ita igitur et quando a simoniacis loca consecrantur, ipsi pro temerario ausu debita ultionis vindicta percutiuntur: ea vero per sanctificatae aquae aspersionem | ab episcopis reconciliata debito f. 109. jure sanctificantur. similiter ordinati a simoniacis pro temeraria[1] praesumptione sacrorum digna ultionis vindicta percutiuntur; et post peractum paenitentiae tempus, digno paenitentiae fructu quasi quodam igne anxiati spiritus sanctificati, sola per manus episcopi impositionem reconciliationis benedictione indigent. sanctificatio quidem nulla existit, nisi per fidem dominicae passionis et assignationem dominicae crucis. sicut enim in veteri testamento sine sanguinis effusione non fiebat sanctificatio, ita et in novo testamento sine crucis assignatione nulla fit sanctificatio. crux quippe ipsius dominicae mortis est signum atque ostensio.

Hac igitur ratione multum distat inter gentilem et simoniacum. gentilis quando sacrat, neque ipse est qui sacrare debet, neque sacrat cui debet, immo cui non debet, idolo videlicet, et omnino aliter quam debet. simoniacus quando sacrat, licet ipse non sit qui sacrare debet, tamen sacrat cui debet, deo videlicet, et omni eo ritu quo debet. revera quidem concedi oportet: *Si recte offeras, recte autem non dividas, peccasti.* tamen et concedi oportet, quod multo vicinius saluti peccat quisquis intra fidem christianam positus peccat, quam is qui omnino extra fidem christianam extat. unde dominus in evangelio: *Sicut Moyses exaltavit serpentem in deserto, ita exaltari oportet filium hominis; ut omnis qui credit in eum non pereat, sed habeat vitam aeternam.*

---
[1] temerario MS.

qui ergo credit in deum potest non perire, si fidem habeat, quae sine operibus mortua existit; at vero qui non credit nulla ratione non potest non perire: *sine fide* enim, sicut ait apostolus Paulus, *impossibile est placere deo.* altare ergo illud, de quo in libro Machabeorum legitur quod gentes construxerant, Judas Machabeus et populus qui cum eo erat jure a solo prorsus destruxerunt; quia ubi nulla sanctificatio fuit nulla prorsus emundatio esse potuit.

Ut igitur et nos responsionis nostrae summam colligamus, paucis attende. dicimus tecum quia simoniacus revera haereticus est, dicimus tecum quia communicandum sibi non est; sed communicare dicimus unum cum illo esse voluntatis assensu atque actione. si idcirco regulariter atque canonice subditi eum amovere possunt, tolerandus non est, immo omnino amovendus est. si autem competenter id facere non possunt, patienter tolerandus est, et sine periculo in his quae fieri licet a subditis ei obedientia exhiberi potest atque debet. sub Nabuchodonosor, qui erat infidelis atque idolatra, vixit per annos multos imperiis ejus parendo Daniel propheta, vir fidelis atque verus Israelita. si ergo obicis mihi auctoritatem apostoli: *Quae communicatio fideli cum infideli?* par pari referimus: obicimus et nos auctoritatem ejusdem apostoli: *Qui potestati resistit, ordinationi*[1] *dei resistit.* et fortassis utraque sic servatur auctoritas, nec alteri altera repugnat, f. 110. si communicare alicui dicimus unum cum illo esse voluntatis assensu atque actione. hoc enim modo cavere possumus ne aliquibus in maligno positis communicemus. ad cumulum vero hujus cautelae atque observantiae plerumque praecipitur a quibus fieri debet, et quibus id observare licet, ne cum ejusmodi ulla prorsus communio vel in cibo vel in potu vel in colloquio habeatur. ad praesens enim loquimur non de illis sub quorum censura existunt simoniaci, at de illis quos necesse est ⟨esse⟩ sub illis, et quorum causae non interest judicare de illis, sed judicari ab illis.

Item dicimus tecum quia simoniacus nil accipit, nil tradit. sed id idcirco dicimus quia aliter quam debet accipit, injuste accipit, ad perniciem et ad judicium sibi accipit; aliter quam debet tradit, injuste tradit, ad perniciem et ad judicium sibi tradit: tamen et ille tradit et iste accipit quae in sacris actionibus ab homine tradi possunt et accipi.

Refert quidem, et plurimum refert, inter simoniacum et sine ordinibus laicum. namque laicus absolute nihil omnino accipit;

---

[1] ordinatio MS.

Heb. xi 6.

whereas a Gentile consecration is nought.

Summary of reply.

There is a duty of subjection for those who cannot remove such persons.

Cf. 2 Cor. vi 15.

Ro. xiii 2.

Communion with them is only wrong if it implies assent.

They receive nought and give nought, in the sense that they receive and give amiss.

But they differ from laymen, who receive not at all.

simoniacus vero et aliquid ab ordinante accipit et nihil ab ordinante accipit. quamvis enim ad perniciem accipiat, aliquid tamen accipit, quia ordines sacros accipit; sed idcirco dicitur quia nihil accipit, quoniam propter quod debet et ad quod debet ordines sacros non accipit: neque enim propter deum accipit, neque enim ad suscipiendam dei gratiam ordines sacros accipit. idcirco dicimus quia nihil accipit, quia dicere solemus rem non esse quae aliter est quam debet esse, et aliquid non fieri quod aliter fit quam debet fieri[1]. unde frequentissimo usu loquendi dicimus ei qui aliud quam debet dicit, Nihil est quod dicis[2]. quamvis enim revera aliquid dicat, revera aliquid faciat, quia non dicit illud aliquid quod debet dicere, nec facit illud aliquid quod debet facere, dicimus quia non dicit seu facit aliquid, quoniam tantundem valet ac si non faceret ullum aliquid; immo melius esset non fecisse aliquid, quam fecisse illud aliquid quod non debuit. si enim malum est non fecisse quod debuit, multo gravius malum existit et non fecisse quod debuit et fecisse quod non debuit.

**Marginal note (left):** This common use of the word 'nought'

Accipe in scripturis quoque multa hujusmodi locutionum exempla. in epistola ad Corinthios dicit apostolus: *Si habuero omnem fidem, ita ut montes transferam, caritatem autem non habeam, nihil sum.* quamvis enim aliud aliquid existat, quia non est aliud aliquid quod debet esse, nihil hoc est, non aliquid dicit se esse. Item in epistola ad Galathas: *Qui autem putat se esse aliquid cum nihil sit, se ipsum seducit:* cum nihil, hoc est non aliquid, sit, quia non est illud aliquid quod debet esse. unde in psalmo dicitur: *Homo cum in honore esset non intellexit, comparatus est jumentis insipientibus et similis factus est illis.* ac si diceret: Destitit esse homo, | quando destitit facere quod facere debet homo *f.* 111. et ad quod factus est homo. unde scriptura: *Deum time, et mandata ejus observa: hoc est omnis homo.* si igitur homo est qui ratione utitur, deum timet, et mandata ejus observat; qui ratione abutitur, deum non timet, et mandata ejus non servat, hominem esse eum contradicit scriptura, licet gerat speciem hominis et formam. eo itaque modo dici potest quia simoniacus nil accipit, nil tradit; quia quod accipit, aliter omnino quam debet accipit; quod tradit, omnino aliter quam debet tradit[3].

**Marginal notes (left):** illustrated from holy scripture. 1 Cor. xiii 2. — Gal. vi 3. — Ps. xlix 20. — Eccles. xii 13.

---

[1] fieri] esse, et aliquid non fieri quod aliter fit quam debet fieri (fieri 2° *supr. lin.*) MS.  [2] dicit MS.  [3] Explicit liber de symoniacis MS (rubr.).

# SELECTED CHARTERS.

THE charters which here follow are for the most part printed for the first time. The originals of six of them are preserved among the abbey muniments (nos. 6, 7, 23, 24, 35, 36). The rest come from Westminster chartularies, and offer for the most part texts of the end of the thirteenth or the beginning of the fourteenth centuries, a few being only of the fifteenth century[1]. I have described these books elsewhere, and will only speak briefly of them here. The Westminster 'Domesday' (as it was called in Q. Elizabeth's time) is a very large folio containing nearly fourteen hundred pages. I have ransacked it again and again, but as it has no index I cannot pretend to have discovered all that may be of interest for Abbot Gilbert's time. Faustina A. III is unhappily no longer in its old home: it passed by some illicit process, now undiscoverable, into the Cottonian collection. Portions of it are copied from the Westminster 'Domesday'; but parts of it are perhaps a little earlier, and certainly offer independent texts. I have, therefore, sometimes given its variants, either as being in themselves of value, or as illustrating the degree of freedom with which scribes copied charters into these large collections. For a few of the charters printed below we depend on the *Liber Niger Quaternus* of the fifteenth century.

I have had no previous experience in the perilous but fascinating work of classifying charters; and I am prepared to find that my ignorance has led me into serious blunders. I have learned much from Dr Horace Round's valuable books, and I have good hope that some of the facts which I am able to offer for the first time will be of interest to him and to other exact students. I need hardly add that I shall be grateful for their aid in correcting mistakes.

For the sake of those who are unfamiliar with such charters and with the problems of classification, I may say that only one of these charters bears a date, and curiously enough that date appears to be a wrong one. We are dependent entirely on the subject matter of each

---

[1] For these chartularies see *MSS of Westminster Abbey*, pp. 93 ff.

charter and the names of the persons granting, addressed, witnessing, or otherwise mentioned. K. Henry I's reign is, fortunately for our purpose, conspicuously marked in two years by the inroads of death. In 1107 quite a number of his old and trusted servants passed away, men who had served his brother and his father, and frequently attested his charters up to that date: and on 23 Nov. 1120 William, his son and heir, with the most promising young men of his court, sank with the White Ship. It is obvious that limits are thus often provided below which charters cannot be placed. The king's frequent absences in Normandy offer further limitations for those of his charters which are issued in England. He appears to have been in England, during the time with which we are concerned, for the following periods[1]:

5 Aug. 1100 (Coronation)—Whitsuntide 1104,
Christm. 1104—Lent 1105,
Aug. 1105—July 1106,
Easter 1107—July 1108,
Whitsun. 1109—Aug. 1110,
July 1113—21 Sep. 1114,
July 1115—Easter 1116.

After this he did not return till Nov. 1120; and meantime Abbot Gilbert had died on 6 Dec. 1117, and Q. Matilda on 1 May 1118.

This will suffice to shew the nature of the problem. I have tried in the notes to make the charters intelligible to those who have no detailed knowledge of the matters and persons referred to. I have frequently referred to the History of Abingdon edited by Mr Stevenson in one of the earliest numbers of the Rolls series: for Abbot Faricius (1100—1117) was an eminent physician, who drew many great benefactors to his abbey and was in high favour with the king: accordingly he secured a quite unusual number of royal charters of confirmation, and these are frequently of service for the illustration of the Westminster charters[2].

I have not included in this series the general charter of Hen. I, confirming the liberties of the abbey at the opening of his reign (D. f. 57 *b*): it is obviously a forgery, and its only interest lies in the problem of its real date and its relation to similar fabrications, of which Westminster possessed a handsome series[3]. These would undoubtedly

---

[1] I state the periods somewhat vaguely, and depend for the statement largely on the investigations of others.

[2] Mr Stevenson made a brave attempt at arranging these in an appendix; but his dates appear to need a careful scrutiny. He accepted too readily the statements contained in the *History*, which are often demonstrably erroneous.

[3] See the Introduction to Flete's *History of Westminster*, pp. 12 ff.

repay the labour of a minute investigation, which ought to reveal the
motives which led men of general excellence and honesty to invent
documents of this kind—documents in which they never appear to
claim anything to which their monastery was not, in their own time at
least, fully entitled. But the subject stands by itself, and does not
belong to our present purpose.

The series includes some charters of the time of Gilbert's predecessor
Vitalis (1076—19 June 1085), and some also of the time of his successor
Herbert, who was not appointed until January 1121. They illustrate
what has been said earlier in this volume, or they are of value for
purposes of reference. I have not undertaken to give all charters that
belong to Gilbert's time: the task of discrimination is often very
difficult. Some important documents have been printed and com-
mented on above, and may for convenience be named here: The
Piriford charter granted 'post descriptionem totius Anglie' (p. 29);
two writs of Abbot Gilbert concerning Sanctuary (p. 37); the grant
of Totenhale to William Baynard (p. 38); 'Firma monachorum' (p. 41).

I have expanded the abbreviations, except where expansion seemed
quite unnecessary, or where (as generally in the case of proper names)
there was good reason for keeping the abbreviated form.

1. D. f. 678.

W. rex Angl' S. vicecom' et fidelibus suis de Exssexe salutem.
Sciatis quia ego concessi sancto Petro Westm' terram et mariscum
qui vocatur Tillabyri, quem Goffridus de magna villa dedit eidem
ecclesie pro anima uxoris que illic jacet. T'. Ricardus fil' Gisleberti
comitis et R. de Oleyo.

[c. 1071—85.] For Geoffrey de Mandeville, see above pp. 32, 39,
and below, charters nos. 2—7, 10, 12, 15, 16, 20, 35, 36.

For Suain of Essex, see pp. 49 f. and no. 2. Suain had ceased to be
sheriff of Essex before the Survey was taken; so had Ralph Baynard also.

On the other hand, as Geoffrey's wife Athelais was buried in the
cloister (see below, no. 15), it is hardly likely that the charter is earlier
than Abbot Edwin's death in 1071.

Richard fitz Gilbert (Richard de Bienfaite) was the son of Gilbert
count of Brionne, the lord of Herluin who founded the abbey of Bec.

Robert de Oleio appears as a benefactor of Abingdon (*Hist. Ab.*
Rolls S. II 25). He attests nos. 4, 5, below. He died c. 1094, and was
succeeded by his brother Nigel de Oleio (see below, no. 21). Robert's

daughter Matilda was married to Milo Crispin: Nigel had a son Robert de Oleio, the younger, who succeeded him.

2.  D. f. 520 *b*.

Willelmus rex Angl' Walchelino episcopo et Hugoni episcopo et Radulpho Baynard et Rannulpho et Goffrido vicecomitibus et omnibus baronibus suis Francis et Anglis de Suthereya et Estsexia salutem.   Sciatis ⟨me⟩ concessisse deo et sancto Petro et Vitali abbati et monachis Westm' illas quatuor hidas in Totingas quas Sueyn ibidem dedit, et quas Ailnoth de Lond' nepos ejus nunc tenet de sancto et monachis illius ecclesie.   praeterea concedo illis terram de Lundon' et molendinum de Stratforde cum tota terra sibi pertinenti, unde praedictus Ailnod' predictam hereditavit ecclesiam, teste Odone episcopo Baioc' et Rob' comite de Morit' et Willelmo filio Osberni.   Valete.

[1076—85.]   Walkelin bp of Winchester was consecrated 30 May 1070, and died 3 Jan. 1098.   Hugh bp of London, consecrated in 1075, died 12 Jan. 1085.   For Ralph Baynard, see above, p. 38.   Rannulf appears as sheriff of Surrey in the Survey.   'Goffridus' is probably Geoffrey de Mandeville.

The attestations do not belong to this writ: for Vitalis came in 1076, whereas W. fitz Osbern was killed in 1071.   They must be regarded as recited in the writ, which itself is not attested, but ends with 'Valete.' I have therefore placed after 'ecclesiam' a comma only.

Odo bp of Bayeux and Robert count of Mortain were half brothers of the Conqueror.   Odo was arrested in the Isle of Wight towards the end of 1082.

Edward the Confessor by a Saxon charter (D. f. 529) grants the four hides in Tooting which Suain held of him and gave to the abbey. Hen. I's grant of them to Abbot Gilbert is printed below, no. 21.   The abbey of Bec held an adjoining property (Tooting Bec), which was given by Richard fitz Gilbert and his wife Rohaise (*Monast.* vi 1052 f.).   Of Ailnodus or Aelfnoth we read in the Survey in regard to Tooting: 'Suen tenuit de rege Edwardo.   hanc terram recepit Wallef comes de Suen post mortem R.E., et invadiavit pro ii markis auri Alnodo Lundoniensi, qui concessit sancto Petro pro anima sua, scilicet quod ibi habebat.' And in the Telligraphus of Will. I (D. f. 50) we have: 'Aelfnothus civis Lundoniensis, qui ibidem monachus effectus fuit.' (Cf. First Charter of Will. I, D. f. 52 *b*.)   For Suain see also nos. 1, 8.

3. D. f. 181.

W. rex Angl' Walchelino episcopo Winton' et omnibus baronibus et ministris suis Francis et Anglis de Sutrega salutem. Sciatis me concessisse et confirmasse deo et sancto Petro et abbati Vitali et monachis Westm' illas tres hidas quas Gaufridus filius comitis Eustachii pro Beatrice uxore sua ibidem libere donavit, annuente tamen Gaufrido de magna villa: unam videlicet in Belgeham et duas in Waletona juxta Mordon'. et precipio quod predictus abbas et monachi Westm' has prenominatas tres hidas perpetuo teneant bene et in pace, libere et honorifice, quietas de murdro et geldo vel danegeldo; et defendo ne aliquis eis super hanc meam regiam libertatem et concessionem injuriam vel torturam faciat. T.' Wluoldo abbate et Gaufrido de magna villa.

[1076—84.] 'Wluoldus' is probably Wulfwold, abbot of Chertsey († 1084). Comp. with this charter Round, *Feud. Eng.* 330 : 'the Mandeville fief in Surrey, where we read of "Aultone":—"De his hidis tenet Wesmam vi hidas de Goisfrido filio comitis Eustachii; hanc terram dedit ei Goisfridus de Mannevil cum filia sua" (i 36).' Combining this statement with our charter, we get the interesting fact that Godfrey of Bouillon, who took the cross in 1096 and was elected king of Jerusalem in 1099, had married Beatrice, the daughter of Geoffrey de Mandeville.

For his brother Eustace count of Boulogne (junior), see below no. 26.

4. D. f. 100 *b*.

Willelmus dei gracia rex Anglorum G. de magna villa et vicec' et Willelmo cam' et omnibus civibus et ministris suis London' salutem. Sciatis me concessisse deo et sancto Petro et Vitali abbati et monachis ecclesie Westmon' pro salute anime mee et amore pie memorie cognati mei predecessoris regis Edwardi in civitate Londonia omnes terras quas idem rex predicto loco sue sepulture dederat, et quas ego postea addideram, vel quas ipsi in eadem urbe ante tenuerant quicunque eas dedisset, cum saka et sokna et toll et theam et miskennige et sceawinge; et ut libere et quiete et honorifice habeant nundinalia et argisteria, id est mercatoria loca, cum seldis et scoppis et redditibus suis, et macella sua cum consuetudinibus et rectitudinibus suis theloneoque suo, que sint ad illuminacionem ecclesie, sicut idem constituit. preterea hiis concessionibus meis adjeci ut omnes mercatores noti vel ignoti,

incole vel advene, hujus vel alterius cujuslibet patrie, qui temporibus predecessoris mei, videlicet regis Edwardi, descenderunt
sive applicuerunt in soca seu seldis vel hwervis sancti Petri ad
hospitandum, ad easdem nunc revertantur; et ibi sint bene et
honorifice, et firmam pacem meam habeant in eundo et in redeundo.
et firmiter prohibe(o) quod nemo vicecomitum, procuratorum,
exactorum vel ministrorum meorum eos disturbet, neque injuriam
vel contumeliam faciat; et nullus se intromittat inde omnino, nisi
per abbatem et monachos suos, sicut idem benignissimus rex
Edwardus per cartas suas concessit atque confirmavit. et ideo
videte, sicut amorem meum diligitis, ne inde clamorem audiam
pro recti penuria, super x libr' forisfacture. Testibus, Walkelino
Winton' episcopo, Willelmo Dun' episcopo, H. comes de War',
R. com' de Mall', Yvone Tailebois, Roberto de Ol', Rog' Big', apud
Westm' in pentec'.

[1081—5.] William of St Carileph was consecrated to Durham
3 Jan. 1081. Vitalis died, probably, in 1085.

Geoffrey de Mandeville was sheriff of London and Middlesex.

William the chamberlain is referred to in *Hist. Abingd.* ii 128 as
'Willelmus regis camerarius de Lundonia': he had land close to
Abingdon, which he held for the service of a knight; but, when Robert
invaded England in 1101, he refused to provide the knight, and the
abbot had to find one instead. He is mentioned (*ibid.* 54) as present
when a grant was made on the altar at Abingdon by William de Curci
on 23 Oct. 1105. A Middlesex grant is addressed to and attested by
him at London, 1100—1 (no. 20, below, see also nos. 17, 39). In the
Ramsey chartulary we find 'Will. camerarius regis' at Brampton
attesting a royal writ in 1110 (Rolls Ser. i 148); and 'Will. camerarius
London' (1114—30; *ib.* i 142): but we cannot be sure that we are
always dealing with the same man.

In the Telligraphus of Will. I (D. f. 50 *b*) we read: 'Willelmus
camerarius meus pro concessa sibi fraternitate et beneficiis memorate
ecclesie, et pro monachatu cujusdam Huberti sui familiaris amici, quem
vice sua pro dei amore ibidem monachum fecerat (gave three hides in
Kingsbury, co. Middles.).' Though that charter is not genuine, the
tradition may be true.

Henry, earl of Warwick, was son of Roger of Beaumont: he died
20 June 1123. He usually attests after Robert, count of Meulan, his
elder brother. Robert († 1118) was the father of Robert, earl of
Leicester.

Ivo Taillebois sometimes attests simply as 'Ivo dapifer.' He has a bad name in the Pseudo-Ingulphus as a robber of Croyland abbey. See below, nos. 9, 27.

For Robert de Oleio, see above, no. 1.

Roger Bigod († 15 Sep. 1107) was 'dapifer' under Will. II and Hen. I. He is 'not traced in English records before 1079' (Maunde Thompson, *Dict. Nat. Biog.*). He was succeeded by his son William, who was drowned in 1120; then by his second son Hugh ('dapifer' in 1123).

I have some doubt as to the genuineness of this charter: the style 'dei gratia' is suspicious (but cf. no. 9). The much larger charter which immediately precedes it (D. f. 99) is certainly fictitious: it is partly founded upon this; it also bears a very close resemblance to the charter said to have been granted in the same year (1081) by Will. I to St Peter's, Ghent (see Round's *Cal. of Doc. preserved in France* I 502).

5. D. f. 529, Faust. A. III, f. 64.

W. rex Angl' M. London' episcopo et G. de magna villa et omnibus ministris suis ac fidelibus Francis et Anglis de Lundon' salutem. Sciatis me concessisse deo et sancto Petro Westm' et G. abbati donum quod Aluuardus de Lundonia eis dedit pro anima sua; id est, ecclesiam sancte Marie que dicitur Niwecirke, cum omnibus rebus ad eam pertinentibus, sicut idem Aluuardus melius et plenius eis concesserat. et volo et firmiter precipio ut bene et quiete et honorifice et libere et absque omni calumpnia et inquietudine et sine cujuslibet reclamatione, cum terris et domibus, cum saca et socna et toll et team et latrone, et cum omnibus rebus et consuetudinibus et legibus eam teneant. et defendo ne aliquis inde illis aliquam torturam faciat. Testibus, Walchel' Winton' episcopo, Willelmo Dunelm' episcopo, et R. de Mell', et R. com. de Warwic, et R. de Oleio, et R. Bigodo, apud Westm'.

[1086.] Maurice was appointed bishop of London at the Christmas court of 1085 at Gloucester, and was consecrated [5 Apr. ?] 1086 at Winchester. The king knighted his son Henry at Westminster 'in hebdomada Pentecostes': later in the year he crossed to Normandy, not to return. Probably, therefore, Whitsuntide 1086 is the date of this charter.

It is wrongly ascribed to Will. II in the rubric of D.

The witnesses are the same, save for the omission of Ivo Taillebois, as in the preceding charter. ' R.' (earl of Warwick) should be ' H.'

For other charters relating to this church of St Mary see nos. 10, 11; and for the controversy regarding it see the detached note *On the early charters of St John's Abbey, Colchester* (pp. 158—166).

6. *Mun.* 2001.

Sciant presentes et futuri, universe sancte matris ecclesie fideles et filii, quod ego Goffridus de magnavilla concessi et mea liberali donatione donavi deo et sancto Petro et ecclesie Westmonasterii, necnon et sancte Marie de Hurleya, pro salute et redemptione anime mee et uxoris mee Leceline, cujus consilio gratia divina providente hoc bonum inchoavi, et pro anima Athelaise prime uxoris mee matris filiorum meorum jam defuncte, necnon et heredum meorum omnium mihi succedentium, eandem ecclesiam sancte Marie de Hurleia in Bearrocsira, cum tota predicta villa de Hurleia et cum toto circumjacenti nemore eidem ville adjacenti, sine participatione aut divisione cujuscunque hominis in ipsa parrochia manentis aut aliquid tenentis; excepta terra solummodo Aedrici prepositi, et excepta terra rusticorum de parva Waltham, quam in mea manu ad me hospitandum retinui. concessi quidem, dico, et firmiter donavi ecclesie eidem de Hurleia cum toto dominio meo libere et quiete in campis et silvis, pratis et pascuis, pasturis et molendinis, aquis et piscariis atque piscationibus et cum omnibus appendiciis suis, id est ecclesia de Waltam cum una hida terre et dimidia que sibi subjacent, et cum socna capelle de Remenham, et cum omnibus aliis rebus et decimis et possessionibus in vivo et mortuo sine parte et divisione, cum omnibus consuetudinibus et libertatibus illi antiquitus debitis, ita libere et quiete ab omnium hominum inquietudine et exactione, sicut dominus meus rex ea mihi dedit et concessit. dedi etiam predicte ecclesie cum supradictis . ea die qua feci eam dedicare, Osmundo episcopo Saresberiensi presente cum multis aliis magne auctoritatis viris et personis, terram Aedwardi de Watecumba in dotalicium libere et quiete cum omnibus sibi pertinentibus. qua vero die supradictus episcopus venerabilis pontificali auctoritate, assistentibus secum magne auctoritatis et dignitatis personis, confirmavit omnes donationes meas quas eidem sancto loco pro anime mee et omnium heredum meorum salute eterna libere contuli; scilicet, in omnibus maneriis que in dominio meo eo tempore erant, terciam partem decime totius annone mee, et duas partes decime totius pecunie omnium maneriorum meorum sine parte in vivo et mortuo, et totam decimam pasnagiorum meorum in porcis et denariis sine parte, et totam decimam caseorum sine parte, et totam decimam lini et lane sine parte, et totam decimam pullorum equorum et vitulorum et pomorum et vinearum sine parte, et totam decimam omnium aliarum rerum mearum, de quibuscunque juste et recte debet deo decima reddi. insuper igitur in unoquoque manerio totius dominii mei dedi prenominate ecclesie mee de Hurleia unum rusticum qui octo acras terre habeat libere et quiete ab omni consuetudine, et in parco meo unam porcariam cum terra porcarii. his etenim addidi adhuc in insula de Hely unam piscariam que reddit unum millearium et dimidium siccarum anguillarum, et unum presentum anguillarum, quadraginta videlicet grossas anguillas : et in villa que Mosa vocatur tria concessi extra prenominata millearia siccorum alleccium. Turoldus quidem dapifer meus concessit eidem ecclesie, et dextera sua super altare confirmavit cum oblatione Radulfii filii sui, duas partes decime totius annone sue de Wochendona et totam decimam totius pecunie sue in vivo et mortuo sine parte; et in Bordesdenæ totam decimam totius annone sue et totius pecunie sue sine parte. Aedricus prepositus meus totam decimam totius annone sue et totius pecunie sue ibidem donavit in vivo et mortuo sine parte. ego vero ad expletionem hujus tanti boni, et ad sustentationem solummodo conventus monachorum in eadem ecclesia deo imperpetuum servientium, gratia disponente divina impetravi a domino meo rege Willelmo hec omnia ad honorem dei et ad salutem anime mee et omnium heredum meorum mihi succedentium pro loci integritate eterna et stabilitate confirmari, et quod locus ille, locus quoque regio munimine insignitus, in protectione mea et defensione semper sit precipuus et mei capud honoris, ab omnium hominum inquietudine liber et quietus. feci itaque in eadem die qua dedicata est ecclesia, ab eodem episcopo et ab abbate Westmon' Gilleberto, cum multis aliis magne auctoritatis viris et personis, omnes infractores seu diminutores hujus mee elemosine excommunicari, ut sit habitatio illorum perpetua cum Juda maledicto proditore domini, et viventes descendant in eterne perdicionis baratrum cum Dathan et Chore cum maledictione eterna, nisi emendaverint digna satisfactione. contestor igitur omnes filios meos, heredes videlicet, et omnes posteros meos per tremendum dei judicium et per omnipotentiam ejus in celo et in terra, ne ipsi faciant aut fieri sinant ullam infractionem huic mee donationi; immo augeant et stabiliant illam, ita ut deus augeat et stabiliat dies et vitam illorum in eterna beatitudine, et habeant partem in hac mea elemosina mecum in celesti requie. Test'. Idem episcopus Osmundus. Gill' abbas Westm'. Lecelina domina uxor mea. Will' de magnavilla. Ric' de magnavilla. Hugo mascherell'. Turoldus de Wochend' dapifer. Goffridus de Wochend'. Walt' mascherell'. Acelinus capellanus. Agamundus persona de Wochend'. Goduuinus de turroc capellanus. Roulf de Hairun. Hacinulf de Greneford. Rob' nepos ejus. Engheram pincerna. Richerius miles. Rog' Blundus. Wimundus de blangeo. Aedricus prepositus. Alfricus cementarius. cum aliis multis inenarrabilibus magne auctoritatis et dignitatis viris et personis in eadem die apud Hurleiam assistentibus. Ex hac vero donatione mea et institutione, consilio proborum sumpto virorum, tria acta sunt brevia: unum apud Westmonasterium, aliud apud eandem ecclesiam de Hurleia, tercium mihi et heredibus meis succedentibus, pro loci integritate eterna et stabilitate reposui.

[1085—6.] See above, p. 33. It is interesting to note that Ralph, the son of Turold the dapifer of Geoffrey de Mandeville, is the first youth dedicated to the priory at Hurley. The expression 'mei capud honoris' is a technical one: 'the chief place of my Honor.' William de Mandeville was Geoffrey's son and heir, and father of the notorious Geoffrey de Mandeville, earl of Essex: see below, nos. 15, 20. Richard de Mandeville was a younger son.

Hugo Mascherell is the first witness to Geoffrey de Mandeville's grant of Eye (no. 15), and he is there followed by his brother Roger. A younger Hugo Mascherell occurs in a charter of Hen. I, *temp.* Abbot Herbert (D. f. 579 *b*). The priory of nuns at Wix (co. Essex) was founded by Walter Mascherell, Alexander and Edith, the children of Walter the deacon, who held the manor at the Survey: the charter was granted c. 1125—35. Can we assume any connexion with the Walter Mascherell who attests here?

'Goduuinus de turroc': 'Turruc' was held by the count of Eu at the Survey (Essex, p. 63).

Ralph de Hairun and Richerius attest no. 15.

'Alfricus cementarius' was no doubt the master mason who was engaged on the building of the new priory.

For notes on the localities mentioned in this charter, see *St Mary's, Hurley*, by the Reverend F. T. Wethered.

7. *Mun.* 3780.

G. de mandavilla Ædrico preposito suo omnibusque hominibus suis de Uualtham salutem. Sciatis quod prior et monachi mei de Hurleia mihi graviter conquesti sunt de hoc quod boscum suum absque eis et eorum licencia tam male vastatis et destruitis. unde vobis mando et super feoda vestra precipio et defendo ne amodo vos neque de aqua sua intromittatis, neque in bosco suo extra sepes vestras sine prioris aut suorum documento quicquam capiatis. si que vero ad domos vestras reficiend[as] necessaria vobis fuer[int] et sepes [in]de precipio [ut] vobis necessari[a] prioris vel suorum documento habeatis. quia omnia que in terra et in aqua et in omnibus rebus pro anime mee atque meorum salute ipsis dedi et concessi, volo et firmiter precipio ut ipsi habeant ita b[ene] et quiete [et] [sicut] ea dedi ac concessi deo et ecclesie mee de Hurleia, die qua feci eam dedicare. Valete.

[c. 1086—1100.] No precise date can be given to this charter. For Edric the prepositus, see the preceding charter. The spelling 'Mandavilla' is of interest.

8. D. f. 526 *b*.

G. abbas et conventus Westm' concedunt Rotberto filio Suenonis ut ipse teneat de sancto Petro et de abbate pro lx sol' per singulos annos terram, scilicet Wateleyam, quam pater suus dedit sancto Petro pro anima sua, et de qua terra ipse Rotbertus cum sua matre fecit donacionem super altare sancti Petri in eodem die quo sepultus est pater suus, videntibus baronibus suis Godobaldo, Turaldo et Willelmo fratre suo et multis aliis, in presencia abbatis et monachorum. et tam diu sic eam teneat, donec pro predicta terra det cambium iiij li, quod abbas et monachi gratanter accipere debeant. hii sunt termini den': in ramis palmarum xxx sol', in festivitate apostolorum Petri et Pauli xxx sol'.

[c. 1087.] This transaction probably took place immediately after the death of Suain: perhaps soon after the Survey, in which he still appears as holding lands in Essex, though no longer sheriff. See above, pp. 49 f., and nos. 1, 2.

9.  D. f. 523.

W. dei gracia rex Anglorum Hug' de Bello campo et fidelibus suis Francis et Anglis de Buchingeham salutem. Sciatis quod Gillebertus abbas Westm' meo precepto deracionavit coram baronibus meis, episcopo Dunolm', episcopo Winton', Eudone dapifero, Ivone Taillebosc, Roberto dispensatore, terram de Burnham et Sippenham per donum patris mei. et ego concedo ut cum omnibus consuetudinibus terram illam solute et quiete habeat. T.' episcopus Dunhelmi et episcopus Winton'.

[Sep. 1087—early in 1088.] Probably granted before Odo's rising in 1088, which was joined by William of St Carileph, the bishop of Durham. But it might be after William's restoration to his bishopric, 3 Sep. 1091.

The style 'dei gracia' may be due to the copyist: see above, no 4.

Hugh de Beauchamp held lands at the Survey chiefly in Bedfordshire. He had three sons, Simon, Pain (m. Rohaise) and Milo: so Dugdale, *Baronage* I 224, who concludes that Walter de Beauchamp, of Elmley, was of the same family. Hugh is mentioned as having been witness of a grant made by Robert Dispensator, whose niece Walter married (see below, no. 27).

Eudo dapifer was son of Hubert de Rie, a Norman noble said to have been sent by Duke William to K. Edward. For his story, see *Monasticon* IV 604. He succeeded W. fitz Osbern as dapifer to Will. I, and served also under Will. II, whom he had greatly assisted by securing Dover and other ports on the Conqueror's death. Will. II granted him Colchester, where he founded a monastery in 1096. At the beginning of Henry's reign, he was suspected of favouring the claims of Duke Robert; but Henry feared to strike him on account of his powerful connexions. For he had married Rohaise, daughter of Richard fitz Gilbert and his wife Rohaise (sister of William Giffard who became bp of Winchester). By the intervention of the bishop and of Peter de Valognes, who had married Eudo's sister, he regained the royal favour. He was buried at Colchester on the same day as his nephew Walter Giffard, the last day of Feb. 1120; for the last fifteen years of his life he was blind, and apparently resided at his castle at Préaux, where he died. It is difficult to distinguish between fact and fiction in Eudo's story; but it may be taken as practically certain that he died at his castle in Normandy in the winter of 1119—20 (Round, *Eng. Hist. Rev.* XVI 728). No. 18 below is addressed to him.

*Deracionavit* = 'made good his claim to': cf. no. 12. For Burnham and Sippenham, see above, p. 48, and below, no. 37.

10. Faust. A. III, f. 76.

Willelmus rex Angl' Mauricio Lond' episcopo et Gaufrido de magna villa et vic' et omnibus baronibus Lond' Francis et Anglis salutem. Sciatis me concessisse deo et sancto Petro Westm' ecclesiam Niwecerch' liberam et quietam et solutam ab omni calumpnia, sicut Agelwardus clericus predicto apostolo dedit, et sicut pater meus per breve suum concessit. et prohibeo ne aliquis eis inde aliquam torturam faciat, vel aliquis aliquam intromissionem habeat, nisi per concessionem abbatis et monachorum. T.' G. episcopo de Const', W. episcopo Dunelm', R. Bigot, apud Winton'.

[Sep. 1087—early in 1088.] The bishops of Coutances and Durham joined Odo's rising in 1088. The MS has 'Henricus' for 'Willelmus'; but this is impossible, for Bp Geoffrey died in 1093. The rubric assigns it to Henry II, but it must be Will. II. For the charter of Will. I, here referred to, see above, no. 5.

For Bp Maurice, see above, no. 5.

11. D. f. 529, Faust. A. III, f. 64.

W. rex Angl' Francis et Anglis de Lundon' salutem. Sciatis me concedere sancto Petro Westm' ecclesiam sancte Marie Newecirce et omnes res pertinentes ad eam, quam Aluuardus de Lundon' ei dederat. et precipio ut ita solutam et quietam habeat sicut pater meus precepit per breve suum. T.' com' Alanus et Milo Crispinus et Rogerus Bygod.

[1087—1100.] Count Alan, of Richmond (Yorks.), was a Breton follower of the Conqueror.

For Milo Crispin, see above, p. 17: the next two charters are also attested by him.

In both chartularies this writ is wrongly assigned to Will. I, see above, no. 5. With the address comp. the Rutland charter of Will. I, D. f. 621: 'W. rex Angl' Francis et Anglis salutem[1].'

[1] This charter, which grants to Abbot Gilbert the churches held by 'Albertus Lotharingus,' is quoted in full from *Monasticon* [I 801] by Dr Round in his interesting identification of this Lotharingian cleric (*Commune of London*, 37). Under Will. II these churches are held by 'Osbernus clericus' (below, no. 14).

12.   Faust. A. iii, f. 55, Lib. Nig. f. 25.

Willelmus rex Angl' Hugoni de Bokel' et vicecomiti et omnibus fidelibus suis de Middelsexa salutem.   Sciatis quod volo et firmiter precipio quod terra de Gyveneya que est pastura de manerio de Stanes, quam Vitalis abbas tempore patris mei contra Walterum filium Oteri deracionavit ad opus ecclesie sancti Petri Westm', sit in pace; ita ut nullus illi molestiam aut inquietudinem inde faciat; neque abbas Gislebertus ejusdem loci alicui inde respondeat nisi coram episcopis et baronibus justificatoribus, qui fuerunt ibi ubi ipsa terra deracionata fuit.   neque ullo modo consentire volo ut aliquis inde quicquam tollat aut minuat; sed in ea concessione et stabilitate qua a rege Edwardo donata est sine aliqua imminucione permaneat.   Testibus Alano comite, Rogero Bygod, Milone Crispino, Goffrido de magna villa, et pluribus aliis.

[1087—1100.]   The *Hist. Abingd.* (Rolls S. ii 7) tells us that Walter fitz Oter was keeper of Windsor Castle early in the reign of Will. I; and that he had then appropriated certain land, which he long afterwards restored to that monastery (*ib.* 29) when the new church was consecrated, c. 1095.

Of Hugh de Buckland we read in the *History of Abingdon*, ii 43: ' et Berchescire vicecomes et publicarum judiciarius compellationum a rege constitutus'; *ib.* 117, 'qui non solum Berchescirae, sed etiam aliis vii sciris praeerat vicecomes, adeo erat nominatus vir et carus regi.' He was still living in May 1114 (*ib.* 147), but in 1119 William de Buckland was sheriff of Berkshire (*ib.* 160).   See below, nos. 20, 27, 29, 37 and 38.

13.   D. f. 129.

G. abbas Westm' concessit Guntero homini suo et heredi illius manerium Hendon' in feudo firme, pro una plenaria septimana firme quoque anno.   Testes : Milo Crispinus, Gislebertus Pipardus, Robertus prior et conventus monasterii in capitulo.

[1086—1102.]   The lower limit is given by the appointment of Robert to the abbey of St Edmund in 1102: see above, p. 29.

Shortly before his death in 1107 Milo Crispin made a grant to Abingdon abbey, which was placed on the altar by ' Gillebertus Pipardus,' his dapifer (*Hist. Ab.* ii 97).   Somewhat later ' Gillebertus

Pipard' occurs with 'Hugo fil' Milonis' as present at Waddesdon (co. Bucks.) when a grant is made to the same abbey (*ib.* 109). As the name is uncommon, we may note that Walter and Robert Pipard attest a Bec charter c. 1147 (Round, *Doc. pres. in France*, p. 121).

For *una plenaria septimana firme*, see above, p. 42.

14. D. f. 621, Faust. A. III, f. 65.

W. rex Angl' W. vicecom' salutem. Mando et precipio tibi ut facias omnem rectitudinem abbati Westm' de ecclesiis de Rotelanda, quas Osbernus clericus tenet de illo; et omnes consuetudines quas ecclesie per rectum habere debent, fac eum habere, sicut habuerunt tempore patris mei. T.' Rannulfus Passæflamblart.

[1087—99.] Ranulf Flambard was consecrated to Durham 5 June 1099. The form of the attestation is noteworthy: for he usually attests as 'Ranulfus capellanus' before he became the bishop of Durham.

For these Rutland churches, see above, no. 11 (note).

Faust. A. III reads *Hosbertus*, and *Ranulfo passeflambard'*.

15. D. f. 103, Faust. A. III, f. 281 *b*, Lib. Nig. f. 5 *b*.

Ego Goffridus de magna villa pro anima mea et pro anima conjugis mee Athelais in claustro sancti Petri sepulte, qui etiam juxta eam sepeliendus sum; pro animabus quoque filiorum filiarumque mearum; dedi sancto Petro Westmon' maneriolum quod juxta ecclesiam ejus habebam, scilicet Eye, in perpetuam hereditatem, sicut illud unquam melius tenui. et hoc donum deo et sancto Petro cum uxore mea Letselina concessione filii mei Willelmi quem mihi heredem facere disposui, quos etiam hujus elemosine participes fieri per omnia volo, super altare predicti apostoli Petri presentavi in presencia Gisleberti abbatis et monachorum et multorum militum meorum et suorum: et continuo per Radulfum de Hairun de predicto manerio sanctum Petrum saisiri feci. hujus igitur concessionis testes sunt Hugo Maskereal, Rogerius frater ejus, Willelmus fil' Martelli, Richerius, Radulfus de Hairun, Goiffridus nepos ejus, Willelmus nepos Turaldi, Goffridus miles ejus, Leuricus Cnivet, Goffridus et multi alii.

[1087—97.] As the next charter confirms this, and as Hen. I in no. 20 speaks of the grant as made by his brother, I have assigned the same limits to this charter as to the next.

Hugo Mascherell, Roulf de Hairun and Richerius miles attest the Hurley foundation charter, no. 6.

For the burial of Athelais, see no. 1.

16.  **D. f. 103, Lib. Nig. f. 5 b.**

Willelmus rex Anglorum baronibus suis et omnibus fidelibus Francis et Anglis de Middelsexa salutem. Sciatis me concessisse deo et sancto Petro Westm' et Gisleberto abbati manerium de Eye, quod Goffridus de magna villa et uxor ejus dederunt eidem ecclesie pro animabus eorum. et volo et concedo ut omnes leges et consuetudines quiete et solute in illo manerio habeat sanctus Petrus et abbas; hoc est, sacam et socam, toll et theam, latronem et omnes consuetudines in via et extra, in festo et extra. et defendo ne aliquis sit ausus ei vel suis hominibus inde super hoc aliquam injuriam facere. T.' Walchelinus episcopus et Haim' et alii, apud London'.

[1087—97.]  See Henry I's confirmation, no. 20.

Walkelin bp of Winchester died 3 Jan. 1098.

Haimo dapifer was brother of the famous Robert fitz Haimo, for whom see Professor Tout's art. 'Fitzhamon' in *Dict. Nat. Biogr.* They may have been sons of 'Haimo vicecomes,' who holds lands in Kent and Surrey at the Survey. Both brothers attest K. Henry's letter inviting Anselm to return in 1100. Robert died in 1107, but Haimo was still living in 1113.

17.  **D. f. 254.**

W. rex Anglorum P. vicecomiti et omnibus ministris suis sal'. Sciatis me concedere abbati Gisleberto in manerio de Feringes soccam et saccam in omnibus rebus, in via et extra viam, in festo die et extra, latronem et omnes illas leges et consuetudines quas et Vitalis abbas et alii antecessores ejus tempore regis Edwardi habuerunt. T.' abbas Beccensis, W. camerarius et alii.

[1093.]  Peter de Valognes was sheriff of Essex at the Survey. An earlier grant, which gives Fering and three houses at Colchester which belonged to Harold, as part of the exchange for Windsor, is addressed to Suain as sheriff (D. f. 254). The mention in the present grant of its having been held by abbots under K. Edward is an error more likely to have been made under Will. II than under Will. I. It would appear therefore to belong to the period between 6 March and 5 Sept. 1093, when Anselm was still refusing to accept the archbishopric.

For William the chamberlain, see no. 4.

18. D. f. 363, Faust. A. III, f. 78 *b*.

H. rex Angl' Eudoni dapifero et Herberto camerario salutem. Precipio quod conventus Westm' et Winton' et Gloecestrie in omnibus festivitatibus quibus in eisdem ecclesiis coronatus fuero plenariam de me habeant liberacionem, et earum cantores unciam auri habeant, sicut Mauricius episcopus Lundon' testatus est tempore predecessorum meorum eos habuisse. T'. Willelmo electo Wint' apud Westm'.

[1100.] Probably issued on the occasion of Henry's coronation at Westminster, 5 Aug. 1100. It was the habit of William the Conqueror to wear his crown at the three great festivals, and in this he probably continued the practice of his predecessor.

William Giffard was appointed to Winchester immediately on Henry's accession and before his coronation. He was present at the council held at Westminster, 20 Sep. 1102; but refusing to be consecrated by Gerard, abp of York, he was banished. He accompanied Anselm to Rome in 1103. Shortly afterwards he appears to have been restored: he was one of the bishops who urged Anselm to return in 1106. He was consecrated 11 Aug. 1107, and died 25 Jan. 1129. He had been chancellor to William Rufus, and continued to act for a short time under Hen. I. See below, no. 21.

Herbert the chamberlain is mentioned below in no. 27 as witnessing a grant c. 1087—97 ('Herbertus camerarius regis de Winton'). See also *Hist. Abingd.* II 43 (end of Will. I's reign): 'regis cubicularius et thesaurarius'; and *ib.* 54 (c. 1102).

19. Faust. A. III, f. 67.

Henricus rex Anglorum Gisleberto vicecomiti de Suthreia salutem. Mando et precipio ut dimittas esse quietam terram sancti Petri Westm' et abbatis Gisleberti que est in dominio meo infra parcum et forestam de Windlesor', et nominatim viii hidas de manerio de Piriford quod pater meus concessit eidem ecclesie amodo semper liberas ab omni geldo et scotto et omnibus aliis rebus. et nominatim clamo eas quietas de novo geldo propter hidagium et de omnibus aliis geldis sicut pater meus et frater concesserunt per brevia sua. T'. R. Bigot apud Bisselegam.

[1100—1107.]   Gilbert of Surrey was sheriff of Surrey, Cambridge-shire and Hunts. in 1114 (Round, *Commune*, 122). This charter (attested by Roger Bigod, see no. 4) shews that he was sheriff of Surrey at least as early as 1107. A charter regarding Battersea granted to Abbot Herbert, probably in 1121, is also addressed to Gilbert as sheriff (D. f. 168). Fulk, his nephew, was sheriff not later than 1126 (Round, *ib.* 121).

Possibly the phrase ' de novo geldo propter hidagium ' may help to fix the date of this charter more precisely.

The charter of William here referred to is the well-known Piriford charter printed above, p. 29 (note).

20.   Faust. A. III, f. 73 b, Lib. Nig. f. 6.

Henricus rex Angl' H. de Boch' et W. camerario et W. de magna villa et omnibus fidelibus suis Francis et Anglis de Middelsex' salutem.   Sciatis me concessisse deo et sancto Petro Westm' et Gilleberto abbati donum quod Goffridus de magna villa et uxor ejus dederunt eis pro animabus eorum, terram dico de Eye. et volo et precipio ut bene et honorifice teneat ipse abbas, et sicut Willelmus frater meus concessit per breve suum.   Testibus Matild' regina et W. cancellario apud London'.

[1100—1.]   Q. Matilda was married and crowned 11 Nov. 1100. William Giffard was chancellor until he was succeeded by Roger (afterwards bp of Salisbury) in Sep. 1101.

This charter suggests that William de Mandeville had succeeded his father as sheriff of Middlesex.   About the same time William was in charge of the Tower of London, where Ranulf Flambard was im-prisoned in Aug. or Sep. 1100, till his escape about Feb. 1101 (Ord. Vit. bk 10, c. 18).

The charters referred to in this confirmation are printed above, nos. 15, 16.

21.   D. f. 529, Faust. A. III, f. 67 *b.*

H. rex Angl' W. Giffardo episcopo Winton' et omnibus baronibus suis Francis et Anglis de Suthregia salutem.   Sciatis me dedisse deo et sancto Petro et abbati Gileberto et monachis ecclesie Westm' iiij⁰ʳ hidas in Totinges, ut eas ita bene et plenarie et honorifice teneant et habeant sicut habuerunt tempore patris mei et antecessorum meorum.   et prohibeo super forisfacturam meam ne ullus eis inde injuriam faciat, neque abbas inde alicui nisi ante me respondeat. T'. Roberto comite Mellent' et Nig' de Oleio, apud Winton'.

[1100—East. 1116.] The lower limit is given by the king's departure for Normandy in the year before Abbot Gilbert's death. The writ may have been addressed to William Giffard before his consecration in Aug. 1107.

I give the chief variants of Faust. A. III to illustrate the freedom with which charters were copied into chartularies : om. *suis, concessisse* (for *dedisse*), *Gisleberto, Rodberto comite de Mellent et Nigillo de Oleyo.*

For Robert count of Meulan († 1118), see no. 4; and for Nigel de Oleio, no. 1.

22. D. f. 254, Faust. A. III, f. 74.

H. rex Angl' omnibus baronibus et ministris suis de Esex' sal'. Volo ut sanctus Petrus de Westm' ita quietam et liberam habeat cum omnibus consuetudinibus omnem terram de Ferynges et de Okendune sicut pater meus concessit et dedit. et precipio ut super hoc nullus ei injuriam faciat. T'. Willelmo de Curceio apud Havering'.

[1100—c. 1109.] William de Curci was a benefactor to Abingdon Abbey: in confirming a grant of his, 23 Oct. 1105, the king speaks of him as 'dapifer meus' (*Hist. Ab.* II 54). He attests at Westminster, Whits. 1107 : also at Winchester, Matilda's charter (*ib.* 116) between July 1108 and May 1109 (or between Aug. 1111 and the summer of 1113): also other charters c. 1105—7 (always by his full name, and not as 'dapifer').

This seems to justify our placing this charter early in Henry's reign: but as William de Curci was succeeded by a son of that name (*ib.* 54 f.), it may conceivably be later.

Orderic Vitalis has much to say about Richard de Curci (of Courci-sur-Dives), and of his son and grandson, both named Robert: but nothing of the English branch of the family.

For 'Okendune' see above, p. 49.

23. Ch. xxx (copies in D. f. 482, Faust. A. III, f. 75 *b*).

H. rex Angl' omnibus vic' suis in quorum vicecomit' elemosina pauperum Westm' habet terras sal'. Sciatis me clamasse liberam

et quietam terrę elemosinę de Westm' de placitis et querelis et
sciris et hundr', et murdr', et a scotis et auxiliis, et de wardp' et de
omnibus occasionibus et consuetudinibus: scilicet terram Padinton'
et Fenton' et Cleigate; et quicquid habuit in villa vel silva de
Ditona tempore regis Eadwardi et patris mei, sicut carte eorum
testantur, volo ut plenar' habeat. T'. Math' regina, apud Lund'.

[1100—16.]   There is nothing to fix the date within narrower limits.
For Fanton (co. Essex) see above, p. 49.   In the Domesday Survey the
monks of Westminster were accused of holding it *per falsum breve*.

24.   Ch. xxix (copy in D. f. 482).

H. rex Angl' omnibus vicecomitibus in quorum vicecomitatu
elemosina pauperum Westmonasterii habet terras sal'.   Sciatis me
clamasse liberam et quietam terram elemosine de Westmonasterio
de placitis et scotis et auxiliis et omnibus querelis et omnibus aliis
consuetudinibus: scilicet terram Patintonæ et Fantona et Clai-
gata; et quicquid habuit in tempore regis Edwardi in silva Dittonę
et in omnibus aliis locis, volo ut habeat.   et defendo ne aliquis
inde injuriam faciat: quia hoc facio pro anima patris et fratris
mei, et pro salute anime mee et Mathildis regine uxoris mee et
subolis mee.   T'. Math' regina, apud Lond' post purific' sancte
Marie.

[Feb. 1103—16.]   The queen's first child was born in Aug. 1101, but
died in infancy; the second was Matilda, born in Aug. 1102: William
was born the next year.

A third charter combines the privileges of this and the preceding
one (D. f. 482), ' precatu regine,' ' T'. ejusdem regine apud Lond'.'

25.   D. f. 525.

Domino suo episcopo R. et baronibus Lincoln' Hugo de Euremou
salutem.   Sciatis me reddidisse sancto Petro Westm' manerium de
Dotinton'; quia manerium quod pro illo dederam sancto Petro
rex a me accepit, et comiti Eustachio reddidit; nec volo ut causa
mei ecclesia dei ullo modo dampnum habeat.

[1102—3.]   See note on the next charter.

Robert Bloet, bp of Lincoln, was consecrated 12 Feb. 1094, and died
10 Jan. 1123.

26.   D. f. 525, Faust. A. III, f. 74.

Henricus rex Anglorum R. episcopo Lincoln' et R. filio Rannulfi et omnibus baronibus suis Francis et Anglis de Lincolnesire salutem.   Sciatis quia me presente et concedente Hugo de Euremou reddidit sancto Petro Westm' et abbati Gisleberto manerium de Dotintune, quod ab eodem abbate coram fratre meo rege Willelmo ipse Hugo acceperat in cambium pro manerio de Ducesuuorthe quod abbati Gisleberto dederat.   sed ego manerium de Ducesuuorthe comiti Eustachio reddidi, et inde Hugoni cambium dedi ; et propterea Hugo sancto Petro manerium suum reddidit.   T'. episcopus Lincoln' R., Henricus comes de Warwihc, Gislebertus filius Ricardi, Willelmus de Werewast et multi alii apud Westm' in pentecosten.

[Whits. 1102—3.] 'Dochesworde' (co. Camb.) belonged at the Survey to Eustace count of Boulogne, senior: see further, *Feud. Eng.* 463.   Early in 1088 Count Eustace junior received Odo into Rochester castle, capturing him ('calliditate episcopi,' it was said) when he came to demand its surrender to Rufus.   The king afterwards took the castle, and banished them both.   Eustace took the Cross in 1096, returned in 1100, and married Maria, sister of Q. Maud, at the end of 1102 (Sim. of Durh. Rolls S. II 216, 227, 232, 235, mainly from Florence of Worc.).   It was doubtless about this time that Hugh de Euremou restored Doddington to the abbey, as the king had given back to Eustace his old manor of 'Dochesworde.'   See above, p. 46.

Hugo de Euremou attests an Abingdon charter, dated in Lent 1111 (*Hist. Ab.* II 73).

Gilbert fitz Richard of Clare (or, Gilbert of Tunbridge) was the son of Richard fitz Gilbert (†c. 1090), for whom see no. 1.   He is first mentioned as fortifying Tunbridge castle against Rufus, 1088 (together with Roger his brother); next as warning Rufus against an ambuscade, 1095.   He settled in Wales 1107(?): attests his mother's charter, 1113; died 1114 (or 1117) after a long illness (Round, *Dict. Nat. Biogr.*).

William Warelwast was much out of England from the autumn of 1103 until Anselm's return.   He was consecrated to Exeter in August 1107.

I give the following variants from Faust. A. III: *Angl', Ranulphi, Lincolnescire, Gilleberto, Dudinton', Ducesworth, manerium suum sancto Petro, R. episcopo Lincoln', Warewik,* om. *multi*: all the attestations are in the ablative case.

R. C.                                                                                    10

27.　D. f. 313 *b*.

Robertus dispensator reddidit in vita sua sancto Petro Westm'
pro anima sua terram et manerium Cumbrinton, quod de beneficio
ejusdem ecclesie emerat a Gisleberto fil' Toraldi : et insuper reddidit eidem ecclesie terram quam de abbate Gisleberto ejusdem
monasterii ad firmam tenebat in manerio ipsius ecclesie, quod
dicitur Wich et est membrum manerii de Persore.　Testes hujus
reddicionis sunt : episcopus Walchelinus, Urso frater ejusdem
Roberti, Herbertus camerarius regis de Winton', Ivo Taillebosc ;
et homines ipsius Roberti, Godardus, Robertus de Echinton, Hugo
de Holauessæl ; de aliis baronibus regis, Hugo de Belcampo,
Willelmus Bainardus, Petrus de Valunnis, Willelmus camerarius,
Hugo de Bochelanda, Otto aurifex, et multi alii clerici et laici ;
homines ipsius abbatis, Otbert de Surreia, Willelmus clericus,
Girardus frater ejus, Hugo de Coleham, Richerius.　hanc red-
dicionem presente episcopo Walchelino et predictis testibus posuerunt super altare sancti Petri uxor ipsius Roberti et Urso frater
ejusdem Roberti per duo candelabra argentea, unum turribulum,
unum pallium, unum tapete.

[1100—c. 1108.]　This memorandum was probably drawn up when
application was being made for K. Henry's confirmation (which here
follows).　Robert Dispensator, the brother of the notorious Urse
d'Abetôt, had bought the manor of Comberton (co. Worc.) from Gilbert
fitz Thorold, who appears as holding it at the time of the Survey.
Robert also held in farm from Abbot Gilbert a member of the Pershore
manor, called Wich.　Both these properties he had given back to the
abbey in his lifetime.

As the leading witness to this restoration, Bp Walkelin, died 3 Jan.
1098, and as the properties had come into Robert's hands after 1086,
we may date the restoration somewhere within the first ten years of
Will. II's reign (probably towards the end of that period).

For Herbert the chamberlain, see above, no. 18 ; and for Ivo Taillebois, no. 4.

Robert de Echintone came from Eckington, the next village to
Comberton: it is abbey land in Domesday (Aichintune), and the patron-
age of the living is still with the Dean and Chapter.

For Hugh de Beauchamp see no. 9 : for William Bainard, above,
p. 39 : for Peter de Valognes, no. 19 : for William the chamberlain,
no. 4 : and for Hugh de Buckland, no. 12.

For Otto the goldsmith, 'lord of Gestingthorpe,' and his descendants, hereditary masters of the mint, see Dr Round in V. C. Hist. *Essex*, I 351. He appears in the Survey as *Otto aurifaber*. He was employed by Rufus to make his father's tomb at St Stephen's, Caen: 'auri et argenti gemmarumque copiam Othoni aurifabro erogavit, et super patris sui mausoleum fieri mirificum memoriale precepit,' Ord. Vit., bk viii, c. 1). He appears in a charter [1104—7] printed in *Hist. Rev.* XXIV 427: 'Othoni aurifabro de Lond'.'

For Hugh de Coleham, see above, p. 30. A knight named Richerius attests Geoffrey de Mandeville's charters, above, nos. 6 and 15.

28. D. f. 313 *b*, Faust. A. III, f. 74.
    H. rex Angl' Ur' de Ab' et baronibus suis de Wirecestrascira salutem. Sciatis me concessisse sancto Petro Westm' terra de Cumbertona, quam Robertus dispensator dedit ecclesie sancti Petri de Westm': et volo et precipio ut bene et honorifice teneat, et nullus ei injuriam faciat. T'. Rob' Linc' episcopo apud Windres'.

[1100—c. 1108.] This charter must be dated after Robert's death and before that of Urse his brother. But neither of these dates appears to be known. If we may assume, from the fact that Robert's restoration was made at Westminster on his behalf by his wife and brother, that he himself was sick and dying, we should place his death not later than 1097. He attests the grant of the city of Bath to Bishop John (1094—97), printed by W. Hunt in Somerset Record Society, *Bath Cartulary*, I, no. 38. His non-appearance in the list of reliefs demanded on the vacancy of the bishopric of Worcester in 1095 (*Feud. Eng.* 309) might be due to his recent death having left his fief in the king's hands. This however is but conjecture; and it may be that there are known facts to the contrary. The date of Urse's death, I gather, is not earlier than 1108 (*Feud. Eng.* 170).
    Variants of Faust. A. III are: *Abet*', *Wircestrascira, deo et sancto Petro, terram, Rodbertus, R. episcopo Linc*', *Windelsoras*.

29. D. f. 516 *b*.
    H. rex Angl' H. de Bokelande et vic' omnibusque fidelibus ac ministris suis Francis et Anglis London' salutem. Sciatis me concessisse deo et sancto Petro ac monachis Westm' illas terras quas tres filie Deormanni pro salute animarum suarum et sepulturis suis, et ut plenam haberent ejusdem ecclesie societatem,

consilio et voluntate Ordgari fratris earum, in Lundon' eis dederunt. unde volo et firmiter precipio ut bene quiete honorifice
et absque omni calumpnia, cum saca et soca, consuetudinibus et
legibus, illas teneant. et defendo et omnimodis prohibeo ut nullus
molestiam aut torturam illis inde faciat. T'. R. canc' et G. de
Clinton' et R. Basset.

[1107—c. 1115.] The upper limit is given by Ranulf as chancellor
(see no. 35), the lower by the address to Hugh de Buckland, who seems
to have died c. 1115 (see nos. 37, 38).

'Orgarus filius Deremanni' (as well as 'Orgarus le Prude') was
one of the members of the Cnichtengild who gave their soke to Holy
Trinity Priory in 1125 in return for the privilege of fraternity. It is
interesting to see that his three sisters had already linked themselves
in a similar way to the abbey of Westminster. For further notes on
this family see Round, *Commune*, 106.

It would appear from *Dict. Nat. Biogr.* that the first occurrence of
Geoffrey de Clinton's name hitherto known is in a charter of 1121—3.
The charter here printed shews him to us seven or eight years earlier.

For 'R. Basset' see the next charter.

30. D. f. 101.

Henricus rex Angl' episcopo † G. † London' et archid' et toti
capitulo sancti Pauli sal'. Precipio quod abbas et ecclesia sancti
Petri Westm' et presbyteri eorum habeant et teneant ecclesias
suas quas pater meus eis dedit: ligneam scilicet capellam sancte
Margarete de Eschep, cum parochia et cum terra et domibus ad
eam pertinentibus; et medietatem lapidee capelle sancti Magni
martiris cum tota parochia; et ecclesiam sancti Laurentii cum
omnibus sibi pertinentibus; et ecclesiam sancti Jacobi super
ripam : ita bene et in pace et honorifice, sicut melius tenuerunt
tempore patris mei, et meo actenus, sine calumpnia, et temporibus
Hugonis et Mauricii episcoporum. et prohibeo ne super hoc breve
inde placitent. T'. Matild' regina et R. Basset apud London'.

[July 1108—East. 1116.] Probably issued to Richard de Belmeis
soon after he entered on his bishopric. 'G' is a scribe's error for 'R',
as is shewn by the similar writ issued to Gilbert the Universal (cons.
22 Jan. 1128, †10 Aug. 1134), where 'G' is right, and 'Ricardi' is added
to 'Hugonis' and 'Mauricii' as one of the predecessors (D. f. 101 *b*).

Ralph Basset is probably the witness here: see below, no. 39.    But
it might be Richard Basset.

This charter is of special interest for its reference to London
churches held by the abbey in the Conqueror's reign.


31.    Faust. A. III, f. 74.

Henricus rex Angl' Ricardo episcopo de Lundon' sal'.    Mando
tibi ut facias plenum rectum abbati Westm' de hominibus qui fre-
gerunt ecclesiam suam de Winton' noctu et armis.    et nisi feceris,
barones mei de scaccario faciant fieri, ne audiam clamorem inde
pro penuria recti.    T'. &c.


[July 1108—1127.]    As the witnesses are not given, we cannot say
whether this belongs to the time of Abbot Gilbert or to that of Abbot
Herbert.    Winton' is for Wineton (Wenington): see above, p. 49.


32.    Faust. A. III, f. 79.

Henricus rex Angl' Ricardo de Monte salutem.    fac habere
abbati Westm' x solidos de elemosina mea, sicut est in rotulis
meis.    T'. episcopo Sarum apud Canoc.    Et hoc quoque anno.
Teste eodem.


[? c. 1110—East. 1116.]    Richard de Monte was sheriff of Oxfordshire
in 1111 (*Hist. Ab.* II 119 f.): so that the abbot here referred to is not
improbably Abbot Gilbert.

'Canoc' is for Cannock (co. Staff.).

The writ is of interest for its reference to the king's rolls.

For Hugo de Monte, see below, no. 37.    Gilbert de Monte occurs
in the Northamptonshire Survey, which Dr Round assigns to c. 1120
(with later modifications): see *Feud. Eng.* 219.


33.    Faust. A. III, f. 76.

Henricus rex Angl' omnibus vicecom' et ministris tocius Angl'
salutem.    Precipio quod totum corredium et omnes res abbatis
de Westm', unde homines sui poterint affidare quod sint sue
proprie, sint ita quiete de theloneo et passagio et omnibus consuetudinibus sicut unquam melius fuerunt tempore antecessorum
suorum.    T'. canc' apud Merleb'.

[? Summer, 1113—Sep. 1114.] A charter of similar import and of exactly the same attestation, on behalf of the abbey of Abingdon, is addressed to Hugh de Buckland (*Hist. Ab.* II 79), and is therefore not later than c. 1114. I have therefore assigned this conjecturally to Abbot Gilbert's time.

34.  D. f. 58 *b*.

H. rex Angl justic' vicec' et omnibus ministris totius Angl' et portuum maris salutem. Precipio quod totum corredium monachorum de Westm' et quicquid in victu et vestitu ad usum eorum pertinet, quod homines eorum poterint affidare suum esse dominicum, sit quietum de theoloneo et passagio et omni alia consuetudine. et super hoc nullus illud nec homines eorum injuste disturbet, super x libr' forisfacture. T'. Rann' cancell' per Otuelum fil' comitis apud Turrim Lundon'.

[Summer, 1113—Sep. 1114 (prob.).] For the probability of this date, see the next charter, which bears exactly the same attestation. For Otwel fitz Count, see nos. 35, 36, 37, 40.

35.  *Mun.* 3765.

H. rex Angl' justic' vicec' et omnibus ministris et fidelibus suis per Angliam sal'. Precipio quod prior et monachi ecclesie sancte Marie de Hurnleia teneant omnia tenementa sua que tenent de feud' Gaufridi de Magnavilla in quocumque fuerint comitatu, in bosco et in plano, in terra et in aqua, in ecclesiis et in decimis, in possessionibus et in consuetudinibus, in libertatibus et in omnibus rebus, et insuper in maneriis que in manu mea sunt de honore ipsius Gaufridi de Magnavilla, tam bene et libere et quiete et plenarie sicut ipse Gaufridus melius et liberius et plenarius ea ecclesie sue de Hurnleia pro anima sua dedit in elemosina et concessit et carta sua confirmavit, die qua fecit eam dedicare, et sicut rex Willelmus pater meus eis per cartam suam concedit et confirmat. quare volo et precipio et firmiter defendo ne ullus super hoc preceptum meum de rebus ecclesie illius se intromittat, nisi per priorem et monachos ecclesie, nec eos inde disturbet, nec injuriam sive contumeliam faciat. T'. Rann' cancell' per Otuelum fil' comitis apud Turrim Lund'.

[Summer, 1113—Sep. 1114 (prob.).] This charter indicates that

Geoffrey de Mandeville had recently died, his Honor being still in the king's hands. He attests an Abingdon charter, apparently granted in Lent 1111 (*Hist. Abingd.* Rolls S. II 73), and Q. Matilda's charter which speaks of the Domesday book at Winchester, and which must be dated either between July 1108 and May 1109, or between Aug. 1111 and the summer of 1113 : see Round, *Feudal England*, p. 143.

If Geoffrey de Mandeville was alive in 1111, this charter must be subsequent to the king's return in the summer of 1113 : and probably it was granted before the king went to Normandy again in Sept. 1114, and at any rate before his prolonged absence from Easter 1116—Nov. 1120[1].

The earliest signature of Ranulf as chancellor is said to be between Easter and Sept. 1107 : he died at Christmas 1122 (*Feud. Engl.* 485).

36. *Mun.* 3587.

H. rex Angl'. Justic'. Vicec'. Baron'. et Omnibus Ministris suis. et hominibus franc'. et Angl' de Berchesir'✓ sal'. Sciatis me concessisse et firmiter confirmasse omnes donationes quascumque Gaufr' de Magnauill' Ecclesie sancte Marie de Herleia pro sua et heredum suorum redemptione et salute libere donauit. et carta sua confirmauit✓ Videl'. totam eandem villam de herl' et circumiacens Nemus eidem ville pertinenti. sine participatione cuiuscumque hominis in Eadem parrochia manentis✓ in terris. et Ecclesiis. in decimis. et possessionibus✓ in bosco. et plano. Campis. et Pratis. Siluis. et Pasturis✓ Aquis. et Molendin'. Piscariis. et Piscationibus✓ Pasnagiis. Porcis. et Denar✓ cum tota tercia parte Decime totius annone Omnium Maneriorum totius dominii sui. et cum duabus partibus decime totius Pecunie omnium Maneriorum dominii sui in viuo. et mortuo✓ et Cum omnibus aliis Rebus sine participatione cuiuscumque hominis de quibuscumque decima deo dari debet. Excepta solummodo terra Aedrici prepositi et .VII. Rusticorum de parua Waltham✓ quam in sua Manu ad se hospitand' retinuit. Concedo igitur et inper[p]etuum confirmo Ecclesie eidem de Herl' Ecclesiam meam de Waltham cum una hida terre et dimid' que ad Ecclesiam illam de Waltham pertinet. et ecclesie de Herl' subiacent✓ et totam terram illam Edwardi que dicitur hwatecumba.

---

[1] Since writing this I have observed that Geoffrey de Mandeville and Haimo Dapifer attest Hen. I's Savigny charter at Avranches, 7 Mar. 1113 (Round, *Doc. pres. in France*, p. 287) ; but I retain what is said above for the sake of its references, and as not being inconsistent with the fresh evidence.

et ecclesiam eiusdem ville cum Omnibus sibi pertinentiis in bosco. et Plano⸓ et Pasturis. tanquam eiusdem supranominate ecclesie de herl' dotalicium⸓ ita bene. et libere. et quiete. et plenarie in Omnibus rebus. sicut idem Gaufr' ea Ecclesie sue de herl' dedit. et concessit⸓ et per cartam patris mei et suam confirmavit. Concedo etiam et confirmo. ut Eadem ecclesia de herl' habeat Porcariam suam in parco libere et quiete. et in Omnibus maneriis dominii sui quicunque ea tenuerint⸓ unum Rusticum qui Octo Acras terre habeat. et cum Omnibus donationibus suis aliis-quas in insula de Heli. uel in villa que Mosa uocatur-ecclesie de Herl' contulit. siue etiam Decimas quas Turoldus dapifer in Wochendona. et in Bordesdena. et Edricus eius prepositus ibidem pro animabus eorum contuler'. et Omnia alia quecunque ecclesie prefate ab eodem Gaufr' seu ab alio quocunque viro ibidem sunt collata et concessa. Quare uolo et concedo. et firmiter precipio. ut Ecclesia eadem de herl' omnem habeat libertatem et firmam pacem. in bosco. et plano. in terra et in Aqua. per totam terram suam. et habeat Socam. et Sacam. et toll. et team. et Infangheneδof⸓ et terra et homines ecclesie eiusdem quocunque loco sint per Angliam. sint liberi. et quieti de Shir'. et Hundr'. de placitis. et querelis⸓ Geld'. et Daneg'. Scottis. et Auxiliis omnibus et de Omnibus operationibus et occasionibus⸓ et exactionibus. et Assisis⸓ Excepto solummodo Murdro. et probato latrocinio. Quodsi huiusmodi forisfactura super terram ecclesie euenerit. precipio⸓ quod Prior et Monachi inde suam plenarie habeant curiam. et defendo ne in Aliis locis quocumque modo placitent⸓ nisi in eadem Curia sancte Marie. et sua. De aliis uero placitis uel forisfacturis-q' super terram ecclesie. et Prior' con-[tigeri]nt. si quis de hominibus suis in forisfactura mea Justo iudicio et causa Aperta missus fuerit de .xx. manchis. adquietet se ante iudicium per .v[i.] denar'. et post Iudicium⸓ per .xii. denar'. et semper iudicetur. per iudicium Curie sancte Marie et Prior' ecclesie. Preterea uolo. et firmiter precipio. quod dimittatis esse in pace imperpetuum .vi. hidas ecclesie eiusdem de Dominio Prior' et Monachorum de omnibus Geld'. et Daneg'. [et th]eloneo per Angl' q[......]r dominicum conredium et usum pertinet. et Passagiis etiam per Angl'. et Assartis que de Dominica terra eorum sint⸓ et ex Omnibus Actionibus [....] pertinent et consuetudinibus. Defendo etiam et firmiter precipio ne francos suos plegios recenseant alibi Annuatim Prior et monachi nisi in eadem Curia sancte Marie et sua⸓ et ut nullus. neque Vicec' neque Minister [aliquis] super hanc

libertatem quam pro animabus patris et matris mee. et pro salute
et redemptione anime mee eis concedo et confirmo: eos amodo
placitis aut occasionibus. aut homines suos grauet aut laboret: aut
iniuriam uel contumeliam faciat. Quoniam eidem ecclesie omnia
pertinentia pro mea et m[a..]mee salute et Imperatricis filie mee
peticione et pro anime sue redemptione: ex omni exactione et
consuetudine regia. et Omnium hominum in[quietudine] soluta et
libera finabiliter clam[....]a. T'. eadem Imperatrice. et Rog.
episcopo Sar'. per Otuelum fil' Comitis. Ap' Turrim Lund'.

[ ? ] If this charter is genuine, it cannot be dated later than Easter
1116, when the king left England. For when he returned in 1120,
Otwel fitz Count, the son of Hugh earl of Chester, was one of those
who perished in the White Ship.

But the charter is granted at the request of Matilda the Empress,
and is also attested by her. Now Matilda left England in 1110, before
she was eight years old. She was crowned at Mainz as Empress in
1114, and after the Emperor's death she returned to England in 1126.

If, then, the evidence of this charter is to be accepted, Matilda must
have visited England between 1114 and 1116. But of such a visit we
have no other record.

We approach the charter therefore with some suspicion. And first
we ask whether it is probable that a charter to Hurley Priory should
have been granted ' at the request of the Empress,' who even at Easter
1116 was not yet fourteen years old ?

Next, we observe that in one sentence Henry makes the grant ' pro
animabus patris et matris mee et pro redemptione anime mee '; and in
the next sentence ' pro mea et m[a..] mee salute, et imperatricis filie
mee peticione et pro anime sue redemptione.' It would be absurd to
read ' matris ' again in the second sentence ; and in any case we look
for some mention of Matilda, Henry's queen. The 'a' is almost certain ;
and we might perhaps read ' marite,' instead of the more usual ' uxoris.'

We must consider together with this charter the much shorter
charter (no. 35), in which K. Henry confirms the properties of Hurley,
when the Honor of Geoffrey de Mandeville has come into his hand
through Geoffrey's decease. This occasion of that confirmation is a
natural one. The date of it must be placed between July 1113 and
September 1114, or else between July 1115 and Easter 1116. It is
attested, like the short Westminster charter (no. 34), by Ranulf the
chancellor *per Otuelum fil' Comitis apud Turrim Lund'*.

I confess that the fuller charter (no. 36) looks to me as if it had been composed at a time when the Empress Matilda had come to be a more important figure in England than she could have been in 1116 ; at a time when it had become worth while to suggest that Henry had been moved by her to grant special privileges to the priory of Hurley in addition to the ordinary confirmation of its properties. The writer has bungled in the phrases by which he describes the king's motives : he has avoided the risk of using the chancellor's name (Ranulf died at Christmas 1122), and has preferred the safer name of Roger bishop of Salisbury ; but he has retained to his ultimate confusion the addition *per Otuelum fil' Comitis apud Turrim Lund'.*

Henry II's charter of confirmation (*Mun.* 3751) follows closely upon the lines of this charter, and expressly refers to the charter of his grandfather. I gravely suspect that it was for his benefit that the forgery was made.

The handwriting appears to me to offer no decisive evidence ; and the charter still retains a broken red seal which arouses no suspicion.

37. D. f. 528.

Hec est convencio inter G. abbatem et conventum Westm' et Willelmum de Bocholanda. s. G. abbas et conventus Westm' dant et concedunt Willelmo de Bocholanda et heredibus suis in hereditate terram de Sipenham et de Burnham in feudo pro l solidis per singulos annos pro omni servicio preter commune geldum regis : et terram de Tecewrde et de Tunge similiter concedunt ei et heredibus suis pro lx solidis per singulos annos pro omni servicio preter commune geldum regis : et placeam que est ante domum suam similiter concedunt ei pro iiij$^{or}$ denariis in feudo. s. Celceiam tenebit in vita sua pro iiij$^{or}$ libris quoque anno pro omni servicio preter commune geldum regis ; et post mortem ipsius Willelmi remanebit Celceia in dominio ecclesie Westm'. et de feudo de Tecewrde et de Tunge, quando rex Angl' communiter accipiet xx solidos de milite, Willelmus de Bocholanda adquietabit ecclesiam Westm' de xx solidis. et de Celceya in Nativitate domini reddet xl solidos, et in die Ascencionis xl solidos ; et de feudo suo in Annunciacione sancte Marie lv solidos et ij denarios, et viij dies ante festum sancti Michaelis lv solidos et ij denarios.

Hii sunt testes : Rotbertus episcopus Lincoln', Bernardus episcopus de sancto David, Otuerus fil' comitis, Clarebaldus medicus, Radulfus fil' Algodi, Radulfus diabolus, Ricardus de Rami cur',

Ricardus de magna villa, Hugo de monte, Asciulus de Taneyo, Sagrinus, Osbertus de Bernivilla, Warinus de Hamesclape, Hugo de Midelton'; de familia abbatis, Willelmus capellanus, Willelmus fil' Fulconis, Gilebertus frater ejus, Herbertus dispensator, Picotus, Rotbertus de Beslun, Willelmus camerarius, Willelmus Germinus, Ricardus fil' Herberti, Oini et Tovius Ganet, et multi alii.

[1115—1117.] Bernard was appointed to St David's 19 Sept. 1115, and consecrated in Westminster Abbey by desire of the queen, whose chaplain he was.

It is probable that this grant was made after the death of William's father, Hugh de Buckland, who was alive, as we have seen, in 1114; see nos. 12, 20, 29.

For Radulfus fil' Algod, a member of the Cnichtengild in 1125, see Round, *Commune of London*, 102; for Otwel fitz Count, above, no. 36; for Richard de Mandeville, above, nos. 6, 20; for Hugo de Monte, no. 32 (note).

Richard de Rami cur' may be Richard son of Guy de Raimbercurt (*Feud. Eng.* 220).

With Warin de Hamesclape comp. Michael de Hanslape (*ib.* 220).

With 'Oini' (the first letter is uncertain) comp. Oini and Wini (both genitives) in *Hist. Ab.* II 53, 100, 138, 144 (but as he died before 1117, I do not suggest identification as probable).

Tovius Ganet attests a later charter (D. f. 528 *b*).

For Burnham and Sippenham, see above, p. 48, and no. 9.

38.   D. f. 516 *b*.

M. Angl' regina Ricardo episcopo et vic' et omnibus baronibus London', Francis et Anglis, salutem. Sciatis me dedisse et concessisse deo et sancto Petro et Gisl' abbati de Westm' hoc quod Hugo de Bochelanda tenebat de me in Londonia super hwervum ejusdem abbatis, cum soca et saca et cum omnibus aliis consuetudinibus quas ego ibi habebam. et hoc facio pro incolumitate anime et corporis Henrici regis domini mei et mea et filiorum nostrorum. T'. episcopo Lincoln' et com' David, apud Westm'.

[c. 1115—1117.] David, the queen's brother, afterwards king of Scotland, became count of Huntingdon in 1114. For Hugh de Buckland, see above, no. 12: his death may be implied by *tenebat*.

*Hwervum* seems to mean 'wharf' (see no. 4).

39. D. f. 363 *b*.

H. rex Angl' Willelmo camerario et Alberico de Ver et omnibus vestris successoribus camerariis et vicecomitibus Lond' salutem. Date de firma London' sacriste sancti Petri de Westm' i obol' quaque die ad emendum lucernam que ardeat coram sepulcro regine Math' a die festi sancti Michaelis proxima transacta usque in sempiternum. T'. Rogero Salesberiensi episcopo et Roberto Linc' episcopo et Rann' cancellario et Radulfo Basset apud Westni'.

[c. 1121.] Probably issued soon after the king's return at the end of 1120. Q. Matilda had died in his absence, 1 May 1118. Ranulf the chancellor died at Christmas time 1122, and Bishop Robert a few days later (Round, *Feudal England*, 485).

For William the chamberlain, see above, nos. 4 and 20; and for Ralph Basset, nos. 30, 43. For Aubrey de Ver, see no. 43, and Round, *G. de M.* 388 ff. This Aubrey de Ver was the son of Aubrey de Ver, and became his heir through the death of his eldest brother Geoffrey de Ver. Geoffrey on his death-bed gave property at Kensington to Abingdon Abbey, in gratitude for the medical services of Abbot Faricius: and Henry's confirmation of this gift is addressed to Maurice bishop of London and Gilbert abbot of Westminster (*Hist. Ab.* II 56).

40. Faust. A. III, f. 75.

Henricus rex Angl' Rodberto de Bertherol et omnibus baronibus de honore qui fuit Otueri fil' com' salutem. Sciatis me dedisse et concessisse deo et sancto Petro et monachis Westm' ecclesiam de Sabricheswrd'. et volo et firmiter precipio ut bene et in pace et quiete et honorifice teneant cum terris et decimis et omnibus rectitudinibus et omnibus rebus ipsi ecclesie pertinentibus, et ita ne aliquis illos inde disturbet vel injuriam faciat super forisfacturam x libr'. Test' cancellario et Gaufrido de Clinton'.

[? c. 1121.] This would appear to have been issued shortly after the death of Otwel fitz Count, while his Honor was still in the king's hand. See above, no. 36.

'Robert de Berquerola' occurs in *Harley Roll* C 8 (of early government of London): see Kingsford's edition of Stow's *Survey* II 382 (note on ' *Robert Bar Querel* Prouost ' in latter part of Hen. I's reign).

41. Faust. A. III, f. 75.

Henricus rex Angl' justic' et vicecom' et omnibus baronibus et ministris suis Angl' salutem. Precipio quod totum corredium

et omnes res quas ministri monach' Westm' qui sunt apud
Sabricheswrd' affidaverunt suas esse dominicas sint quiete de
toll et passagio et omni consuetudine. T'. cancell' &c.

[? c. 1121.] This was probably issued at the same time as the
previous writ.

42. Faust. A. III, f. 67 *b*.

Henricus rex Angl' Rodberto episcopo Lincoln' salutem. Precipio quod teneas plenariam convencionem Herberto abbati et
monachis Westm' de manerio suo de Leosne quod de illis tenes,
sicut firmatum fuit inter te et Gilebertum abbatem et eosdem
monachos tempore fratris mei; et ita quod inde amplius clamorem
non audiam. Teste Rogero filio Ricardi et aliis multis apud
Wodestoke.

[1121—Chr. 1122.] I insert this for the sake of its reference to
Abbot Gilbert, and also as a contribution to the somewhat obscure
history of the relation of Westminster to the manor of Leosne.

Roger fitz Richard was one of the many sons of Richard fitz Gilbert:
see above, no. 26, and for the pedigree, Round, *Feud. Eng.* 472 ff.

43. Faust. A. III, f. 78 *b*.

Henricus rex Angl' R. Basset et Alberico de Ver sal'. Facite
ita habere abbati Westm' estallos suos in novo opere sicut solebat
habere in veteri, et sicut precepi, ne audiam inde clamorem pro
penuria recti. T'. &c.

[Prob. 1121—30.] Though this probably belongs to Abbot Herbert's
time, I have added it here in order to correct a misapprehension
regarding it. It appears in the cartulary under the rubric of Henry II,
and has been accordingly supposed to give proof that 'novum opus,' or
new building, was being carried on in the church in that reign under
Abbot Laurence. Some have referred it to the chapel of St Catherine
in the infirmary, which doubtless belongs to that period. But a glance
at the writ shews that, like several others in Faustina A. III, it has been
erroneously entered under Henry II instead of under Henry I.

What 'novum opus' is here meant must remain uncertain: and it is
very doubtful whether choir-stalls are intended, as has hitherto been
assumed. Possibly some rebuilding was going on under the king's
directions outside the abbey; and the stalls may be market-stalls, or
even stables.

# ADDITIONAL NOTE A.

## ON THE EARLY CHARTERS OF ST JOHN'S ABBEY, COLCHESTER.

Three charters are printed above which relate to St Mary New-church in London: one is granted by Will. I (no. 5), two are granted by Will. II (nos. 10, 11). The first of the three has been already printed (*Monasticon* I 302). Besides these the grant of this church to West-minster is included in what is called the First Charter of Will. I (Cotton Charter VI 3 = D. f. 52 *b*), a long document reciting grants of properties, which though not genuine contains a good deal of valuable tradition : 'deinde quidem ecclesiam sancte Marie que Newecirke appellatur, cum terris et omnibus rebus ad eam pertinentibus, quam Alfwardus cogno-mento Grossus in predicta urbe pro salute anime sue ei dederat, sicut idem melius et plenius prenominato sancto contulerat, omnimodis im-mutabiliter concessi.'

The donor appears in these various charters as
   (1)   'Aluuardus de Lundonia' (nos. 5 and 11)
   (2)   'Agelwardus clericus' (no. 10)
   (3)   'Alfwardus cognomento Grossus.'

On the other hand we notice the absence of this church from the interesting charter (no. 30) in which Hen. I confirms [1108—1116] the grants of London churches made by the Conqueror: to wit, the wooden chapel of St Margaret Eastcheap, half the stone chapel of St Magnus Martyr, the church of St Laurence and the church of St James 'super ripam.' Moreover there is extant[1] a charter of Abbot Herbert [1121—1136(?)], in which he assigns to the sacrist among other revenues 'Niwecirce in Lundonia, quando auxiliante deo illa diracionari poterit ad honorem et proficuum hujus ecclesie.' From this it is clear that Westminster had lost its hold on the property: nor does it appear ever to have regained it, in spite of its express inclusion in a bull of Adrian IV to Abbot Gervase (D. f. 7*b*: et omnes ecclesiasticas possessiones quas habetis in London': scilicet Newechurch' et ceteras ecclesias cum omnibus libertatibus et dignitatibus ad easdem pertinentibus).

---

[1] Printed in *Monasticon*, I 307 from Harley Charters 84 F. 46: a late copy is also preserved (*Mun.* 3435), and it is also found in D. f. 408 *b*.

The charters of Will. I and Will. II (D. f. 529) are followed by a charter of Hen. I [after 1121], which is stated in the rubric to refer to the same church:

*Carta regis H. primi de ecclesia sancte Marie Newekirke.*

H. rex Anglorum vic' et baron' de Lundon' salutem. Precipio quod abbas Herbertus et monachi sancti Petri Westm' teneant bene et in pace ecclesiam sancte Marie quam Goslanus eis dedit cum terris eidem ecclesie pertinentibus. et precipio ne aliquis se intromittat nisi per abbatem. T'. R. Basset apud Windlesh'.

With this must be read a charter of Stephen to Abbot Gervase (D. f. 61):

S. rex Angl' justic' et vicec' et baronibus et omnibus ministris suis London'. Precipio vobis quod sicut me diligitis custodiatis et manuteneatis omnes terras et tenuras G. abbatis de Westm' filii mei sicut meas dominicas; et ad posse vestrum faciatis ei habere redditus suos et debita que ei debentur, et nominatim ecclesiam sancte Marie ei faciatis habere, quam Gislanus ei dedit, cum terris appendentibus: et tantum inde faciatis quod gratis inde vobis sciam. T'. Ad' de Beln' apud Westm'[1].

When we take this with the confirmation by Pope Adrian, we can hardly doubt that St Mary Newchurch is referred to: but 'Goslanus,' or 'Gislanus,' introduces a new element of perplexity.

So much for the Westminster side of the controversy, to which justice has not hitherto been done[2]. We find the rival claimant in the abbey of St John the Baptist at Colchester, the important chartulary of which was printed from Earl Cowper's manuscript for the Roxburghe Club in 1897. The historical value of some of these Colchester charters was pointed out by Dr Round in an article in the *English Historical Review* (XVI 721—30). With the question of the authenticity of most of the earliest charters he dealt severely. It is necessary for our present purpose to take a further step in the path of criticism which he has marked out; and in doing so we shall discover that the monks of Colchester not only deprived their Westminster brethren of one of their churches, but also stole their very choicest thunder.

The chartulary opens with the foundation charter of Eudo Dapifer. Of this it is sufficient to say with Dr Round, that 'it obviously is not genuine in the form in which it is transcribed.'

---

[1] Adam de Beln' attests a Lincoln charter at Oxford, Feb.—Dec. 1146 (*Eng. Hist. Rev.* XXIII, 727). 'Adam de Balnai' appears in a document relating to the Cnichtengild soke as present at Westminster in the second year of K. Stephen (Round, *Commune* 99).

[2] See, e.g., Mr Kingsford's brief dismissal of it in his valuable edition of Stow's *Survey* (II 317).

The next item (p. 4) relates how Gilbert a monk of Bec, having been made abbot of Colchester, found that the muniments of his church were grievously defective, and caused a charter to be written out and sent across the sea to Eudo and his wife, who were living at Préaux, begging them to obtain its confirmation from King Henry; which accordingly they did at a council at Rouen in the year in which Henry's son William was married (i.e. 1119). The charter was read out by a Norman clerk, who however came to a standstill at the long list of English words in which certain privileges were granted. The king thereupon took the document out of his hands, and read out and explained the terms in question[1]. We shall not comment on this story further than to say that there is good reason for believing that Eudo could not have been present on this occasion, though the king is represented as conversing with him.

The document which next follows is the pretended charter which the king is said then to have granted. One thing certain about it is that it was written, as we have already gathered, by a Colchester monk. But before we consider the sources upon which he drew for his phraseology, we must look at the sixth item in the chartulary (p. 11), which Dr Round accepts 'as the original confirmation by the king of Eudo's foundation of the house,' and which he thinks was almost certainly written in 1104.

That charter falls into four main divisions:

(1) A preamble of 17 lines: 'Quia inter multa bona opera—castitate copulavit.'

(2) A confirmation of the church and monastery founded by Eudo, with a list of properties granted to the same.

(3) A grant of privileges, briefly stated in these words: ' Huic ecclesie et cuncte ejus possessioni eandem libertatem et easdem leges quas habet ecclesia sancti Petri Westmonasterii in perpetuum possidere constituo.'

(4) Then follow the attestations, introduced by: ' Quod subsequenter dominice crucis karectere ad confirmationem subsigno ✠ annuente eodem domino nostro Jesu Christo, qui vivit et regnat et gloriatur in individua trinitate per omnia secula seculorum.'

We may suppose that the charter was composed in the abbey and brought to the king for confirmation. This will account for its peculiar

---

[1] 'Legit itaque cartam Johannes Baiocensis, clericus nobilis et regis consanguineus; cumque ventum esset ad consuetudines Anglice scriptas, cessavit, profitens nescire quid essent: tunc rex ipse (erat enim optime litteratus) cartam accepit, legit, et iis qui aderant exposuit.'

phraseology. But it remains very difficult to conceive that Henry I should have granted privileges in so vague a form as the statement that St John's Abbey at Colchester was to have the same liberties and customs as St Peter's Abbey at Westminster. There may be parallels to this of which I am ignorant: but, until they are pointed out, I must confess my inability to believe that this clause stood in the original charter granted by that prudent king.

Another ground of suspicion occurs to my mind. This charter, as we shall presently see, grants St Mary Newchurch in London to the abbey of Colchester, and the charter is attested by Gilbert abbot of Westminster. We have already noted that Abbot Herbert, Gilbert's successor, still looked forward to establishing Westminster's claim to this church ('quando auxiliante deo illa diracionari poterit'): but this could hardly have been a possibility, if Gilbert Crispin had attested a royal charter giving it to Colchester some twenty years before. On the other hand, we have a clear motive for the introduction of Gilbert's attestation, if the charter be not in its present form a genuine document.

We may now return to the pretended charter of 1119 (p. 4). This falls into the same four divisions.

(1) The preamble: 'Quia inter multa bona opera—castitate copulavit.' This is repeated from the charter of 1104.

(2) The first clause here is the same, save that 'Mahaldis' has become 'Matildis,' and for the words 'pro memet ipso et uxore mea Mahalde regina,' we now have 'pro memet ipso et uxore mea Matilde regina atque pro filiis meis[1].' The list of properties has considerably increased, as might be expected in the first fifteen years of a new foundation. Otherwise the phraseology is copied from the former charter with slight changes. The first items may be set side by side, as they stand in the two charters, to call attention to the past tense used of Eudo, who as Dr Round has noted does not attest the later charter:

| 1104. | 1119. |
|---|---|
| Manerium Wileye et manerium Picheseye, excepto feudo Ranulfi de Mundona et excepta terra Alwini Socheman. | Manerium Wileye et manerium Mundone et manerium Picheseye. hec tria maneria integra sicut Eudo ea de me tenebat, excepto in Picheseya feudo Ranulfi de Mundune et excepta terra Alfuuini Socheman. |

---

[1] As both Matilda and William were born before 1104, we might have expected such a phrase in the former charter: cf. 'subolis mee' in no. 24, above.

11

(3)   It is the third section that gives its special character to this charter.   The brief clause which granted the privileges enjoyed by Westminster is repeated thus : ' Huic ecclesie et cuncte ejus possessioni concedo eandem libertatem et easdem leges quas habet ecclesia sancti Petri Westmonasterii.'   But the time for vagueness has gone by, and the charter goes on to define the privileges thus: ' Primum videlicet ut tantus honor,' &c.: a passage occupying 53 lines of the printed text, and granting exemption from all episcopal and judicial control, rights of sanctuary, customs cited by their English names, &c.

The whole of this long passage, from ' ut tantus honor ' to ' penitencia satisfecerit,' is copied out of the so-called Third Charter of Edward the Confessor.

In one single point the privilege claimed by Colchester falls short of the privilege claimed by Westminster.   For Colchester claims, on behalf of any one who takes sanctuary: *membrorum suorum ac vite impunitatem consequatur*: but in the Third Charter of St Edward we read (in what purports to be the original with St Edward's seal, ch. xx; in the Westminster 'Domesday'; and in the *Monasticon* which quotes from Faust. A. III): *immunis sit omnino ac plenam libertatem consequatur.*

It is obvious that the Westminster privilege here is much larger than that which is claimed for Colchester; and yet there can be no doubt that the Colchester fabricator had St Edward's Third Charter as his authority.

Now an examination of ' Domesday' shews that the text has been tampered with at this point, since the chartulary was written; and portions of letters can still be seen which correspond with the Colchester reading.   When we turn to the ' original ' ch. xx, all seems in perfect order—except possibly the abbreviated *omnino* which looks darker and a little crooked.   It so happens that the word *omnino* comes earlier in the charter, and has there a different abbreviation; and a minute inspection reveals slight differences in the shapes of various letters, though not a trace of the obliterated letters can be detected.

It is possible that this Westminster alteration would never have come to light but for the Colchester forgery.   When was it made ? It cannot have been made when the long charter of K. Stephen was forged (Ch. xxxiii): for this refers to the privilege of St Edward, and gives the earlier form at this particular point.   It cannot have been made when the ' Domesday ' chartulary was written (c. 1303): for the earlier form was then copied, and it was subsequently erased to make way for the later form.   It is not unlikely that it belongs to the great period of strife as to sanctuary in the reign of K. Richard II.   Abbot

Litlyngton then pleaded the cause of Westminster at the Parliament at Gloucester with good success.

We go on now to the fourth item in the chartulary (p. 10), which also purports to be a charter granted by Henry I at Rouen in 1119. Its prefatory rubric declares it to be an abridgement of the fuller charter, more suitable for carrying about. Its genesis however is best explained by setting side by side with it a charter granted by the same king to Herbert, who became abbot of Westminster in 1121.

| WESTMINSTER. | COLCHESTER. |
|---|---|
| Henricus rex Angl' archiepiscopis, episcopis, abbatibus, comitibus, optimatibus, vicecomitibus, omnibusque ministris et fidelibus eius Francis et Anglis in illis comitatibus in quibus sanctus Petrus de Westm' habet terras et homines, salutem. | Henricus dei gratia rex Anglorum et dux Normannorum archiepiscopis, episcopis, abbatibus, comitibus, baronibus, et omnibus vicecomitibus in quorum vicecomitatibus sanctus Johannes Baptista de Colecestria terras habet et homines, et omnibus fidelibus suis Francis et Anglis totius Anglie, salutem. |
| Sciatis me concessisse deo et sancto Petro et Herberto abbati Westm', pro salute anime mee et Edwardi regis cognati mei et antecessorum et successorum meorum, | Sciatis me concessisse deo et sancto Johanni Baptiste de Colecestria et monachis ejusdem loci cuncteque eorum possessioni eandem libertatem et easdem leges quas habet ecclesia sancti Petri Westmonasterii : scilicet sakam |
| sacam et socam, toll et theam et infangenethef et flemenesfirmth', miskenninge et sceawinge, | et sokam, et toll et team, mundbryce, burhbryce, miskenninge, sceawinge, hleastinge, frythesocna, flemenefirmthe, wærgyldweof, uthleap, forfeng, feohfeng, feordwite, feohtwite, weardwite, hengwite, hamsocna, forsteall, infogenatheof, et omnia jura qualiumcunque causarum et omnes alias leges et consuetudines que ad me pertinent, in terra et in aqua, et in urbe et extra, in domo et extra, in villa et extra, in placito, in soko et saka, in theloneo, in furis apprehensione et emissione, in sanguinis effusione, et in omnibus aliis rebus in omni tempore et in omnibus locis. |
| et pacis fracturam et domus invasionem et omnes assultus in suo jure, in via et extra, in urbe et extra, in festo et extra, et omnes leges et consuetudines in aqua et in terra tam plene et tam | Has ergo omnes leges et consuetudines concedo deo et sancto Johanni Colecestrie in perpetuum possidere, in aqua et terra tam plene et tam libere sicut egomet illas melius habeo. |

11—2

libere et tam firmiter sicut predictus rex
Edwardus illas unquam melius concesserat et sicut per privilegium carte sue
confirmavit.

Et nullo modo volo consentire ut
aliquis hanc ecclesie sancti Petri concessam a nobis libertatem ullo tempore
infringere presumat, aut in aliquo de
omnibus que ecclesie juris fuerint se
intromittat, nisi abbas et monachi ad
utilitatem monasterii.

T'. R. archiepiscopo < Cantuar' et
G. archiepiscopo >¹ Rothom' et R. episcopo London', W. episcopo Winton' et
R. episcopo Sar', R. episcopo Lincoln' et
Ranulpho cancellar' et Johanne Baioc',
com' David, R. filio regis et W. Tan-
cardivilla, W. de Alben' et N. de
Albeneye, G. de Clinton' et R. Basset,
apud Windlesor'.

Et nullo modo volo ut aliquis hanc
ecclesie sancti Johannis concessam a me
libertatem ullo tempore infringere presumat.

Testibus Radulfo archiepiscopo Cantorberie et Gaufrido archiepiscopo Rotho-
magi et Turstino archiepiscopo Eboraci
et Rannulfo episcopo Dunelmie et Ber-
nardo episcopo de Sancto David et
Ranwlfo cancellario et Henrico comite
de Auco et Waltero Giffardo comite et
Willelmo comite de Warenna,
apud Rotomagum, in mense et anno
quo Willelmus filius regis desponsavit
uxorem suam filiam comitis Andega-
vensium.

It appears from a comparison of these two charters, that the
Colchester compiler, when he had written the words 'sakam et sokam,
et toll et team,' observed that the Westminster charter did not give so
full a list of English privileges as had been copied from St Edward's
Third Charter into the longer Colchester charter of 1119. He therefore
returns to the more complete list with the words 'mundbryce, burhbryce,'
etc., and then takes a succession of phrases out of the longer charter
until he comes back to Abbot Herbert's charter at the words 'omnes
leges et consuetudines.' It is interesting to see that he thus per-
petrates a 'doublet': for he has first 'in terra et in aqua' from the
longer charter, and then 'in aqua et terra' from Abbot Herbert's
charter.

Further criticism of this shorter Colchester charter is unnecessary.
But we may note with interest the style of the king, and also the
designation 'archiepiscopo Cantorberie,' which may point to Normandy.

The fifth item (p. 11) is a bull of Pope Calixtus II [1119—24], which
is said to be a confirmation of what has preceded. I do not think

---

¹ Cf. a similar charter of liberties in London granted at the same time and place
(D f. 101).

it is likely to be genuine. In any case it is of no special historical importance.

I pass on to the charter of William Rufus (p. 18). Dr Round has already said enough to condemn this as a forgery. I would only add that, besides the two manors which were not granted till about twenty years after his death, the king is also made to confirm the questionable possession of 'ecclesia de Niewechirche.'

To St Mary Newchurch we must, in conclusion, return. It is granted to Westminster by a charter of Will. I and by two charters of Will. II: but in Abbot Herbert's time it had somehow been alienated. He still hoped for its recovery, and his successor Gervase got a confirmation of it from Pope Adrian IV—a sign, at the least, that Westminster persisted in claiming it.

St John's Colchester however had evidently got hold of it, and defended its claim by a forged charter of Will. II; a forged charter of Hen. I dated 1119; a forged foundation deed of Eudo Dapifer; and, as we shall see, a forged charter of Richard bishop of London. I am inclined to add to this list of forged evidences the charter of Henry I which bears the attestation of Abbot Gilbert of Westminster in 1104: but I refrain from a positive statement on this point.

It is in the forged charter of Eudo alone that any details regarding the gift or the donor appear. There we read: 'ecclesiam sancte Marie de Westchepinge Lundonie, que vocatur Niewecherche, concedente Ailwardo grosso presbitero[1], qui in eadem ecclesia ex donatione antecessoris mei Huberti de Ria personatum consecutus fuerat; postmodum vero juri personatus sponte renuntiavit, pensionarius ecclesie sancti Johannis de eadem ecclesia factus' (p. 3). On this Dr Round remarks: 'One would hardly expect Eudo to describe as his *antecessor* Hubert de Rye, who was his father. Moreover, so far as I know, we have no other evidence of Eudo's father preceding him as a holder of lands in England[2].'

The forged charter of Bishop Richard (p. 82) has been exposed by Dr Round, who has set side by side with it the story of the monks (p. 50) on which it is based. Of this latter I will only remark that it introduces the name of 'Gunduinus monachus Becci.' Now the list of Bec shews us a 'Gundwinus' as entering the monastery c. 1085, and also a 'Gunduinus' c. 1112[3]. So we are dealing with a real person. Indeed

[1] Compare the 'Alfwardus cognomento Grossus' of the fictitious First Charter of Will. I, quoted above, p. 158.
[2] *Eng. Hist. Rev.* xvi 726.
[3] Porée, *Hist. du Bec* i 630, 632.

the names mentioned in these Colchester documents, whether as attesting charters or otherwise, are surprisingly accurate, and seem to prove that the compiler or compilers of these forgeries must have had a number of genuine documents, which, though insufficient for the purposes contemplated, furnished the necessary historical setting. There must have been genuine charters of Eudo Dapifer and of Henry I when the abbey was founded, and there may have been a confirmatory charter of the king in 1119 granted at Rouen either just before or just after Eudo's death. We may doubt whether either of the king's charters contained any reference to St Mary Newchurch or to the Westminster privilege: we may be certain that neither of them cited the exposition of that privilege in the terms of the Third Charter of St Edward. The real charters would be superseded by the forgeries, and perhaps even destroyed as conflicting evidence of a very compromising character.

The long charter of Hen. I (1119) reappears on p. 14 as granted afresh by Hen. II, and in a considerably extended form (especially in regard to the Westminster privilege) on p. 42 as granted by Rich. I. The short charter of Henry I (1119) reappears on p. 30 as granted by Stephen. A charter of Hen. III (p. 56) refers to Richard's charter, and gives an interesting interpretation of three of its English terms; this is supplementary to an *Inspeximus* of Richard's charter, which is printed immediately after it. If we could accept the charter of Henry II as genuine, we should have a valuable starting-point for discussing the date of St Edward's Third Charter: but the position which it occupies in the Colchester chartulary is not in its favour.

# ADDITIONAL NOTE B.

## A CHARTER OF KING ETHELRED.

### (Westminster 'Domesday,' f. 80 *b*.)

*Telligraphus ejusdem regis de quadam parte terre in loco qui dicitur Berewican, cum libertate ejusdem terre.*

Regente perpetualiter summo celorum opifice cunta, que convenienti dum non erant condidit serie, qui jure tripudiando in electorum agmine triumphatur, cui voluntarie supera atque infima deservire conantur per cromata ne nos pellacis circumveniendo vapide insidiatoris astutia imparatos mole pressos inmisericorditer ut sui moris est excruciet ex omni mentis conamine cordisque auditu prout vires divina opitulante clemencia nostræ animadvertendum est alma quid apostolica cotidie intonat tuba dicens: Ecce nunc tempus acceptabile, ecce nunc dies salutis; et item: Dum tempus habemus operemus bonum ⟨ad⟩ omnes, maxime autem ad domesticos fidei.

Quam ob rem ego Ædelræd dei favente clementia Angligene nationis imperator quandam telluris portionem, id est duas mansas terre in loco qui celebri vocabulo at Berewican appellatur ad monasterium beatissimi Petri celestis clavigeri in loco nobili qui Ⅎestminster nominatur pro anime mee remedio ad sustentac⟨i⟩onem fratrum deo inibi deservientium in perpetuam confirmo hereditatem quatinus ipsa congregacio pervigiles pro me jugiter intercessiones exsolvat solertique industria deo ejusque apostolo felici habitu deserviat. nam ejusdem loci abbas vocitamine Ælfwi ipsaque familia hanc prefatam terram a me cum centum auri obrizi mancusis comparavit, ea etiam interposita condicione ut trescentas pro me missarum oblaciones offerant, totidemque Davitici cursus modulationes pro me mente devota persolvant.

Sit autem hec prefata terra deo ejusque apostolo donata ab omni secularis gravidine servitutis exinanita cum universis que ad dictam pertinere noscuntur in magnis sive modicis rebus, exceptis tribus, expeditione videlicet pontis arcisve recuperacione. si quis autem, quod non optamus hoc nostre munificencie donum pervertere conamine stolido studuerit, collegio privatus perpetue felicitatis aerumpnam hauriat atrocissime calamitatis mortis, nisi ante terminum presumptionem hanc temerariam legati satisfaccione emendare studuerit.

Istis terminis predicta tellus circumcincta clarescit.

Ærest of þan hlape into theoburnan. norð anglang teoburnan to Cuforda. of Cuforda to pætlinga stræte. east andlang stræte to þam setle. of þam setle on hinan croftes ge mære. þanon souð to þan ealdan stræte. of þare stræte eft to patlinga stræte. andlang strate to þare ealden perhrode. þanan to þas ealder mannes ge mære. þanan suð rihte to akemannestræte. pest andlang stræte to cyrringe. þanon eft on þone hlape.

Anno dominice incarnacionis .m̊.ij. indictione .xv. anno vero prefati regis Aedelraedi .xxiiij. scripta est hec scedula hiis hierarchis consentientibus, quorum nomina inferius caraxantur.

✠ Ego Aedelraed rex Anglorum hoc donum dedi et confirmavi. ✠ Ego Aelfric archiepiscopus Dorovernensis ecclesie concessi. ✠ Ego Aelfhean episcopus corroboravi. ✠ Ego Wulfstan episcopus impressi. ✠ Ego Aelfstan episcopus adnotavi. ✠ Ego Aelfhean episcopus consensi. ✠ Ego Aedelric episcopus imposui. ✠ Ego Adulf episcopus adquievi. ✠ Ego Aelfpeard abbas. ✠ Ego Aelfsige abbas. ✠ Ego Kenulf abbas. ✠ Ego Ƿulfgar abbas. ✠ Ego Godpine abbas. ✠ Ego Aelfric dux. ✠ Ego Aeðelmaer minister. ✠ Ego Ordulf m̄. ✠ Ego Ƿulfgeat m̄. ✠ Ego Ƿulpheah m̄. ✠ Ego Ƿulfric m̄. ✠ Ego Eadric m̄. ✠ Ego Æðelric m̄. ✠ Ego Ulfhcitel m̄.

In discussing the 'berewic of the vill of Westminster called Totenhala' on p. 40, I was unwilling to introduce a further complication by referring to the above charter of K. Ethelred which grants 'two manses in the place called *at Berewican.*' But it is possible that this charter may have some bearing on the problem; and in any case I am glad to print it here, as it has never, I think, seen the light, and its ancient boundaries deserve to be studied in connexion with those given for the abbey estate in the well-known charter of K. Edgar.

That charter of K. Edgar confirms to Westminster Abbey *five manses*, which belonged to the church in the time of K. Offa. These *five manses* are confirmed by K. Ethelred in the general charter which precedes the present one (f. 80). Here K. Ethelred adds *two manses* 'at Berewican.'

K. Edward the Confessor confirms *seventeen manses and a half* ' circa illud monasterium': in some of his charters they are called *hides.*

The following translation of the boundaries in K. Ethelred's charter is kindly given me by Professor Skeat.

First from the mound to Teoburne: northwards along Teoburne to Cuford. From Cuford to Watling street: eastwards along (the) street to the dwelling-place. From the dwelling-place to Hinan-croft's boundary. Thence southwards to the old street. From the street back to Watling street: along (the) street to the old gallows. Thence to the Alderman's boundary: thence southwards straight to Akeman's street. Westwards along (the) street to Cyrringe. Thence back to the mound.

On the text Professor Skeat makes the following notes:

The copy seems to be a Norman scribe's copy, as it has a few mistakes which an A.S. scribe would hardly make.

l. 1. *Theoburnan*: error for *Teo—*. *anglang*: for *andlang*.

l. 3. *hinan croft* had better be left as Hinan-croft, which is quite safe. It cannot here mean 'hence,' as that would require *hinan on* (not *on hinan*).

l. 3. *souð*: Norman for *suð*. An important spelling, as *ou* for *u* is seldom found before 1300.

l. 4. *strate*: miswritten for *stræte*; quite inadmissible: *strete* was possible.

l. 5. *ealden*: for *ealdan*. *perhrode*: for *þearhrode*. *þanan*: better *þanon*. *ealder*: better *ealdor*.

In view of these notes it is interesting to add—what the Professor did not know at the time—that the copy was made about the year 1306: this being the approximate date of the Westminster 'Domesday.'

I add the following valuable comments from a letter which Professor Skeat has also written:

It is only safe to take *Hinancroft* as a proper name. It probably means 'croft of the hind' or farm-servant. But the history of the word 'hind' is imperfectly known, and this is the earliest example of the form *hinan*, with a final *n*.

It is even possible that *Hinan* is the gen. sing. of *Hina*; *ealder mannes* is the gen. of *ealderman* ='alderman'; 'old' would be *ealdes* or *ealdan*.

You will see that I give an older boundary, about 959, which seems to go round the other way, and coincides for a short distance. 'From Cuford along Tyburn' instead of 'along T. to C.' [see below].

I find several points of interest.

1. *Teoburne* is the old form of *Tyburn*, which ought rather to have come out as *Teeburn*.

2. *Cuford*=Cū-ford=Cowford. It keeps *Oxford* in countenance!

3. Mention of Akemann Street, which went to Akemannes-ceaster, i.e. to *Bath*.

4. *Cyrringe*: inferior spelling of *Cerringa*, gen. pl. of *Cerringas*='the sons of Cerr,' in very early times pronounced Kerr, riming with the German *Herr*. It is the same name as Charing in Kent, which is mentioned A.D. 799.

This is important, as it is by far the oldest mention of *Charing* in London.

Places like this are found in all three forms: (1) nom. pl. *Cerringas*, (2) gen. pl. *Cerringa* (later -*ge*), (3) dat. pl. *Cerringum*. They indicate family settlements.

The older boundary to which Professor Skeat refers is that of K. Edgar's charter. It is printed in Birch, *Cartularium Saxonicum* III 261, and less satisfactorily by Widmore and in the *Monasticon*. I print it here from the ultimate source, Ch. no. v of the Westminster muniments, which if not the original is certainly an early copy.

Ærest up of temese. andlang merfleotes. to pollene stocce. spa on bulunga fenn. of ðam fenne. æft ðær ealdan dic to cuforde. of cuforde upp andlang teoburnan to þær[e pide] here stræt. æfter ðære here stræt. to ðære ealde stoccene sče andreas cÿricean. spa innan lundene fenn. Andlang fennes sud on temese. on midden streame. andlang stremes be lande 7 be strande eft on merfleote.

l. 3.   Birch prints *teobernan* (a misprint).
l. 5.   The scribe has omitted the *a* of *streames*.

An expanded form of this charter is found in Ch. no. vi, a faulty transcript of which is printed in an appendix by Birch (III 693). To that transcript is apparently due the form 'Bulinga,' which has obtained a wide currency. But 'Bulunga' is the reading of the charter; and its only actual variants from Ch. no. v, so far as the boundaries are concerned, are the following:

l. 2.   Om. *of cuforde.*
l. 3.   *stret* (bis): ðære (secundo loco)] *there.*
l. 4.   *cÿricean*] *on Holeburne: Lundane: suð.*
l. 5.   *middan.*

Once again I have to thank Professor Skeat, who has given me the following translation:

First, up from the Thames along Merfleet to Pollene-stock. So, to Bulungs' fen. From the fen, following the old dike, to Cuford. From Cuford, up along Teoburne, to the wide army-street : along the army-street to the old foundation[1] of St Andrew's church. So, within London-fen. Along the fen southwards to the Thames to midstream [i.e. giving rights over the nearer half of the river]: along the stream, by land and by strand [i.e. along the edge, for those on foot], back to Merfleet.

[1] See note in Earle, *Land Charters*, p. 465.

# INDEX

Wrdesfelde 33 n.
Wulfric, the king's moneyer 34
—— Bordewayte 38
Wulfwold, abbot of Chertsey No. 3
Wulnoth, abbot of Westminster 36

Wulstan, bp of Worcester 27, 31

York 38; abps of, *see* Gerard, Roger,
Thomas II, Turstin; precentor of, *see*
Hugh

CAMBRIDGE: PRINTED BY JOHN CLAY, M.A. AT THE UNIVERSITY PRESS

# NOTES AND DOCUMENTS RELATING TO WESTMINSTER ABBEY

**No. 1.    The Manuscripts of Westminster Abbey.    By J.** ARMITAGE ROBINSON, D.D., Dean of Westminster, and M. R. JAMES, Litt.D., Provost of King's College, Cambridge.    Royal 8vo.    pp. viii+108.    5s. net.

" The Library of the Dean and Chapter of Westminster contains now but a small batch of manuscripts, and these have for the most part no connexion with Westminster Abbey.    They represent however the last of three quite distinct collections, of which the first was dispersed or destroyed at the dissolution of the monastery, and the second perished by fire in 1694. It so happens that of both these earlier collections a considerable amount of evidence is preserved in various quarters.

The Westminster Muniments contain a good deal of scattered information as to the care of books both in monastic times and in the later period, and this has been drawn together here as a small contribution to the history of the Abbey.

The division of responsibility for this little book is indicated by the initials in the table of contents.    The Dean and Chapter are under a great obligation to the Provost of King's for having placed his unrivalled experience in these matters at their disposal.    They hope that this may be the first of a series of studies bearing on the history of the Church of which it is their high privilege to be the guardians." *Preface*

**No. 2.    The History of Westminster Abbey by John Flete.** Edited by J. ARMITAGE ROBINSON, D.D.    Royal 8vo.    pp. viii+152.    5s. net.

" The only medieval writer who has attempted a history of Westminster Abbey is John Flete, a monk of the house from 1420 to 1465.    Sulcard indeed, nearly four centuries earlier, wrote its story, then for the most part legendary, in the days of William the Conqueror.    Widmore, three centuries after Flete, availed himself of Flete's labours, and also diligently investigated the treasures of the Muniment Room : he compiled a history, accurate, judicious and concise, which has been the foundation of all subsequent work.

The present edition is an attempt to do tardy justice to a writer, who, though he displays no graces of style and not the most rudimentary sense of humour, has devoted vast pains to his task, has copied actual documents in attestation of his statements, and refrains from guessing where he can find no evidence.

To have accompanied this edition with adequate notes would have meant an indefinite postponement of its publication, and would have demanded an intimate acquaintance with monastic institutions to which the present editor can make no claim.    A trustworthy text is the first and immediate need. This is what is here attempted.    Some introductory remarks deal with the growth of the legend of the consecration of the Church by St Peter ' in the spirit'; with the authenticity of some royal charters and papal bulls ; with the relics and indulgences, the effigies of the Norman abbots, and the ancient tapestries of the choir." *Extract from Preface*

## Cambridge University Press
London: Fetter Lane, E.C.
C. F. CLAY, Manager

For EU product safety concerns, contact us at Calle de José Abascal, 56–1°,
28003 Madrid, Spain or eugpsr@cambridge.org.